WAHIDA CLARK PRESENTS

DIARY OF
A PIMP'S WIFE

WAHIDA CLARK
P R E S E N T S
INNOVATIVE PUBLISHING

BY
KAREN JOY

Featuring
Mr. Cheeks

Wahida Clark Presents Publishing
P.O. BOX 383
Fairburn GA 30213
1(866) 910-6920
www.wclarkpublishing.com

Library of Congress Cataloging-In-Publication Data:

Diary of A Pimps Wife
Audiobook ISBN: 978-1-957954-29-5
Paperback ISBN: 978-1-957954-27-1
Ebook ISBN: 978-1-957954-28-8

Library of Congress Control Number: 2023900244
KEYWORDS
1. Pimp 2. Real life stories 3. True Crime 4. Stories of women 5. Biographies and Memoirs 6. Books about rappers 7. Women's non-fiction 8. Friendships 9. Drama 10 . Street life

Cover design by Temper Tantrum Tina
Interior Layout by Nuance Art, LLC
Editor: Chase Bolling, Alan Nixon
Book design by www.werkthatart.com
Printed in United States

WAHIDA CLARK PRESENTS

DIARY OF
A PIMP'S WIFE

WAHIDA CLARK
PRESENTS
INNOVATIVE PUBLISHING

PREFACE

This book is based on my personal experiences and is written in anachronic order. The chapters flash back and forth in time covering the years between 2008 to 2013. Everyone knows the love of money is the root of all evil. The book chronicles the trials and tribulations of an up-and-coming pimp named AZ who lives in Long Island with his common-law wife, Karen Joy. Prior to becoming a pimp, AZ worked one dead-end job after another. He even tried to become a rapper. Nothing worked for him until the summer of 2008. AZ's love for money led him into a dangerous, treacherous pimp game. At this time, he and I had separated to pursue different dreams. While I strived to build a country club, he trained to be a ruthless pimp.

KAREN JOY

INTRODUCTION

In today's society, there's a social stigma regarding pimps, prostitutes, and the commercializing of sex because it's a known form of human sex trafficking. The exploitation is based on the trafficker selling a victim to a customer to perform sexual acts. The profile of a trafficker is either pimp-controlled, gang-controlled, forced marriage, or sex for survival.

Pimp-controlled trafficking is when the victim is controlled by a pimp. Pimps can be male or female. When they are female, at times, they're referred to as madams. Victims are either controlled physically, psychologically, or emotionally. A pimp will use various tactics to gain control over his victims. Generally, they use force, drugs, or financial means. In the initial phase, a pimp looks to gain the trust of his victims and seeks out their weaknesses. In this stage, they are most interested in making their victim dependent on them. Whatever the victim is lacking the pimp will pretend to fill that void. This includes but is not limited to love, employment, a place to live, or financial stability. If this doesn't work, pimps may even resort to kidnapping to obtain victims. Once the victim is controlled, a pimp will move to the next step and coerce the victim into performing sexual acts for money. This is called prostitution. A pimp's job is to maintain the business between the prostitute and the customer.

3

Prostitutes are people who sell their bodies for money. They can be male or female and are sometimes referred to as whores, hookers, escorts, and ladies of the night. Customers are known as johns or tricks. They become tricks when they're swindled for money in place of being serviced. It's a dangerous risky business. A pimp's primary function is to protect the prostitute against any harm which may occur. Prostitutes are raped, robbed, and unfortunately sometimes killed in the line of duty. Not all prostitutes have pimps.

Some handle their own affairs and are not controlled by other people. They perform sexual acts to obtain basic commodities such as food, shelter, and clothing. This is sex for survival.

I think strip clubs, adult film companies, Playboy TV, porn sites, escort agencies, and the whole damn adult entertainment industry are pimps. Hugh Hefner, rest his soul, was idolized for the

Playboy brand, though society labels the less lucrative players as sex traffickers. There's only a negative perception of them. Realistically, prostitution is the oldest profession in the world. Today, selling sex has thrived into a multi-billion-dollar industry. I don't necessarily condone the sex trade. I'm merely stating there's a double standard based on the economic status of the seller. Now that we've covered a blueprint of the game, let me introduce some players.

The book chronicles the trials and tribulations of an up-and-coming pimp named AZ. He lives on Long Island with his common-law wife, Karen Joy. Prior to becoming a pimp, AZ worked one dead-end job after another. He even tried to become a rapper. Nothing worked for him until the summer of 2008.

Everyone knows the love of money is the root of all evil. AZ's love for money led him into a dangerous treacherous pimp game. At this time, he and I had separated to pursue different dreams. While I strived to build a country club, he trained to be a ruthless pimp. His first conquest was a female exotic dancer named Shi, a beautiful twenty-three-year-old Filipino girl. When they first meet, her charismatic charm, sarcastic wit, and mysterious aura instantly attracted him. Shi was perfect for the tricks of his trade. Falling for his beguiling ways, she was quickly sucked into a web of lies and deceit. Before long, the two were as inseparable as Bonnie and Clyde.

When Shi suffered a tragic accident in Miami, I reluctantly let them come live with me at the country club in New York. Against my will, AZ continued to build his stable. I went along with it believing I could save the women and my investment. This was regrettable.

A few years passed and AZ's luck continued. He came across a bourgeois, pampered eighteen-year-old girl named Nina whose parents died, leaving her with an aunt and uncle. Preferring to hang out, pop pills, and smoke weed all day, she got kicked out on the streets. Once homeless, Nina stayed at a local trap house with some drug dealers. A dealer they called Uni introduced her to AZ. Knowing Nina was extremely marketable, AZ lured the pretty young girl in with promises of a life of luxury. The bubbly teenager was easily persuaded by the wolf in sheep's clothing. Nina became AZ's number one money maker.

Last but not least, there was sexy Lexy. She was an innocent runaway dropped off in AZ's lap by a more experienced hooker named Roxy. Like Nina, Lexy was very gullible and eager to learn the game. The naive eighteen-year-old had a baby face and a heart of gold though in time she grew into a whiny, bipolar pest. Her insane jealousy over AZ drove him crazy. The sweet Hispanic girl eventually turned into a force to be reckoned with.

Now that you've met the players, come travel with me through this dark, spiraling tale of sex, drugs, and money. My only hope is that this book serves as an outreach tool bringing awareness to the perils of human sex trafficking. I've learned not to judge others because their sin is different from mine.

Dear Diary, it's July 8th, 2010.

Hello, World. Thank you, God, for another day of life.

Waking up groggy from a deep sleep, I squint with one eye open. Thick red curtains hang over my bedroom windows keeping daylight out. The room is dark, but the cable box reads one o'clock in the afternoon. I fumble around the bed to find the remote. Turning on the TV, Will Smith's Movie, *Enemy of the State*, is playing on FXTV. It's one of my favorites. Sitting up to watch, I hear loud moans coming from the other room. I crawl out of bed and go to investigate.

I see two silhouettes squirming around in the living room on the black leather sofa bed. The female's legs are jack-knifed wide open with a man thrusting in and out. *Oh Lord, what have I allowed my sanctuary to become?* Embarrassed, I duck behind the wall and then quickly run to release my urine. The night before, AZ fell asleep out here. Apparently now he has company.

Coming out of the bathroom, I hear them scurry up the steps. The flushing toilet must've spooked them. AZ is now a full-blown pimp. Stupidly, I allow him to live in my house thinking the fast money will make our estranged relationship better.

Just my luck, the hustle-and-flow pimp is a poor businessman.

CHAPTER I
A MACK IN TRAINING

I cross paths with AZ in the year 2003, while managing a rap artist on Select records named Computa. AZ and his childhood friend, KG, are producing beats for the label during this time. Believing AZ is a nice guy, I soon find out he has a dark side. He spent most of his younger years in and out of group homes and jails. I, on the other hand, was cut from a different cloth. I was conceived in Harlem when my mom fell in love with a married man. My dad, James Edwards, was relentless in pursuit of her banging body and exotic features. My father was a master tailor. In the ghetto, he was considered an affluent black man. His shop was located on 116th Street across from the Malcolm X Shabazz Mosque. His clientele came from both sides of the track. He sewed clothes for wealthy businessmen, police officers, street hustlers, and number runners. To me, his cup runneth over. Growing up, I didn't know I was poor. Life was good in the hood.

Unfortunately, my parents parted ways when love didn't live there anymore. I was only five years old when my mom moved us to the South Bronx. Inspired by my father's hard work ethic, years later I went to New Paltz college earning a bachelor's degree in business administration. After graduation, I hooked up with a shy handsome police officer. We shared many of the same dreams and aspirations. Settling on Long Island, we built a four-bedroom home with intentions of marriage. Regrettably, the strain of commuting back and forth to work in the city pulled us apart. Many nights he remained in the city projects with his side chick. It was only a matter of time before his infidelity would cost us everything. Tossing his cheating ass out on the street, ironically, I meet and start dating a pimp. Life is strange that way. I was introduced to AZ by a mutual acquaintance at Select Records named AL. He was the A/R who set up our first meeting.

On the day of our meeting, I was super-excited. AL and I sat waiting in my 1997 burgundy Maxima in the 7-Eleven parking lot. Thirty minutes would. pass before our contact arrived.

"That's him!" AL says, watching the huge green SUV turn into the parking lot. The windows of the vehicle were down with loud music blaring out of the speakers. A clean-shaven guy wearing dark shades skillfully maneuvered into the space beside us. AL stuck his head out of the window to greet him.

"Hey KG."

"Hi, AL!" the guy smiled revealing a missing front tooth.

"I finally got you to come to Long Island," he says, sarcastically. "Yeah, but it's business as usual," AL sighs, glancing at me.

"This is Joy, Computa's manager." Smiling, I lean across the front seat so the guy can get a better look at me. He takes off the dark glasses, glaring at me closely. "Nice to meet you, Joy. My name is KG," he says, in a soft-spoken manner.

"Hi, KG, the pleasure is mine," I say to him, politely. He puts the shades back on and turns his attention to AL again.

"I want y'all to follow me to pick up my partner, AZ. He's not too far from here."

"Oh, I know AZ. Let's do it," AL says, suggesting I follow the SUV out of the parking lot.

Driving about twenty minutes to the town of Bellport, I turned into a driveway behind KG. He honked the horn and a medium-built, dark-skinned guy opened the front door.

"I'll be right out!" the man hollered, then disappeared back inside.

A few minutes later, he reappeared wearing a filthy beige snorkel with faded blue jeans and dirty white Nikes. He was also in bad need of a haircut. KG and AL were smoking cigarettes in front of my car. The guy walked over, cracked a gapped tooth smile, and shook their hands. My first impression of him was not very good. I thought the guy was a hot mess.

In the weeks to follow, KG and I got along very well. However, AZ and I constantly argued over every little thing. Nonetheless, Fred Munao, the label owner, agreed to underwrite the cost for a single. My artist Computa was now in his early twenties and hadn't released a record since signing with the label at the age of sixteen. The task of getting him into work mode was almost impossible. Al, however, was elated to A&R the project. He hired Mr. Cheeks of the Lost Boyz to feature on a single called, "Itty Bitty Hustlaz". Computa and Mr. Cheeks did a few shows together to promote the song, but it was ultimately a dud. We continued pushing Computa, but he was young, wild, and distracted. He was lyrically talented but far more interested in women and flossing than a music career. Nobody could get Computa to focus. That was part of the reason his project was shelved in the first place. After months of disappointments, I finally severed business ties with Computa. Subsequently, KG, AZ, and I, moved on to do business with Mr. Cheeks.

The love-hate relationship I had with AZ continued on. I was a person of integrity with good character. AZ, on the other hand, was a savvy street hustler who used grimy business tactics to get ahead. Growing up on the block in Brentwood molded him into a sheisty con artist. If AZ told people one thing, he always did the opposite. That type of behavior didn't sit right with me. It made us clash at every turn.

As time went on, I got to know AZ better. Apparently, he had a passionate, more sensitive side which blindsided me. Opposites usually attract and inevitably we began to date. Allowing AZ to move in with me was a mistake on many levels. Four years passed before he and I realized we were not meant to be together. The constant bickering over money and other differences was too much for us to bear.

The opposite qualities, which were once the attraction, were now the repellent.

AZ finally decided to move out. One day, while I was in the basement cleaning up his illegal mess, someone knocked loudly at the front door. I tiptoed slowly up the steps hoping it was not the police. Peeking through the blinds, I breathed a heavy sigh of relief. It was KG's two brothers, Born and Shaq. They were accompanied by their nephew, Shah boo, and a friend named Dre. I was happy to open the front door for the fellas.

"Hey, guys! What brings you around today?" I say cheerfully to them.

"Where's AZ?" Shaq grumbles, rudely pushing me aside and heading straight for the basement.

The rest of us quickly followed him.

"Where's the weed plants?!" Born shouts at me once we're downstairs.

Shrugging, I nervously back away from him. His big black, burly frame leans over me breathing heavily.

"How should I know?" I say, looking at him puzzled. *After all, this is your ridiculous project.*

"Where's that nigga, AZ?!" he asks, chest heaving in and out.

I didn't know where AZ was, and I was becoming frightened by his outburst. For weeks, I heard the men in the basement joking about having pounds of weed at harvest time. Today, looking around, that was not the case. There was nothing here but twenty pots of dirt and some leaves scattered on the floor.

Bright lamps hung overhead emulating the sun. With no weed in sight, the fellas grew even angrier.

Shaq was a stocky man, almost six feet tall. I was somewhat intimidated when he looked at me with bloodshot eyes.

"You better call that nigga and find out where my shit is!" Shaq says sharply through clenched teeth with a lisp.

"Yeah, you better call him or we gonna tear this place up!" Sha Boo growls, tugging on a piece of equipment hanging from the wall. He was a younger more ferocious version of his uncle. At this point, the men begin cursing and tossing things around the basement to make their presence felt. Their behavior made me really uncomfortable. Feeling like a victim of a home invasion, I threw my hands up in submission.

"Guys, I don't know where AZ is! But he's not going to be very happy when he finds out you came here bullying me!" I said, trying to make sense of it all.

For a second, they stopped to think about it. I looked at Dre, who was the civil one.

"How would you feel if AZ were at your house doing this to your woman?" I asked, still visibly shaken, hoping my words had an impact.

Dre's shoulders slumped. His body language told me I had won him over.

"Yeah, fellas, there's nothing here. We might as well leave," he said, making them listen to him. Obviously disappointed, they throw a few more items around and then stormed up the steps. When I heard the front door slam, I ran upstairs behind them and locked the deadbolt. Shaking uncontrollably, I went straight to the landline and called AZ. His phone rang repeatedly.

"Hello! Who is this?" Some chick asked, finally picking up his phone. Hearing her voice and a bunch of girls giggling in the background made my temper boil. I sucked my teeth and slammed the phone down in her ear. AZ called me right back.

"Hi, Bae," his voice played calmly over the receiver. This time there was dead silence in the background. I didn't bother to say hello because he brought the worst out of me. I tore right into him.

"Listen, you asshole! Your boys just left my house threatening me about some weed! They came here throwing shit around like the feds. They say you owe them some money! They are pissed at you and so am I! My electric bill is sky-high! Where are you?!" I yelled at the top of my lungs.

AZ also had a bad temper. Though, smartly, he controlled himself.

"What are you talking about?! Why did you let them in?! Next time they come there don't answer the door!" he yells, then quickly composes himself. "Listen, babe, don't worry about them." The smooth operator prepares his lie. "I'm in Florida working on some big things for us. I got an opportunity to make some crazy money. I can't talk about it right now, but when I'm straight, I'll send some money. You have to trust me on this. I love you," he says, then quickly hangs up on me.

I was steaming mad when the call ended. In the back of my mind, I knewAZ was lying. Getting money from his cheap ass was almost impossible.

During the next six months, things calmed down. The goons never came back, and AZ called several times to string me along. He never sent any money but eventually pieced together a full story. Supposedly, when he left my house, he moved into KG's studio. He only took a few items and the clothes on his back. The weed plants and most of his belongings still remain deeply hidden in my basement. That was probably the pungent odor I smelled coming from downstairs.

Prior to his leaving, AZ carefully hung the plants upside down in a dark closet. It's a process that allows the tetrahydrocannabinol or THC to flow into the buds. THC is the main mind-altering ingredient found in the cannabis plant. The buds have to cure before they're mature enough to smoke. That's the reason AZ didn't take the weed with him.

After AZ moved out of my house, he became down on his luck. One day, he and KG were listening to some beats at the studio when the door swung open. Their friend, Kal, walked in.

"Hey, guys, what's up?!"

"Yo, Kal, what's good?" AZ leaps to his feet embracing Kal. KG leans back in the chair, giving Kal a pound. "What brings you around today?" KG asks, grinning wide.

"Nothing much, just came by to check on my guys," Kal giggles and squats on the sofa next to AZ.

The men knew something exciting always happened when Kal came around. Kal was dark-skinned, very tall, and one hundred thirty pounds soaking wet. He was a fur coat, gaudy jewelry-wearing, BMW-driving, flashy type of guy. The easy-on-the-eyes lady's man was also known for carrying a gat. AZ met him years earlier at the radio station while promoting Mr. Cheeks. The two men kept in touch after that. The guys joke around for a few minutes then Kal got straight to business.

"Okay, fellas, listen to this." Kal stands up, rubbing his palms together. "For the past week, I've been with these birds at the Marriott hotel in Manhattan. They have plenty of money, and they're not being cheap with it!" he says, pausing for their reaction.

AZ and KG's eyes grow wide. They lean in close hanging on his every word.

Kal bounces around the room, happy to give more details. "These girls are spending money like crazy! They are buying champagne, jewelry, and expensive clothing. Whatever I want, they buy it!" Kal smirks, winking at them.

KG's forehead wrinkles. "Where you meet these girls? he asks, turning back to the keyboard, playing a few notes. AZ's head cocks to the side. He's already scheming on the money.

"My cousin introduced me to them. He ran into the girls on the street in Manhattan. They're from out of town looking for a good time. My cousin gave them directions to some local nightclubs. It's two girls and a guy, all in their early twenties. The Asian girl is mad sexy. The chubby white girl, not so much. Whoever gets her will have to take one for the team," Kal says, making them all laugh.

"How much money are we talking about?" AZ asks, eyes narrowing with greed.

"Oh, they caked up. You don't have to worry about that! The one they call Queen seems to be the boss. She's spending two to three thousand dollars daily. Me and my cousin have been eating lovely," Kal says, grinning at them wide. "I am trying to figure out how to walk away with some of that money. My cousin is leaving tonight. He got to get back to his wife. I need help executing a plan. You guys in or not?" Kal asks, holding out his hand for a pound.

"Oh, we definitely checking it out," AZ says, slapping his palm. The men then make plans to meet the girls later that night.

———

Stepping off the elevator at the Marriott, their feet sink into plush red carpet. The swanky five-star hotel was very impressive with its trendy architectural design and textured wallpaper. AZ lifts his nose into the air and sniffs out the money like a bloodhound

"Damn, this hotel is dope!" he says, admiring the decor.

"I want y'all to meet Queen first. She's the one to focus on," Kal whispers in his ear on their way down the hall.

Walking past four doors, they stop at the last one on the right. Kal begins rapidly knocking. The guys hear light footsteps approaching from the other side. Someone jokingly knocks back.

"Who is it?" Kal asks, playing along. A girl cracks open the door and teasingly pokes her leg out.

"Oh, you want to play today!" Kal says to her, licking his lips.

"Come in," she giggles, backing away from the door. The girl is wearing nothing but a cut-off tank top and booty shorts. Her thick thighs, small waist, and perky breasts complement a pretty face. She is gorgeous from head to toe. *This must be Jenna; she's as pretty as Kal said she was.* AZ thinks to himself.

"Hey, Jenna. Where is Queen?" Kal asks, walking to the back of the room, peeking into the refrigerator.

"I'm glad you came back," she says, smiling at him.

"I told you I was coming back. I went to pick up my boys. This is KG and AZ," Kal says while the fellas curiously look around the suite.

"Hello!" Jenna says to them. KG gives her a friendly nod. AZ's baseball cap is tilted over his eyes. He smirks, mumbling something underneath his breath.

"Have a seat. Queen is in the shower," Jenna says, motioning for them to sit on a sofa by the wall.

"Where's the food at? I'm starving," Kal says, digging in the refrigerator and taking out a small bottle of juice.

"We ordered Chinese food from the restaurant downstairs. There's nothing left unless you want the scraps in the garbage," Jenna giggles, flopping into a chair matching the sofa. She seductively crosses her legs with the fellas admiring every move.

"Oh, you a comedian now," Kal says, laughing with her. He swallows the juice and looks out the window at the people below. Being this high up makes the people look like crawling ants to him. Kal feels on top of the world. Suddenly, the adjoining room door swings open.

"Hello, everybody!" Queen says, sashaying into the room playing her role of an heiress. The big girl is wrapped in a white bath towel which can easily be a blanket. Her chubby face sits under brown frizzy shoulder-length hair. AZ and KG stare at each other. She's the complete opposite of Jenna. Not their idea of a queen at all.

"Hello," they mutter, looking at her big glassy eyes. Kal happily goes over to kiss Queen on the cheek.

"Champagne, anyone?" she smirks, raising a bedazzled goblet high into the air.

Unbeknownst to them, Queen is from Virginia. She's in New York and spending money recently received from a settlement. Kal's under the impression Queen is the daughter of a rich mobster. She hides behind this lie for protection, knowing no one in their right mind would rob the daughter of a reputed crime boss.

"Sure, we'll have a glass," Kal accepts the offer for everyone. AZ and KG just continue staring at her.

"Perfect!" Queen says, batting her long eyelashes at them. "Kal, call room service. Have them send another bottle of Don to the room. Jenna, you come with me," she commands, then exits the room with Jenna on her heels.

AZ leans back clasping his hands behind his head. "So, that's Queen?"

He mouths the words without making a sound. KG winks, taking a Backwood out of the pack to roll a blunt of weed.

"Shh," Kal nods, placing a finger over his lips.

For the next two weeks, the men go back and forth to the hotel room, plotting on the money. Ultimately, their plan works. The girls become so comfortable, they allow KG and AZ to escort them to the bank. Every time they go, Queen withdraws large sums of money. She spends thousands on jewelry and clothing for the guys. Once the money runs out, she comes clean about the inheritance. With only a few dollars left in the bank, Queen is desperate for more money. She schemes on ways to get some. Stupidly, she sends their gullible male companion to rob a local convenience store. The robbery goes terribly wrong. The friend is caught and arrested by the police. The car they drove to New York gets impounded, leaving the girls broke and stranded. Kal, though, conveniently comes to their rescue. He plans a road trip for them to get out of town in case they're implicated in the robbery. The girls naively go along with the plan, having no idea what's in store for them.

"Are we there yet?" Queen asks Kal, looking out the car window at the palm tree lined streets in Miami. Kal's been driving for hours. The girls are now sleepy and tired as they ride past several high-rise condos in the downtown district. Sweltering heat beats off concrete streets until they finally reach their destination on the outskirts of town.

"Yup, we're here!" Kal says, grinning at his prey in the rear-view mirror.

Jenna sits up, flabbergasted by what's in front of her.

"Wow! Is this the place?"

The mansion was surrounded by a fishpond structured like a moat around a castle. The girls leaped from their car seats onto a diamond-glittered driveway, paved straight through twenty yards of manicured lawn.

"Ooh and ah", they said walking past several late model tricked-out cars: a navy blue 750 BMW with a panoramic roof sat next to a pretty pink SLK Mercedes Benz with spinning chrome rims. The silver Porsche Cayenne truck and white stretch Hummer also caught their attention.

"Are we staying here?" Queens asks, eyes wide with admiration. The girls were unaware of Kal's plan to sell them. He never tells them his cousin, Big Will, is a pimp. When Kal calls Big Will about the girl's problem, he is more than happy to help. He quickly sends money for them to make the long trip to his house in Miami. Twenty-four hours later, Kal, AZ, and the girls land in Florida.

"This is just one of his cribs," Kal giggles, nudging AZ's arm on their way down the path. The glitz and glamour are overwhelming for them.

Big Will isn't faking it, he's really making it. AZ looks around taking everything in. This was a lifestyle of the rich and famous to him.

Kal rings the doorbell, ignoring the shiny lion head knockers. Shortly afterward the glass door opens. A tiny blond bombshell stands before them topless in a black thong.

"Hi, brother! Long time no see!" the girl squeals, jumping into Kal's outstretched arms with hugs and kisses. Gawking at the perfect naked body, Kal can't hide his perverse excitement.

"Whoa, Candy! Miss you too," he says, quickly pinching a nipple. "Where's my cousin at? Kal asks, stepping into the foyer.

"We just made the long trip from New York. This is Jenna, Queen, and my boy AZ. They're your new sister wives," Kal says, winking at her.

Candy looks past him at the girls. One girl is fat, and the other girl is even fatter. Big Will is known for the finest stock in town. She doubts either girl will make the cut.

"Nice to meet you. I didn't know daddy was expecting company. He doesn't tell me anything," Candy sighs. "Right this way," she says, tiptoeing barefoot on the black Italian marble.

Following her through a winding foyer, beautifully decorated with crystal ornaments, they enter a breathtaking living room. Their feet sink into thick peach color carpet, coordinated with pleated drapes hanging over ceiling to floor windows. The girls stare at expensive art on the wall.

"Make yourselves comfortable. I'll let daddy know you're here." Candy says, walking away.

Kal smiles, watching her tiny booty wiggle down the hallway.

Jenna and Queen, obediently take their seats on a white leather sectional and watch a sixty-inch flat screen mounted on the wall.

"AZ, this place is the shit. Let me show you around." Kal says giggling.

"Lead the way," AZ says, following him out of the room.

When they're gone, the smell of fresh blood fills the air. Big Will's barbie dolls circle the room like sharks in the water. Jenna quickly catches their eye. She and Queen have no idea Big Will has agreed to pay a handsome fee for them.

On the tour, Kal and AZ discover flat screen TVs cleverly concealed everywhere. There's even a few hidden in bathrooms and behind picture frames on the wall. In the kitchen, they walk past stainless-steel appliances and exit through sliding patio doors. Outside, there's another fully equipped kitchen in the backyard. It has a triple propane grill and dual sinks with a refrigerator underneath. In the distance, they spot a large swimming pool, tiki hut, and wet bar. A flat-screen TV hangs over a state-of-the-art deejay set. Pink stone pavers outline a dance floor and fancy patio furniture upgrades the ambiance to the next level.

"So, what you think, AZ?" Kal asks him.

"I can't believe my eyes. Me and the girls are going to love it here." AZ smiles with a peculiar grin, marveling at the motorcycles on his right.

"I know that's right! Big Will employs a weekly staff to cook and clean. This property is spectacular," Kal laughs, patting AZ on the back as they make their way to the wet bar.

It's dark outside when Big Will emerges from the house hours later. Everyone is under the tiki hut drinking at the bar.

"Here comes this negro now," Kal says to them. They all fall silent, watching the six-foot frame glide cautiously across the backyard. Big Will's shiny bald head gleams under the moonlight. His muscles ripple under a black and yellow Versace shirt. Silk pants and alligator shoes accent his ensemble. The rich cologne reaches them before he does. Kal giggles, hopping off his bar stool.

"Hey, Big Money, I saw that drop-top CLK in the driveway. You gotta let me take it back to New York with me." A sly smirk dawns on Big Will's clean-shaven face.

"Not that one, kid," he says, embracing Kal with a handshake hug.

"I got something special for you!" Kal whispers, winking at him. Big Will ignores the girls and glares directly at AZ. Kal notices the distraction and quickly introduces them.

"Oh, this is my man, AZ. He rode down with us."

AZ walks over taking Big Will's hand into a firm grip. Big Will's diamond-encrusted pinky ring and Pearl master Rolex sparkle under the light. Thick platinum Cuban links, dangle from his wrist and neck. Big Will is rumored to be the most influential pimp in Miami. Queen and Jenna stare at the razor-sharp man with their mouths hanging open. AZ snarls, green with envy. *If this dude can profit off of girls, so can I.* he thinks to himself. Seeing the tension between them, Kal quickly interrupts the men.

"Come, let me introduce you to the product," he whispers in Big Will's ear.

The two of them walk away and go into the tiki hut where Big Will meets Queen and Jenna. AZ's eyes grow narrow. He can hardly believe this corny dude from Queens is controlling such a large empire. He makes a mental note to find out how the game is played. For the remainder of the night everyone chats under the tiki hut getting to know each other better. They drink cocktails and make plans for the girls to stay in Miami. After some time, Big Will leaps off the bar stool, excusing himself.

"Alright everybody, I got to get these girls to work. Kal, let me have a word with you," Big Will says, brushing the wrinkles out of his pants leg. Strolling toward the house, they stop to talk before Big Will enters the sliding patio doors. Once the conversation is over, Kal returns to AZ, disclosing the gist of it.

"Big Will agrees to let us stay a few weeks. However, not without a price. He wants Jenna for the stable. Queen is really not his type. She's too thick and defiant for the game. Jenna, on the other hand, is a China doll. At first glance, he saw the dollar signs," Kal says to AZ. They both look across the bar at Jenna, sipping on her drink. The poor girl was clueless.

20

"Good, then we're in," AZ says to him.

In the weeks to follow, Big Will keeps his eye on Jenna. Within this time, he draws as close as possible to her. He even takes Jenna on a few shopping sprees and out to dinner with the other girls. He allows Queen to tag along so Jenna will feel comfortable.

On the morning of departure, AZ and Kal go to Big Will's room ready to unfold their master plan. Kal goes in the room first, flopping on the edge of the bed. AZ remains in the doorway. Big Will is relaxing in bed naked with Jenna. The fellas understand the importance of making their move when he is vulnerable.

"Hey man, it's time for me to go back to New York. AZ's going to stay here with the girls," Kal blurts out unexpectedly.

Big Will rolls over looking at them suspiciously.

"Nah, man! That's not gonna work," he says, wrapping his large biceps tightly around Jenna's waist.

Kal pauses before sticking the *dagger in him*. "Well, if AZ goes, Jenna goes too," Kal says, without blinking an eye.

Big Will raises an eyebrow, pondering the idea. He knew Jenna was easily worth a million dollars. Game recognizing game, he quickly changes his tone.

"All right, man, whatever you say." Big Will sighs, stroking the side of Jenna's face. Jenna's delighted. She wanted AZ to stay. He served as protection for her.

"Thanks, bro, we appreciate your hospitality," Kal says, reaching out to shake Big Will's hand. He smacks it away, rolling over on his stomach.

"Get out my room and close the door behind you," Big Will says, brooding.

AZ grins, leaving the room behind Kal. He was now officially a pimp in training. A few days later, Big Will had his guy named Sparky send Queen back home to Virginia. She was considered a liability.

The next six months are a blur for AZ who feels like a boy playing with big toys. He even crashes and breaks a few. One time he falls off a motorcycle putting himself out of commission for weeks. Though, overall, he enjoys the company of beautiful naked women and a lavish lifestyle. Big Will comes to respect AZ's swagger and appreciates having him around.

He teaches AZ some tricks of the trade. Although AZ's familiar with bagging chicks, he learns from Big Will to concentrate mainly on white girls. He tells AZ blonde girls are big money-makers. He advises they're also more obedient than black girls. White girls let you pimp, whereas black girls are aggressive and make you pimp. AZ admires the way Big Will transforms the girls from plain Janes into barbie dolls. He sends them overseas, spending thousands on plastic surgery for butt and boob jobs. He keeps the girls on lemon diets and in the gym to remain in great shape. Big Will runs a tight ship and prohibits drugs on the premises. AZ jokingly calls him Doctor Frankenstein and soaks up as much knowledge as possible from the smart pimp.

During their stay, AZ and Jenna build a special bond. She earns thousands of dollars dating rich entertainers, business tycoons, and professional athletes. Big Will brags about her prowess unaware she is sharing money with AZ. Nonetheless, the crafty businessman has many streams of income. When money is slow on the street, he cracks the whip. His connections with porn producers allot the girls gainful employment in the film industry earning them thousands of dollars per sex scene. His *Bad Girl* clothing line also pops. The company manufactures assorted apparel for adult entertainers. The lucrative business venture accrues sales online and in local strip clubs. Often times, the girls work eighteen-hour days. It's hard work but the rewards are very high. The girls drive flashy cars, live in beautiful mansions, wear fancy clothes, and flaunt pricey jewels. No other pimp in Miami moves like his team. They are the envy of the town.

One of AZ's duties is to help build the stable. He goes out on the prowl with Big Will's other workers, Sparky and Gene. Together they search for new prospects. Driving big shiny whips around town easily captivates unsuspecting victims. Becoming a pimp is AZ's dream until reality sets in. After six months, Jenna falls in love with a sugar daddy and leaves the confines of the stable. Without Jenna, AZ has no leverage to stay. He has to return to New York with emp ty pockets.

CHAPTER II
PIMPIN' AIN'T EASY

AZ flew into New York from Miami early spring of 2008. He's broke and living back in the studio with KG again. Barack Obama is campaigning for the Presidency at this time. Every Black man in America is looking for a come-up.

One early afternoon, AZ observes a young lady walking by his room. He jumps off the bed following her down the hall to the recording area. When AZ arrives, his business partners, KG and Chuck, are entertaining the girl. She's on the sofa laughing with them and Dennis, the studio owner.

"Hey, what's so funny in here?" AZ barks, walking into the room. The girl looks over her shoulder, startled by the intrusion.

"Erin, that's just our partner AZ. Don't pay him any attention," KG says to her.

"Hi, Erin, I'm the boss in here. You better pay me some attention," AZ says, smiling at the big blue eyes.

"You scared the heck out of me," she says, blushing from his intense stare.

"Aww, I didn't mean to," AZ says, slipping into the seat beside her.

The group continues talking while AZ focuses on Erin. Her infectious laughter and high energy intoxicate him. Listening to Erin speak, AZ patiently waits for an opportunity to engage her.

"So, Erin, what brings you to the studio?" he asks when the other men turn their attention to the music.

Staring at him with bright blue eyes, she takes a deep breath before answering,

"Dennis is an old friend of mine. I come here often to put work in at the lab," she says, pointing to a small vocal booth behind the plexiglass.

"Oh, so you're a rapper?" AZ teases, feeling her out.

Erin smirks, sucking her teeth at him. "No, silly, I sing in my spare time but I'm really a dancer," she says.

AZ's antennas go up.

"You mean at the strip club?" he asks, hardly able to control his excitement.

"Yeah, I work at Blush. You should come to visit and have a drink with me sometime." Erin thinks she has a fish on the line. Unfortunately, she's inviting a fox into a chicken coop.

"Maybe I will," AZ grins wickedly, mind ticking a mile a minute.

Moving fast, he grabs a pen and paper off the table. "If you ever need some beats, let me know," he says, scribbling some numbers on the paper. "Here's my digits. Give me a call next time you come to the studio."

AZ hands Erin the piece of paper and stands to leave. She squints at the writing.

"Thanks, maybe I will," she says, mimicking him.

"I'm out of here. You guys are too boring for me." AZ jokes, exiting the room.

Walking down the hallway, he could hardly think about anything but Erin. He was so preoccupied with his thoughts that he missed when the guys started talking about embezzling money. Prior to Erin's arrival, his partners were concocting a scheme to take money out of the company. Chuck, the brains of the act, had this idea to falsify tax documents on their Ruggett beats company. Using a guarantor with good credit, he intended to show income and take out several bank loans. AZ had no knowledge of this plan. They knew if AZ was involved, he'd take everything from them.

Weeks go by before AZ hears anything from Erin again. He's in the studio with the music blasting when his blackberry lights up. AZ quickly steps outside to answer the call.

"Yo, who dis?" he says, hearing nervous laughter on the other end.

"It's me, Erin. Remember me?"

"Hi, Erin! Of course, I remember you. Where have you been? AZ eagerly asks her.

"I've been working hard for this money. How are you doing?"

"I'm better now that you called," he says, turning on the charm.

"Is that right? Then why haven't you come to the club to see me yet?" Erin flirts back, hoping AZ would come spend some money on her.

His partners, Chuck and Dennis, are at the strip club almost every night. She believes AZ also has plenty of money to burn too.

Inhaling deeply, AZ decides honesty is the best policy. He'll simply tell Erin he's a pimp. Thinking it's now or never, AZ starts off slowly and shoots his dart.

"You're a big girl. I'm going to keep it real with you. I'm a daddy looking for someone who wants to make some real money." AZ paces nervously back and forth, kicking pebbles around the parking lot waiting for Erin's response. After a long pause, she lets out a loud laugh.

"Where your girls at? You ain't no pimp," she says, catching him off guard.

"I'm talking to one now," AZ laughs, knowing Erin's on to him. "Nah, I really just got back from Miami. I've been sitting low getting my shit together." His statement had some truth to it, so Erin believed him.

"So, what are you looking for? You need a bottom girl to help you recruit?" she asks, suddenly becoming more interested.

It's exactly what AZ needed. Erin was around strippers every day and could easily influence one to join him. He's anxious to get his feet wet but avoids appearing desperate.

"When I come to the club, we can talk about it. How is your music coming along?" AZ asks to change the subject.

"We can talk about music when I come to the studio. I'll start looking for girls right away," she says, staying on topic.

AZ's heart skips a beat. "Alright then; that sounds good to me," he grins, gripping the cell phone tightly.

"Okay, we'll talk later. I have to get back on stage now," Erin says hanging up the phone.

Coming to terms with Erin sets his plan right in motion. AZ stares at the cell phone unable to believe his good fortune.

At work, Erin spots the perfect victim for AZ. She sips a drink at the bar, watching the pretty Filipino dance on stage. Erin's been checking the girl out for a few days now. She seemed timid compared to the other rowdy strippers. After some observation, Erin heads to the locker room to call AZ. He answers the call on the second ring.

"Hi AZ, I found the ideal girl for us. If you're ready, she'll be an easy target," Erin says.

Anxiety takes AZ's breath away. It's been two weeks since he heard anything from Erin.

"I was born ready," he says, nervously choking on his spit.

"How fast can you get to the club?"

"I can be there within the hour," AZ says, quickly ending the call.

Hanging up the phone, his heart races with excitement. He knew tonight was the night. It was either do or die for him. He searched through a bag of clothes on the floor looking for something suitable to wear. Pulling different clothes in and out of the bag, he settles on a sweatshirt and a pair of wrinkled blue jeans. Quickly changing clothes, he sprayed some c ologne, checked himself in the mirror, and walked out of the door.

AZ squints as he walks into the dark, smoke-filled club. He locates Erin on the far side of the room talking to Chuck and Dennis at the bar. After embezzling the money, strip clubs had become their pastime. He makes his way over to the group, oblivious to anyone else in the club. On stage, Shi immediately spots the new fish out of the water. Her eyes lock on his five-foot, ten-inch, muscular body. To Shi, AZ looked nervous in this environment, although something about his dark mandingo features had sex appeal. She found him slightly attractive. The laughing trio fails to notice AZ standing directly behind them.

"Oh shit, look who's here!" Chuck blurts out, grabbing AZ into a bear hug. AZ glances at the big wad of cash in Chuck's hand. His diamond-studded watch and ring also raise suspicion.

"What's good?" AZ says, sitting on a bar stool next to Erin.

"What you drinking?" Chuck asks, then quickly dismisses the idea.

"Forget that. We celebrating with champagne tonight!" Chuck affectionately puts AZ into a chokehold. "Sweetie, bring us over your best bottle of bubbly! My man here never comes to the strip club."

After Chuck hollers to the bartender, he discreetly passes AZ a stack of bills to tip the strippers. AZ takes the money without uttering a word but planned to investigate how Chuck came across it later.

Shi watches the flowing champagne bottles on the other side of the room. After her set on stage, she sashays across the floor to meet the men. Erin sees her coming and pinches AZ to get ready. When Shi approaches them, Erin grabs her by the arm.

"Hi, Shi! How you doing tonight?" Erin says.

Shi narrows her eyes as if to say...*Bitch why are you stopping me?*

Ignoring Shi's mean glare, Erin seizes the opportunity to introduce her. "Shi, this is my friend, AZ."

The sparkling green eyes offer him a gentle smile. She was brightly tattooed with long hair swinging loosely over pierced nipples. To him, she was more beautiful in person than she was on stage. AZ leans back on the stool taking in her full beauty.

"Why they call you Shi?" he slurs, tipsy from the champagne.

"Because I'm Shy," she says, turning around and playfully rubbing her booty against his manhood.

"Whoa!" AZ stumbles off his barstool, dumbfounded by the bold move.

Shi giggles, pleased by the effect she has on him. Embarrassed, AZ frowns at his clumsiness. He's a self-proclaimed pimp, and Shi is out of pocket for treating him this way. Erin chuckles, pretending not to notice the exchange between them.

"I'll let you two get better acquainted," Erin announces, walking away feeling her job was done.

AZ and Shi talked for a while before she got back on stage. By closing time, AZ had convinced Shi to meet him the following day at the studio. Believing AZ is a wealthy record producer, Shi's easily persuaded.

Leaving the Strip club that night, AZ comes straight to my house and packs the rest of his belongings. He sneaks the weed and clothes out in garbage bags to officially begin life as a pimp. For him, meeting Shi is something like the movie *Harlem Nights*. The guy sleeps with the hooker, Sunshine, then calls home telling his wife and kids he's never coming back.

From the start, AZ and Shi's relationship is doomed. AZ acts more like Shi's gigolo boyfriend than her pimp. He moves out of the studio into her cottage right away. Shi gives him money and he lays the pipe. By doing this, he, unfortunately, creates a monster. It's a mistake AZ will regret his entire pimp career.

Their romantic nights don't last very long -- especially after her psycho Italian boyfriend finds out. Angelo is an old sugar daddy Shi's been dating prior to AZ. He is married but considers Shi to be his young mistress. For years, Angelo pampered Shi with the f iner things in life. He spent thousands of dollars to please her. He also pays her rent and car note. When Shi stopped seeing Angelo, he went berserk.

Returning home from work one night, Shi discovers her cottage door ajar. She parks the jeep and steps out to investigate. Creeping down the driveway alone and frightened, she goes to the front door, slightly pushing it open.

"Hello! Is anyone in here?! I'm calling the police!" Shi yells, too afraid to go inside. After several minutes of hearing no noise, she carefully goes into the house and flips the lights on. "Oh, NO! Angelo, what have you done?!" Shi screams out loud.

To her astonishment, the cottage has been destroyed. Looking around, she sees all of her expensive clothes shredded to pieces across smashed furniture. Heartbroken, she goes to the phone, frantically dialing AZ's number. Receiving no answer, she cries softly to herself and bends down to pick up a piece of porcelain at her feet. It was fragments of a lamp given to her by her grandmother before she died. Droplets of Angelo's blood were all over it. Shi assumed he came and did this because she stopped taking his phone calls. Sitting on the sofa, she lit a cigarette as her tears turned to anger.

This damage is unforgivable! The evidence is good enough to call the police on him. Briefly flattered by Angelo's insane jealousy, she decides against it. Instead, she exhales circles of smoke into the air and calls AZ again. This time he answers right away.

"Hey, bae!" AZ says, happy to hear Shi's voice.

"You won't believe what this crazy man did to me," Shi whimpers, looking at the broken lamp in her hand.

"What happened?!" AZ instantly grows angry.

"That asshole Angelo came here and wrecked the place while I was at work. I want to call the police before he comes back."

"Angelo did what?! I'm going to break the little bastard's face. I'm on my way!" AZ says, hanging up hyperventilating.

Everyone in the studio heard the conversation. They all look at him when the call ends. AZ fumes with anger, staring at the floor and thinking about his next move.

"You alright man?" Born asks him. AZ balls his fist, shaking uncontrollably.

"Nah man, this bitch ass nigga broke into my girl's house and tore shit up!"

Born's eyes narrowed.

"Grrr, that's a violation!" he growls, ready for war.

"That shit deserves an ass whupping." KG says, lowering the music on the track board.

"We gonna make him regret he ever met Shi," Chuck says trying to act tough.

They all disregard his idle threat.

"So, what you wanna do?" Lil Ralph says jumping up off of the sofa.

This made AZ even more hyped. He begins breathing heavily, fantasizing about pulverizing Angelo's face. Though within minutes he calms down. Shi already warned him about Angelo being a made man. Thinking logically, he didn't need that kind of smoke. Especially not with the mafia.

"I need to go check on my girl before this clown comes back! Who's with me?!" AZ barks at them.

"I'm down. Let's go knock his ass out!" Born says, itching for trouble.

"I'll go too!" Lil Ralph says.

"I got to finish this beat. Call me if you need me!" KG says, looking dead serious.

"Yeah, we'll be there in a heartbeat if you need us!" Chuck says as the fellas walk out of the studio.

"Shut up, punk! You ain't doing shit! And we taking that damn Armada with us too!" Born laughs, walking out the door.

Eventually, KG tells AZ about the money embezzled from their production company. After it's all said and done, Chuck received several cash loans and luxury vehicles from the scam. The banks never knew what hit them. Now Chuck had no choice but to turn over the keys for the 2008 Nissan Armada to AZ. Either that or get beat up!

Shi was on the cottage steps crying her eyes out when the guys pulled into the driveway. Her face was flushed with tears when AZ hopped out of the Armada with Born and Lil Ralph. AZ walked over, hugging Shi tightly around the waist.

"You okay, baby girl? he whispers in her ear. Shi buries her face in AZ's chest, avoiding eye contact.

"No, I'm not!" Shi snaps at him. AZ helplessly sulks.

A fight with Angelo was not in his plans. He was not there to seek vengeance. His goal was something entirely different.

"Bae, I'm only here to move a few of your things out. I didn't tell the fellas about our drama. It's none of their business. I'll take care of Angelo later," AZ says, squeezing her tightly in his arms. Trusting him, Shi nods her head, wiping tears in his shirt.

"Hi, guys. Thanks for coming. Let me take you inside so we can get started," Shi says dryly, mustering a weak smile for Born and Lil Ralph.

"No problem," Born says winking at her. Even with smeared makeup, Shi was a vision of beauty to him.

Walking inside, the guys see the cottage is turned upside down.

"Damn, this place looks like a tornado hit it!" Lil Ralph blurts out without thinking. AZ shoots him a dirty look.

"Just pick up whatever is salvageable and load it into the truck," AZ says, stepping over rubbish on the floor.

Shi's mouth pops open. She isn't expecting to move out of the cottage. Though, at this point, she is too weak to protest. When AZ's finished loading the last of Shi's clothes into the truck, he comes back into the house for one final look.

"Is that everything, bae?" he asks, sympathetically.

"I think so," Shi says sadly but continues picking through the trash on the floor. Most of her belongings remain in shreds strewn across broken furniture.

"Well let's get out of this dump. The guys are waiting for us in the truck. I have to get them back to the studio."

Shi takes one long look at the place then stomps out the door behind AZ.

Driving to the studio, AZ grins to himself. With Shi's belongings in the SUV, he planned to take her clear across the country. Miami was the perfect place for a pimp to perform smoke and mirrors. Getting Shi out of that cottage is the move he's been waiting for. It was the only way to gain full control over her.

Dropping his friends off at the studio, AZ goes inside to pack some clothes for himself. Returning to the SUV, he drives around the building and parks out back. Underneath the stars was a cozy atmosphere to have his serious talk with Shi.

"Crazy night, huh? AZ says, studying Shi's mood. "You think!" She says, sarcastically.

"You're lucky you wasn't home when that crazy man came there. Men are very territorial. No telling what Angelo might've done to you," AZ says triggering thoughts of fear in Shi's mind. His wicked grin makes her uncomfortable.

Shi pouts, concerned for her well-being.

"I have an idea. Let's get out of New York tonight." AZ says head cocked to the side, grinning. "We can start over somewhere new and exciting! I know a place you can make thousands of dollars at the strip club."

Shi stares in his eyes soaking up every word.

"I told you about Miami. Now let me show you!" AZ says, pulling her into his arms.

"Obviously, I can't go back there. The cottage is in Angelo's name. He leases it for me. What other choice do I have?" Shi says eyes watering from the disappointment of losing her home.

"Aww, baby girl. It's going to be okay. Let's not waste any more time here. If we leave now, we can be in Miami in twenty-four hours!"

Shi shrugs, feeling tired and overwhelmed. AZ attempts to hide his gratification. Though putting the plan into action made his face brighten with enthusiasm. He eagerly starts the engine, drives out of the parking lot, and speeds down the street. A few minutes later, the SUV jumps onto interstate 495. Without having a license, AZ pushes the Armada to eighty miles per hour.

The overhead sign reads, *Welcome to North Carolina*. It's been fourteen hours since AZ and Shi left New York. AZ daydreams while Shi dozes in and out of sleep. Glancing in his rear-view mirror, AZ sees Shi's angelic face peacefully resting on soft pillows. She's wrapped comfortably in bedding from the cottage. He suddenly panics, realizing it's his job to take care of Shi from this point on. He was familiar with Miami though not connected in the pimp game. The only person he could rely on was Sparky. They grew close when AZ lived in Miami at Big Will's mansion. AZ wrinkles his nose thinking about it. Sparky knew exactly where to find Shi a job. *Could he really trust Sparky not to betray him? After all, that was Big Will's right-hand man.* On second thought, he changes his mind about calling Sparky. Big Will's team was always in pursuit of a prostitute. Looking at Shi in the mirror, AZ knew he was very vulnerable with only one girl.

"Hey, sleepy head, wake up! I need you to take this wheel for me."Shi sits up rubbing her eyes when she hears AZ's voice.

"Ahhhh, where are we?" She yawns loudly, looking out the window.

AZ turns up the radio. "Somewhere in Wisconsin" comes blasting through the speakers in answer to her question. T Pain's hit song is played all day long on every radio station.

"That's not funny," Shi says, wiping her eyeglasses with her T-shirt, placing them on her face. "We're in North Carolina," she says, reading the passing sign.

"Yeah, and I need you to drive now. I'm a wanted man in these parts."

AZ frowns, thinking about all the tickets he got from driving Big Will's cars. Without bail money, he couldn't afford that problem now.

"I have to pee. Are we stopping somewhere?" Shi removes the blanket and climbs over the middle console into the front passenger seat.

"A rest stop is up ahead. We can grab something to eat, and you can use the bathroom there. Afterward, you have to drive!" AZ says sharply.

Shi folds her arms, reluctantly nodding her head. AZ gives her a stern look. *Bitch, you should be happy I didn't make you drive this whole damn trip!* AZ knew he better step up his game or he would be the laughingstock of Miami. It was also possible to lose a girl to a more experienced pimp out there.

At eight o'clock at night, they pull into the rest area. AZ deliberately parks far away from the other cars. Shi can't hold her urine anymore. She hops out relieving herself on the side of the vehicle. AZ leans out the passenger window handing Shi her purse.

"Bae, when you're done, go get us some chicken and fries."

KAREN JOY

Shi stands up sucking her teeth, annoyed by the interruption.
AZ smirks, watching her walk away mad toward the food court.
He speculates Shi made at least a few hundred dollars at the club
last night. He planned on cracking for that money when she
returned. It was his duty as a pimp to take every dime she made.

Shi juggles the bag of food crossing the parking lot in high
heels. A gentleman would go help her. AZ just chuckles,
admiring the effort she's making to please him. Once she's
inside of the truck AZ unfolds his plan. Not much of a talker, he
lets his action speak. Finishing his last bite of chicken, he
watches Shi slowly drink the soda. Sucking on her straw arouses
him. He unzips his pants. Reaching over and taking her hand, he
lets it move slowly up and down. Without blinking an eye, she
removes her hand, placing him into her mouth. AZ closes his
eyes, panting heavily. Hearing him moan, she sucks hard like a
professional. He pushes her head down for every inch. Shi
swallows with gurgling sounds.

"Wait, Shi! I don't want to bust."

AZ grabs her around the waist, bringing her across the seat
to him. He pulls up the skirt, sliding her panties to the side. He
swivels his hips into wetness filling her up. Shi breathes hard
thinking it's never like this with Angelo. Eyes closing, she
moans and groans, letting him stretch her open.

"Daddy knows how you like it," AZ says, gyrating with
wicked thrusts.

"Oh, please, daddy, don't stop," Shi begs, straddling wide
and throwing her head back she moans with pleasure and pain.

"That's right, baby girl. Give it to daddy." Breathing heavily,
AZ's voice is hoarse and low.

"Mmmmm." Shi tightens and climaxes.

AZ groans, pushing hard and deep, exploding in ecstasy with
her. Ignoring the passersby, AZ stays inside of Shi's trembling
body. Her eyes burn with passion looking over her shoulder at
him.

36

"Mmmm...that's some good stuff, daddy," Shi says, dismounting him.

Reaching into the food bag, she gets a wet nap and wipes him off.

"Careful with that," AZ grins, feeling himself becoming aroused again though thinks against it because only a square moves with his penis. "Come on, let's get out of here. We got a long ride ahead of us," he says, pulling his pants up. "I need to school you on some things before we get to Miami." He got out of the truck and walked around to the passenger side. Shi's mood was much more jovial now.

"Anything you say, daddy," Shi grins and jumps over the console into the driver's seat.

Trying to remain serious, AZ smiles to himself. Laying pipe always worked for him. He also enjoyed it. Maybe a little too much. In follow-up, he'd give Shi a crash course on the rules of the game. It was a whole different beast from dancing in the strip club. There were many sinister characters lurking out there.

He had to train Shi on how to survive. Any slip up and she'd be charged for the game or worse, kidnapped. He couldn't afford to lose his only bitch. Shi was the breadwinner. AZ looked at her, reasoning she was a smart girl who'll learn quickly.

Shi pulls out of the rest area, merging into traffic. As soon as they get on the expressway, AZ lets the game flow.

"How much money we got in here?" he asks, digging through Shi's handbag. He's smooth like a thief with it, ignoring her disapproving stare.

Some guys are gorilla pimps. They bully, beat, and bruise a chick. Other pimps push drugs into girls to keep them in a fog and out of touch with reality. Lastly, you have the Mack daddy. That was more AZ's style. He liked to portray a smooth lover man. Though don't get it twisted. If a girl kept the money or disrespected AZ, he would put the fear of life in her. Shi, however, believes AZ is a gigolo.

KAREN JOY

Ignoring her frown, AZ comes out of the bag with the money she made from the night before. "In Miami, this is nothing compared to what a bad chick like you can make," he says, pocketing the three hundred dollars. Shi obediently says nothing. AZ's thrilled inside. It's like taking candy from a baby just like Big Will said it would be. AZ proudly sinks back in the seat, quietly drifting asleep for the next couple of miles. Ten minutes later, his eyes pop open.

"Oh, I forgot to tell you something. Miami clubs are fully nude," he says, blinking rapidly.

Shi jerks the wheel startled by his voice.

"Wait! What? I thought you were asleep. Don't scare me like that," she says, staring at him wildly. "I'm not dancing naked. That's illegal!"

AZ's devilish grin lets Shi know she has no choice in the matter. "Watch where you're going!" he barks, ready to grab the wheel.

Taking her eyes off the road too long made him nervous.

"Shi, men in Miami pay big money to see girls naked. It's different from New York. Every club out here competes with each other. Perverts want to feel, touch and taste you. It's your job to provide that fantasy, baby girl."

A glimpse into AZ's eyes convinces Shi. *All men are under the spell of beautiful women, including pimps. Later she'll use this to her advantage.*

"More importantly, Miami is pimp central," AZ goes on to say.

"A working girl should never talk or look at another pimp. Doing so, she may risk being charged by him. That means you will have to pay for his time. If you suspect he's pimping, ask him. A pimp has to tell you. There's rules to this shit,"AZ said as Shi stared at him intently.

"You should be able to identify a pimp. Most will not spend any money on you. They are not tricks. They're in these clubs

38

looking for new product, such as yourself!" AZ raises his voice to emphasize this. "Some pimps are straight forward. They tell you they're pimping and ask you to choose up. This means he wants you to join his hustle. Other pimps are not so direct. They send a bottom bitch to recruit you. She's his main girl, working as his partner to pick up chicks. At first, she'll probably befriend you without telling you she has a pimp. Next, she might invite you to the crib. Don't fall for the okey-doke. It's your job to bring her home to your daddy. Understand!"

Shi nods though doesn't fully comprehend. Listening to the rules, she wonders why AZ's telling her this stuff. *Does he expect me to sell my body? I date customers but that's a little different.*

She thinks to herself. But the stern look on AZ's face has her decide against questioning him.

"Aren't you going to be around to protect me against these pimps and perverts?" Shi interjects, naively. It's the biggest misconception young girls have about the game.

"Of course, I will! I'll always have your back. Nobody is going to mess with my Shi Boogie," AZ says reassuringly.

Obviously, if she's in the field alone and he's at home laying on his ass, he won't be much protection. A pimp will tell a whore whatever she wants to hear to work for him. It's all part of his game. The trickery usually works best with younger girls. Females are more gullible between eighteen to twenty-four. After this they become wiser and stop believing the lies. Pimps will hang out in bus depots, train stations, or anywhere they can find a young girl. He will even go to colleges and high schools for his prey. A pimp lurks wherever there is a damsel in distress. He'll do whatever's necessary to win her over. Beware of this wolf in sheep's clothing!

"Just stay on route I-95 south. Wake me up when you see the sign for Florida," AZ says, laying back and closing his eyes again. He's hopeful Shi's ready to work in Miami.

Shi slows the truck down, letting the speedometer rest at sixty-five miles per hour. Unlike AZ, she's a conservative driver who never likes to speed. It's early morning when she cruises off the road into a nearby McDonald's parking lot. The July sun is scorching hot in Miami.

"Wake up, sleepy head," Shi says using AZ's words.

Opening one eye, AZ looks at the dashboard clock. "I see you made it in good time," he says, kissing her on the lips. Shi winces from the sour smell of weed and alcohol on his breath. "I'm hungry, aren't you?" he says, rubbing his stomach.

"Starving!" Shi says grabbing a bag from the back seat.

Together they hop out of the Armada and go into the fast-food joint for breakfast.

When Shi returns from the bathroom, AZ's already seated in a booth talking on his cell phone. There are two plates of pancakes and cups of coffee on the table in front of him. Preferring an Egg McMuffin, Shi grimaces at the food but sits to eat it anyway.

"So, you telling me Candy left Big Will?" AZ scratches his temple leaning forward on his elbows.

Shi listens carefully to his conversation. Candy was someone she once met when the girl came to New York for a visit.

"All right, all right, Kal. Just give me her number!" AZ frowns, losing patience with Kal. He's heard enough of the babbling. "I'll hit you back," AZ says, hanging up while repeating the number over and over in his head. "Excuse me," he says to Shi, exiting the booth.

She slides to the side letting him pass. AZ walks briskly out of the restaurant. Circling the parking lot with the phone to his ear, he unexpectedly bursts out in laughter.

Shi thinks it's peculiar he's outside making the call. Out of curiosity, she tries to read his lips through the window.

"Hey, bae. What's going on?" she thinks he says.

Candy was Big Will's bottom bitch. Shi wondered what could've happened between them. After a few minutes, AZ opens the restaurant door, waving for Shi to come outside. Only partially done with breakfast, she hops to her feet, grabbing the bags off the seat.

"We making money moves. Chop, chop," AZ grins, holding the door wide open for her. Getting in the truck, Shi expects AZ to say where they're going. When he says nothing about their destination, she lowers the seat, relaxing for the ride.

A slamming door wakes Shi out of her sleep. The Armada is parked inside of a large private garage. AZ is nowhere in sight. There's a pink Cadillac CTS parked next to her. The car is a typical flamboyant Miami whip. It has tinted windows and shiny chrome rims. Shi listens to process sounds coming from outside of the garage. She hears a woman's high-pitched laughter.

"So that's your plan, AZ!" Candy says, letting out a hearty laugh.

"Yup, I got me a bad bitch outside. Shi will make plenty of money here in Miami," AZ says, laughing with Candy. "No but seriously, can you get Shi a job?"

"I don't see why not. Shi is a very beautiful girl. She'll fit right in."

"Good. It'll help with some bills around here," AZ says, walking out of the kitchen with Candy back into the garage. He opens the hatch to get another bag of clothes out of the SUV. Shi sits up, surprising him.

"Oh! You're awake. I didn't want to disturb your sleep. You remember Candy, right?" AZ says to Shi.

Candy walks around the truck and opens the passenger door to give Shi a hug.

"Hey, girl, you're in my part of town now!" Candy says with her squeaky voice echoing throughout the empty garage.

"Miami is a nice place. I'm glad we came," Shi says looking over at AZ, eyeing him suspiciously.

Candy smiles at them and walks back to the house swaying her hips from side to side. "Whew, child, it's hot out here. Y'all come inside when you're done," she says, exiting the garage.

AZ watches her with admiration and then turns his attention to Shi.

"Bae, Candy is going to let us stay here for a while. The mansion is fire. You're gonna love it!"

"Is that right?" Shi frowns at him, rolling her eyes.

AZ pretends not to notice her sarcasm. He's not about to let Shi ruin this for him.

"Forget these bags. Let me show you around the place. It's a beautiful lakefront gated community."

He takes Shi by the hand dragging her into the house. They enter the kitchen, walk across the room, and exit through sliding doors. There's an elevator waiting to take them to the second floor. They step off the elevator into a long hallway. Shi sees one door to the left and two on her right. AZ turns left, passing a staircase with a hanging chandelier.

"Why couldn't we take the stairs, show off," Shi says, sucking her teeth.

"Where's the fun in that?" AZ smirks, squeezing her hand hard.

"When you were sleeping, Candy showed me around. This estate is dope. It has all the amenities we want. There's tennis courts, a spa, and three patio gardens overlooking a sparkling lake. We also have an Olympic size pool and a state-of-the-art fitness center. You can practice your dance moves anytime you want. Miami is everything I promised it would be," AZ raves, smiling at Shi with a twinkle in his eye.

Shi, who's not so convinced with the idea of staying in Candy's house, appeases AZ and agrees, "Wow! I guess you're right. This place sounds fantastic."

"Bae, trust me. You're going to love it here. I promise!"

AZ plants a long, juicy kiss on her lips. In the back of his mind, he was thinking about all the girls he'll bag while living here.

Frustrated without having an exact plan, AZ squints back at himself in the bathroom mirror. The puffy eyes and stubble beard reflect the great time he's having in Miami. The last couple of days playing naked in the pool with Candy and Shi have been a blast. They eat steak and lobster and drink champagne all day. At night they puff, puff, and pass the haze. Now it's time to step up his game. AZ must complete the task of making them both his bitches. It's the only obstacle he faces. Candy can help him overcome it. After all, she did help Big Will build his empire. Working with Candy is a risky move, however. A seasoned whore can steal your girl and pimp her herself. Staring into the mirror, AZ uses long strokes with the razor to erase his beard. Candy and Shi will be home soon from their date. He wanted to look his best when they returned. Stepping back from the sink, AZ gloats at the handsome guy in the mirror. It was a job well done. Once he made Candy choose up tonight, the mansion would be his!

Tossing and turning in bed, Shi wakes to the smell of freshly washed linen and the absence of AZ's warm body. She's back from her date, resting from hours of exhaustion. The client was a rich businessman who requested two girls for an overnight stay. The trick made an offer AZ could not refuse; therefore, Shi was allowed to go with Candy.

Yawning loudly, Shi stretches her lazy body across the bed confirming AZ's not there. He's usually wrapped tightly around her body sweating bullets. Smiling to herself, Shi thinks he might be in the kitchen for a late-night snack. She puts on her slippers and goes to look for him. Halfway down the hall, she gets a strange feeling. There's a light coming from underneath Candy's bedroom door. *What's she doing up this late?* Shi thinks to herself.

"I miss this," AZ groans, voice deep and faint.

"Ugh!" Candy grunts with every deep thrust.

It's barely above a whisper, but Shi hears every word, pressing her ear against the bedroom door. Slightly cracking it open, Shi can hardly believe her eyes. Her mouth pops open. Candy is face-down, ass up on the bed. AZ is steadily pumping from behind.

"AZ! What the hell are you doing?! Stop it!" Shi screams, stumbling backward out of the door. Candy's eyes pop open. She scrambles to cover herself with the blanket at the foot of the bed.

"AZ, you asshole!" Shi yells, running down the hallway.

"Shi, wait! It's not what you think!" AZ fumbles with his boxers to put them on and run after her.

By the time he reaches the room, Shi is screaming, crying, and tearing shit up. Pillow feathers fly everywhere. The mattress is flipped off the bed and she's stomping on his clothes. AZ tries to grab her, but she's too quick. Shi darts out of his reach with a crazed look in her eye.

"What the hell are you doing? You're destroying this girl's house!" he says.

"Fuck you and that bitch, AZ!" she says, hurling pieces of the diamond-encrusted watch he stole from Chuck at him.

"You broke my fucking watch?!" AZ ducks and dives across the bed, tackling Shi.

They fall on the floor rumbling together.

"Shi, you're acting like a fool!" AZ breathes heavily, struggling to restrain her.

He places a knee in her chest, pinning Shi's hands above her head.

"Stupid bitch, what's wrong with you? I'm a daddy nigga! You got me looking crazy in these streets!"

Shi wiggles beneath him. The thought of AZ screwing another woman enrages her.

"Fuck you, pimp! Let me go! I'm getting out of this house! You can have that bitch!" she screams in frustration.

"Okay! I'm letting you go. You better not break nothing else!" AZ says, slowly releasing Shi's arms.

She jumps up, snatches some clothes off the bed, and runs out of the room crying. Once Shi is gone, AZ surveys the damage. The room was in complete disarray. There were holes in the walls and dents on the hardwood floor. Shi literally broke a leg completely off the nightstand. Taking a deep breath, AZ attempts to clean the mess while simultaneously packing their clothes. He props the nightstand against the bed and moves the dresser to cover the holes in the wall. Sitting on the edge of the bed, he wonders where he went wrong. *This stupid bitch thinks I cheated on her. Shi got the game fucked up.*

"Damn! This is all my fault!" he says out loud, kicking a bag of clothes on the floor.

In the truck, Shi curls in a fetal position while AZ tosses bags through the open hatch.

With the last bag inside, he slams the hatch close.

"Hey stupid! I'm going back inside to apologize to Candy," he angrily glares at Shi through the rear window.

She pouts, refusing to look at him. *I know AZ is recruiting a new girl, but seeing him do it is devastating,* she thinks to herself.

Leaping two steps at a time, AZ reaches the second-floor landing. Head hanging low, he dreads the walk down the hall to Candy's room. He listens first before knocking lightly on the door.

"Hey, Candy. You still up?" AZ whispers through the closed bedroom door.

"AZ is that you? Come in."

Opening the bedroom door, AZ's too ashamed to look at Candy who's lying on the bed, half-naked from the waist up.

"You heard the fight?" he asks, lowering his eyes.

"Yeah, I did. Is everything okay?" Candy feigns concern, crawling to the edge of the bed and holding a pillow over her breast. AZ lingers in the doorway, keeping his distance.

"Nah, Shi is wilding. We not gonna be able to stay here anymore. I'll be in touch with you about the damage," he says, quickly leaving the room and closing the door behind him.

"Damage! What damage?!" Candy yells after him.

"I'll call you later about it," he hollers, walking fast down the hallway.

Candy knew AZ wasn't going to call her. He hadn't paid for anything up until this point. Why would he start now?

Riding to the beach in silence without any money, Shi and AZ would have to sleep there for the night. AZ glances at Shi. Even with crocodile tears running down her face, she was still very beautiful to him.

The next day, I received a call from Kal. I was on the computer in my bedroom when the phone rang.

"Hey, what you doin'?" Kal asks, when I pick up the phone.

"I'm working on a new project with Ant Live. What you doing?" I ask him.

Around this time, I was looking for a change in my life. I was searching for property on Long Island to build a country club. I knew it was God's plan to bless me with His favor. I kept receiving signs that big things were coming by His grace.

"Nothing, I'm at this girl's house. She's at work right now, and I'm bored to death. Eventually, I'll be moving out of here. This girl's been getting on my nerves ever since I lost my job at the bus company," Kal babbles in frustration.

It's too much information but I listened anyway. Kal was AZ's friend, and since we were no longer dating, I was curious about the call.

"So, what's going on, Kal?" I ask, wondering what this had to do with me. "I'm just bugging out, thinking things over. Can you come over here so we can talk?" he asks, still being evasive.

"Where are you? Is it that house off of Main Street?"

"Yeah, make a left at the light and come straight down to the beach." "Kal, you have so many women. I can't keep up with them," I say making him giggle. It pleased him to know I thought he was a player. "I'll call you when I'm in the area," I say hanging up the phone.

Thirty minutes later, I pulled into the housing complex and called Kal's phone. Receiving no answer, I parked and waited. Five minutes later, he called me back.

"Hi, Joy Joy," Kal says, nervously.

"What's up? I've been waiting out here for twenty minutes," I say, exaggerating the time.

"I had to wait for this girl to go back to work. She surprised me by coming home for lunch. She'd kill me, finding another woman in her house. I would be kicked out on my ass for sure," Kal says, peeking through the window blind at me.

"You ready?" he asks, jerking his head from side to side, looking up and down the parking lot.

"Ready for what?" I ask, sucking my teeth impatiently.

"When I open this door, you can't hesitate. Get out of the car and come inside quickly. One of her nosy neighbors might see us. You shouldn't have parked in front of our door anyway."

Kal opens the front door for me. Foolishly, I obey his dumb order. I jump out of my car, flying inside like a bat out of hell.

"Damn, man, what's all this secret squirrel stuff about?" I say, laughing loudly, thinking it's safe once inside.

"Shhhh, be quiet. The neighbors might hear you," Kal shushes me, peeking outside to see if the coast is clear.

"I told you we're not getting along right now. I would've come to your house, but I have no gas. Did you bring any trees with you? I'm edgy as hell. I need some smoke to calm down," Kal says, grinning sheepishly.

His jumpy behavior made me nervous too.

"Yeah, I got some bud. I hope this chick doesn't double back on us," I say, sitting on the couch, taking out the weed.

"Hurry up and roll something. I haven't smoked all day."

"Is that the only reason you called me over here?" I ask, annoyed by him rushing me.

Kal smiles and sits on the couch next to me.

"That and I have somebody for you to talk to," he rubs his palms together and picks up the telephone.

"Oh yeah. Who's that?" I ask, trying to figure out who he's calling. Kal continues dialing without answering me.

"Back on your secret squirrel stuff, I see." He places a finger over his lips, silencing me.

"More rolling, less talking," he says, turning his attention to the person on the phone. "Hi! She's here now. Wanna talk to her?" Kal grins, handing me the phone. He can hardly contain his excitement.

"Who's this?" I ask him, wary of the call.

"Just talk to them," he says, without revealing a name.

"Hello, Karen," the female says in a high squeaky voice.

"Hello, who is this?" I ask, looking at Kal curiously.

"Talk to her." He motions for me to continue the conversation.

"My name is Candy. You don't know me, but I've heard a lot about you."

I listened to the woman talk without interruption. I wanted to see where this was going.

"I know AZ and his girlfriend, Shi," she says, making me tense. "I just thought you should know they were staying here with me in Miami."

Whoa! She strikes a nerve. My face twists in anguish. Seeing my reaction, Kal squirms with delight. He hits the speaker button to hear the conversation.

"So, what you telling me for?" I say, trying to conceal my anger.

Candy ignores the question and proceeds, "I told Kal sending them here was a bad idea. The pigs never cleaned up after themselves. All they did was sleep, eat, and shit all day. The lazy bums didn't even pay bills." She hesitates, waiting for my response.

Letting my guard down, I fall right into her trap.

"The bum ass nigga did the same thing here in New York! He left me with a high electric bill and no money. He's good for nothing. I'm glad he's somebody else's problem now," I say, but not truly meaning it.

It hurt feeling abandoned by AZ. In my anger, I let the words flow freely until it was too late to take them back. No sooner than I say it I regret it. Kal talks into the speaker with me.

"Candy, I told you how she felt about him. Right, Joy Joy," he says, looking at me sympathetically.

Candy sighs, "Karen, I'm just telling you this in case he tries to come back. Believe me, it sounds like you're better off without him. I have to go now, but it was nice talking to you," she says, seemingly proud to put a nail in AZ's coffin.

Hanging up, I look at Kal not fully understanding his motive. It was an odd conversation. To me, it's a sucker move on his part. I stay a few minutes longer to finish smoking and then make an excuse to leave. On the ride home, I gasp looking at myself in the rear-view mirror. Analyzing the situation, I figured the whole thing out. *It was a setup! Candy still lives in one of Big Will's mansions. Kal sent AZ and Shi there to trick them. The plan to steal Shi for Big Will didn't work. AZ dodged a bullet by leaving Candy's house. When the plan failed, they called me to completely annihilate him. It was a sneaky, traitorous move. Going forward I had to watch my back where Kal was concerned.*

In Miami, AZ drops Shi off in front of the strip club. He kisses her goodbye and drives away hoping she gets hired there. Counting the money in his pocket, AZ is down to the last few dollars. They've been sleeping in the Armada and washing up at gas stations since leaving Candy's house two days earlier. Tonight, they desperately needed somewhere to stay.

Shi has the jitters standing in front of the strip club. She's nervous about dancing fully nude. Puckering for one last pull on the cigarette, she tosses the butt on the ground. The sign above the door reads, *Boobie Tap Two*. Shi reluctantly opens the front door and goes inside. Walking through the dark lobby, Shi squints to focus. A big hairy hand moves a black curtain aside for her to step through.

"Hello, can I help you?" The husky bouncer stares at Shi in awe. To him, she's a stunning beauty. Her green contact lens sparkled at him under the dim light. Shi knew the effect she had on men. Recognizing the bouncer was caught like a deer in highlights boosts her ego.

"I'm here to fill out a job application," Shi says, flirtatiously flipping long, black wavy hair over one shoulder.

"Sure, right this way." The bouncer hurries to move a second curtain so Shi can enter the empty club.

Two well-dressed men are seated at the bar drinking beers. They watch a lone dancer attempt to spin around a pole on the stage. Shi wrinkles her nose, following the bouncer to the back of the club.

"Wait right here, someone will be with you in a minute," the bouncer says pointing at a small chair for Shi.

She sits in front of a door labeled *Management*.

A half-hour later, a short, creepy bald guy opens the office door. "Hi, I am Jerry, and you are?" he asks, holding his hand out for Shi.

"Hi, I'm Shi. I'm here to fill out an application," she says, happily shaking his clammy palm.

The manager undresses Shi with his eyes, making her even more nervous than she already is.

"Come into my office. Let's see what I can do for you," Jerry says to her.

Shi follows him thinking, *what does that mean?* In the office, Jerry takes out an application from the desk drawer and hands the paper to Shi.

"Have you ever danced before?" he asks, glaring at her over specs sitting on the tip of his nose.

"Yes, sir!" Shi says anxiously.

"Well, this should be easy for you. Do you have some identification?" She searches through her handbag, coming out with a license for him.

"This is New York State issued. Do you have a local address?" he asks looking at the card.

Shi gives him Candy's address angrily thinking she'll never go back there again.

"What hours are you available to work?" Jerry asks copying the license on a machine behind them.

"Anytime!" Shi says enthusiastically.

"Well, unlike clubs in New York, our bar is fully nude," he says turning around to face her. "The girls here dance three records. On the third record they finale with a strip tease becoming fully nude," he says with a weird smirk.

Shi completes the application, awkwardly handing it back to him. After reading it, he sets the piece of paper on the desk. Leaning back in the chair, he clasps his fingers behind his neck.

"That completes the written part," he says to her.

Shi stands to leave believing the interview is over.

"Now take off your clothes," he says, calmly.

"Take off my clothes?!" Shi repeats, thinking she misunderstood him.

"Yeah, is that a problem? I like to see the merchandise.

Oh shit! This fool is trying to screw me. Sweating profusely, Shi doesn't know what to do next.

"Don't you want me to audition in front of the customers?" she asks, backing away toward the door.

"Just pull up your top, honey," he chuckles at her discomfort. "I want to see them titties," the pervert says, leaning forward in his chair.

"Oh, you serious?"

"I am!" He exhales, annoyed by her stalling.

Looking away from him, Shi peels off the top layer of clothing. Half-naked, from the waist up, her pierced nipples poke out at him.

He licks chapped lips, groping his pecker underneath the desk. "Very nice, honey."

"So, do I have a job?" Shi asks, feeling humiliated.

"You can start right now," he grins, satisfied by what he saw. "Your regular shift is seven at night to four in the morning," he mutters, eyes glued on her breast.

Without thanking him, Shi quickly dresses and rushes out the office.

"The locker room is in the back on the right, honey," he hollers after her.

Sitting on a bench in the safety of the locker room, Shi stares in the mirror, calling AZ.

"Hey, bae!" AZ says, picking up on the first ring. Shi was still salty about Candy and wasn't sure about giving AZ every dime she earned tonight.

"How'd it go?" AZ asks, hopeful Shi got the job.

Shi thought AZ dropped her off and left. Actually, he circled the block and came right back, parking across the street. He watched Shi the entire time she smoked the cigarette. He couldn't afford to lose sight of his only investment. It was a trick he learned from Big Will. Always keep your eye on the prize.

"The interview was awkward, but I got the job," Shi says, not wanting to disclose many details.

"That's good! When do you start?" AZ asks, hoping it's tonight.

"I'm working now! I get off at four o'clock in the morning. I'll let you know when to come get me."

"Okay, bae, love you! See you tonight," AZ hangs up with no intention of waiting for Shi's call.

Looking at the dashboard clock, it was two o'clock in the afternoon. He planned to go inside of the club in a couple of hours and take whatever money she had. Reclining the seat, AZ closed his eyes until that time came.

In the dressing room, Shi changed clothes twice waiting for her next set. She wanted to look her sexiest for the men in the club. Dabbing her makeup in the mirror, she hears the deejay calling her name. Walking out on the floor, Shi surveyed the crowd in search of the big spenders. She climbed quickly on stage and did a backflip landing in a split.

"Ouu, Ahh!" Onlookers stand and applaud.

With all eyes on her, the remarkable talent took full control. The superb dancer is a cross between a ballerina and a skillful gymnast. Shi did a series of dizzying spins around the pole. The dance was so impressive a flurry of ten and twenty-dollar bills landed at her feet. Ending the set, Shi came off stage to work customers at the bar. She tossed back shots of liquor, twisting and winding between horny legs. The drunken patrons pushed wads of money between her firm tits and thighs.

AZ overslept. By the time he slipped into the club, it was Shi's last set. He sat in the cut, watching her closely. Scanning the room for more victims, Shi eventually came across his face. They locked eyes and she made her way over to him. "Hey, stranger," Shi slurred from the heavy drinking.

"What's up? AZ mumbles, swallowing his vodka and pineapple juice.

"When did you get here?" Shi asks, seductively rubbing his leg.

She wonders if AZ saw how much money she made.

"I just got here," he said, glancing around to see who's watching them. "I fell asleep in the truck. How much money we got?"

Shi, sitting on the bar stool next to AZ, slipped two folded bills into his palm. After the incident with Candy, she thinks it's best to stash some money for herself.

Looking at the forty dollars, AZ knows it's not enough money to rent a room for the night.

"Shi, do you see those drunk men in the corner?" He points to a crew of rowdy guys packed in a booth.

Shi turns around to look at them.

"Don't be so obvious; just go over there," AZ whispers to her.

Finishing the drink, AZ loses sight of Shi. Suddenly there's a loud commotion coming from that corner. The bouncers run in that direction, but AZ's vision is obstructed. He stands to get a better look. The men in the corner are beefing about some bitch robbing them.

Concerned, AZ moves closer to the ruckus. At this point, all of the bouncers run out of the back door. Looking up, AZ sees an exit sign above the door. He follows the security into the parking lot, discovering police activity outside. In the midst of confusion, AZ spots Shi in the back seat of a squad car with tears rolling down her face. Stricken with panic, he races to the squad car.

"Hey, get back!" The police officer says, pushing AZ in the chest.

"Wait, that's my girl! Why is she in the back of a police car?!" AZ asked, heart pounding rapidly.

His hysterical behavior brings more officers over to the scene.

"What happened to my girl? What's going on?!" AZ insists on answers, but they ignore him and continue blocking his path to the police car. When Shi opens her mouth to speak, AZ sees the blood and missing teeth.

"Oh NOOO! What happened to her teeth?!" Feeling light-headed, AZ buckles at the knees. "She needs medical attention! Let me help her!" he insisted, pushing forward and pleading with the police to let him go.

They aggressively restrained him and showed no sympathy for Shi.

"She assaulted a police officer! She's going to jail!" One officer yelled at him.

AZ watched in agony as they drove Shi away with blood drizzling out of the side of her mouth. That whole night AZ couldn't sleep. Ridden with guilt, he tossed and turned in the back of the Armada. A burning sensation sat in the pit of his stomach. Tears streamed down his face as he pictured Shi in the back of that police car. *Shi's missing teeth is all my fault! If only I hadn't sent her to those guys in the booth! Now I have no money to get her out of jail!* AZ sat up, wiping his eyes. *I got to pull myself together. Shi needs my help. This pity party is over!*

Reaching into the glove compartment, AZ got some weed and a backwood to roll himself a blunt. He rolled the blunt, lit it, and took a few pulls to relax when an idea popped into his head.

"Sparky can help me!" he said out loud.

Sparky has access to all of Big Will's resources for situations like this. It's just part of the game. Grimacing from the pain in his stomach, AZ put the blunt out in the ashtray. *But what part of the game is Shi losing her teeth? Damn, baby girl, I got to get you out of this mess. I'll call Sparky in the morning. He'll know exactly what to do.* AZ laid back, drifted into a hazy fog, and let the weed overtake him.

———————

Sparky's voicemail comes on.

"Hello, your dime, my time. Leave it at the beep."

"Hey, Sparky, it's me, AZ. Hit me when you get this message. It's an emergency, bro. You got my number."

At nine-thirty in the morning, it's sweltering hot in the truck. AZ's a bundle of nerves sitting in front of the courthouse. He watches court officers, judges, criminals, lawyers, and delivery men assume their normal day of business. The cops took Shi away five hours earlier with blood gushing out of her mouth. Cringing from the thought of her pain, AZ wonders if they took her to the infirmary. Frustrated, he begins rolling his third blunt of weed roaches. Jail is the last place he wanted Shi to be. Dade County had the worst police officers in the country. AZ knew this firsthand.

Looking at his cellular, AZ realizes he missed Sparky's call. *Shit, my phone's on silent.* AZ pushes the redial button as fast as his fingers will allow.

"Hey, you alright?!" Sparky answers right away.

"Aww, man, I'm so glad to hear your voice," AZ says, breathing a sigh of relief.

"My phone was off all night. Soon as I got your message, I called right away, but you didn't answer," Sparky says.

"I know, I'm bugging. Had my phone on silent and missed your call. You won't believe what happened to me, man. I had my girl working out here last night. She got locked up, but that's not the half of it. The cops fucked her up, bro. She's hurt really bad, Sparky. I need your help getting her out, man."

Sparky lets out a nervous grunt.

"Ugh, What the hell happened to her?!"

"I really don't know," AZ says sadly.

"Well, I'm home now. Come over. You remember the address, right?"

"I sure do. I'm on my way."

A wave of comfort sweeps over AZ on the ride to Sparky's house. He hasn't seen his boy since the last time he was in Miami. It would be good to see his old friend again, especially under the current circumstances.

Sparky's front door is wide open when AZ arrives. He parks the Armada in the driveway and walks right into the house without knocking.

"Hello! Anybody home?" AZ calls out from the hallway. "In here, AZ!"

Sparky's playing video games when AZ walks into the living room. Sparky was a huge guy, much taller and heavier than AZ. He pauses the game, flashes a big smile, and stands to hug AZ.

"What's up, man? How long you been in Miami? Why didn't you call me when you got in town?" Sparky asks, returning to the game, clicking the controller buttons.

"I came down with my girl. I was trying to get some money before looking you up. You know a nigga had to get right first, but shit went crazy wrong."

A lump forms in AZ's throat. He sits on the sofa to compose himself.

"Man, they hurt her bad, Sparky. They knocked all my girl's front teeth out!"

Sparky drops the remote control, places his hand over his mouth and says, grimacing,

"Wait! What?! That sounds crazy! How the hell did that happen?"

"I still don't know. One minute we're in the club and Shi's entertaining customers.

The next minute she's out back in a police car with her teeth knocked out. Blood was everywhere! The cops wouldn't let me near her. I felt so helpless seeing my girl that way."

AZ frowns, overwhelmed with animosity for the cops. Sparky's eyes grow narrow.

"I hate the cops. So sorry that happened to her," he says, jumping to his feet, and going into the kitchen.

"Let me make some phone calls and see if we can get her out," Sparky yells from the other room.

Exhausted, AZ sits back on the sofa to relax. Shi was relying on him to get her out. No one knew she was in Miami but him. He was grateful for Sparky's help. Sparky returns with the phone in his hand.

"I'm on the line with the bail bondsman. Give him Shi's first, and last name and date of birth. He'll get some information from the courthouse," he says passing AZ the phone. AZ's hand trembles taking it. He answers the bondsman's questions and hands the phone back to Sparky.

"Whatever you can do, man, we appreciate it," Sparky says to the bondsman, walking back into the kitchen.

The men play video games until the phone rings thirty minutes later. Sparky jumps to his feet running into the kitchen to answer it. Watching him pace back and forth talking to the bondsman makes AZ anxious. Sparky finally hangs up the phone and returns to the living room.

"Shi's being charged with assaulting a police officer. Her bail is five thousand dollars. It's going to cost you five hundred dollars plus collateral to get her out. You got that?" Sparky frowns, believing AZ doesn't.

"You know I don't." AZ says, taking a deep breath. "Before Shi got locked up, she only gave me a measly forty bucks. I can't even fill up the gas tank with that amount," AZ grumbles in disappointment.

"Sparky, call that bond guy back. Tell him to make arrangements to get Shi out. I'm calling New York to get that money," AZ sighs, scrolling through his phone contacts.

CHAPTER III
THE MANSION

It's July 15th, 2008. Shi's been in jail all night long. With no money to get her out, AZ must rely on his gift of gab. He and Sparky negotiate over the phone with the bail bondsman. AZ fast talks the guy into accepting one hundred and fifty dollars with no collateral for Shi's release.

However, getting Shi out will still be no easy task. AZ now has to get the money from women he betrayed. His first call is to his baby's mama in New York. She has his youngest daughter and is still very much in love with the creep. With no hesitation, she sends him a Western Union to cover the bond. Afterwards, AZ calls me.

I refuse to pick up the phone when I see his number on caller Id. He calls every fifteen minutes until I finally relinquish.

"What do you want, AZ?!" I yell angrily at him.

"Karen, I'm in trouble," he mutters, trying to spark some empathy from me.

Here comes the bullshit! I think to myself.

"Did you hear me?"

"AZ, what else is new?" I grit my teeth, satisfied he's met his fate.

I was thrilled listening to him beg, knowing he brought so much anguish to everyone else.

"I desperately need your help. Please send me some money."
My stomach knots hearing him say this. I take the phone away from my from ear, staring at it in disbelief. *Is this idiot really asking me for money?*

"Nigga, is you crazy!" I scream, letting out all of my frustration.

This was followed by a slew of curse words.

Expecting this reaction, AZ humbly listens without uttering a word. When I'm finished with the rant, he slowly begins telling me the story. AZ's words weigh heavily on my heart. The heinous attack on Shi is too much for me to bear. It's so shockingly sad, I can't be upset with him anymore. My good nature compels me to help them. I book a hotel room for them to stay at upon Shi's release.

With many nights of prayer and by the grace of God, I came into some money. I was fortunate enough to move into a mini mansion with plans of starting a country club. The newly renovated, six-bedroom, four-bathroom estate sat on seven acres of land in the middle of nowhere. There was no view of the property from the street. Visitors had to come thirty yards through a tree-lined winding driveway just to see the location. The forty-five hundred square foot mansion was painstakingly beautiful.

Entering the house, an open floor plan greeted guests with high cathedral ceilings surrounded by white crown molding. A ceiling-to-floor brick fireplace adorned the large living room. Massive white columns separated colossal windowpanes extending the full length of the room. A sea of hardwood floors covered a master bedroom, sunroom, and guestroom. To my delight, a contemporary kitchen with stainless steel appliances was in the middle of it all. In addition to that, there were two bathrooms on every floor. The jacuzzi in the basement was large enough to seat five people. The master bathroom had a four-jet tub and a stand-alone shower. The guest bathroom was decorated with a fancy glass bowl sink and waterfall faucet. The second floor had three plush carpet bedrooms. A beautiful glass chandelier hung on the sky roof, illuminating a long catwalk. The property was a dream come true. It was the perfect location for my Urban Black Country Club.

A venture capitalist showing interest in the business plan offered to invest a quarter of a million dollars to see the project to fruition. The only catch was I had to help her daughter with a music career. To do this, I needed KG's help. He and I were both Pisces, innovative, and very creative. Reaching out to KG, I had no idea he was at odds with AZ too.

"Hi, KG!" I say enthusiastically when he answers my call.

"Hey, Karen Joy! What's going on?"

KG sounded very upbeat and in good spirits.

"Well, Kay, we haven't spoken in a while. During this time, I've landed a great opportunity that I want to involve you in."

Waiting patiently for KG's response seemed like forever. "Do you hear me?" I finally asked him.

"Yeah," Is all he said with little interest.

"KG, I just brokered a great deal for some prime real estate. I intend to build a country club on the land. The owner wants to get her daughter into the music business. I need your help with some music production."

Again, KG said nothing. I guessed it was going over his head.

"Listen, I want to bring her to the studio. We can see what happens from there," I say as a last-ditch effort.

"Is she spending any money?" KG asks as if missing my whole point.

"Is a quarter of a million dollars enough for you?!" I say to ignite his flame.

"Now you're talking my language. Bring her right over!" KG laughs, giving me some relief.

"I'll set it up and get back to you." "Okay, Karen Joy. Talk to you later."

Sitting on the back porch of the mansion, I gazed at the twinkling stars above. Getting KG's help was only half my battle. The rent was due on the estate in two weeks. My limited funds were hardly enough to satisfy the bill. I had to get some steady income fast. Thinking about a plan made me reach for the phone to call Kal. He was a Virgo like AZ. Both men were cold and calculating. But Kal was more sinister. His phone rang twice before he answered it.

"What up, Joy Joy? I'm out of that bitch's house now!" Kal says, giggling.

"Aww, for real!"

"Yeah, I'm homeless. Living in my car."

Hearing Kal say this gives me the ammunition I need. Smiling to myself, I can hardly contain my happiness.

"You're not homeless. You have a mother to live with."

"Nah, I'm a grown man. I'm not trying to live with my mother, especially without having a job," Kal giggles again.

"Well, I'm staying at this mansion in Middle Island. I'm working on building a country club. Ant live is supposed to help, but he's going to jail. Right now, I'm here all alone," I pause, letting the words sink in.

Kal takes the bait, hook line and sinker. "Huh! You got a mansion?! I need to see the place. If it's right, I got the perfect hustle. My girl, Liza, can pay for the whole spot!" Kal babbles on, but I only half listen.

"That's great. I have many empty rooms over here." I say, trying to maintain my cool. Though inside, I was jumping for joy.

"Dope! I'll call you in the morning for the address!"

Ending the call, I was more excited than he was. I figured Kal was planning to pimp this girl, but I really didn't care. All I cared about was getting my hands on that quarter of a million dollars to start the country club.

The next morning, I sat on the back porch enjoying a beer, soaking in some sun. The doorbell and my blackberry rang simultaneously. On my way to the front door, I answered the unfamiliar call.

"Hello," I said apprehensively.

"Hi, it's me. I really need your help again."

Sensing AZ was in trouble, I didn't want to hang up on the idiot. I covered the mouthpiece and answered the front door.

"Hold on! I'm coming!" I yelled to whoever continuously knocked on the door.

Frowning, I returned to AZ's call.

"What is it this time?!" I asked, not really caring to know.

Like everyone else, I was fed up with his ass.

"Since Shi got her teeth knocked out by the cops, she can't work anymore. We have no more money or place to stay. We've been sleeping in the truck on the beach." AZ blurts out with no shame in his game.

I stare at the phone unmoved by this.

"How is this my problem?" I snap, contemplating hanging up on him.

In addition to AZ leaving me to become a pimp, I still had a very high electric bill from his unsuccessful weed venture.

"Ugh, I wouldn't ask you, but I have nowhere else to turn. We are stranded." AZ grunts pitifully.

"I know that's right. You screw everybody over who cares about you!" I say with a hint of empathy.

"So does that mean you'll help us?!" AZ asked, sounding very relieved.

Like a sucker, I still deeply cared for him. With much regret, I agreed to send him some more money.

Peeking through the opaque glass in the front door, I was ecstatic to see Kal and his friend outside. I eagerly opened the door for them. Kal's goofy grin outshined the young girl standing next to him.

"You don't know how glad I am to see you," I say to him.

"Really? I couldn't tell as long as you had us waiting," Kal laughs, giving me a big hug.

"I'm so sorry. I was on the phone with my problem child, AZ."

Kal shakes his head and glances at his friend. "Joy Joy, this is Liza."

She's the dancer I told you about who works at Blush. Liza, this is Joy Joy. She's my peoples!"

Even with makeup on, Liza was a bland sickly-looking girl with short, blonde, spikey hair that stuck up awkwardly off her head. Offering a weak smile, I was hopeful she earned as much money as Kal said she did.

"Come inside!" I say, damn near ripping Kal's arm out of the socket. Liza strolls in with us.

"What did that fool AZ want?" Kal asks, being nosy.

"AZ's in a jam as usual," I blurt out without thinking.

Kal narrows his eyes at me. "I hope you're not going to help him with all that he's done to hurt you."

"Of course not. I'm not thinking about AZ," I say, dropping my eyes, too embarrassed to look at him.

"Good, 'cause me and Liza are here as long as he's not."

Kal blows Liza a kiss. She smiles at him with a twinkle in her eye. I can tell she's very smitten.

"This place is really nice, Joy," Liza says, admiring the large open space.

"Yeah, it's dope, Joy Joy. How you come across this place?" Kal asks, bouncing around the big empty room.

"That's a different story for a different time. For now, let me show you around the place."

I was pleased they liked the spot. I urgently needed their money.

Kal and Liza ended up staying in the master bedroom on the first floor. I moved into one of the guestrooms on the second floor. Us three, lived peacefully for about two weeks until I received another dreaded phone call from AZ. Everybody was seated in the living room chatting at the table when my cell phone on the kitchen counter rang. The vibration sent an echo through the empty mansion alerting Kal and KG to the incoming call.

"Let me get that," I say, jumping up from my seat to answer it.

"Hey, bae!" AZ says to me when the line connects.

Kal and KG curiously stare at me. I turn my back to them for some privacy.

"Who is it?" I mumble, pretending not to know.

"It's me! Aren't you happy to hear my voice? When I don't answer him, it's obvious I'm not.

"Guess what?" AZ says, remaining upbeat. "What?!" I ask, impatiently.

"I want you to know your man is on his way back to New York! Text me the address to the mansion," he says.

Then the line goes dead. Looking at the cell phone in my hand, a lump forms in my throat. I turn around, Kal and KG are still watching me. Their eyes follow me back to the card table.

"Who was that on the phone?" Kal asks suspiciously.

"It probably was AZ," KG sighs, shaking his head.

"What he want?" Kal asks, inhaling deeply.

By this time, life at the mansion is beginning to unravel. Kal's been trying to pimp Liza but she's playing him. She claims to only make a hundred and fifty dollars at the strip club every night. But he and I both knew that was strange for a dancer. Therefore, one night I went to the strip club and spoke to the bouncer myself. He informed me that Liza earned over a thousand dollars every night. I knew then Kal's pimping game was weak. He was too busy letting her suck the life out of him on the rides home from work to pay attention to her cash. It was apparent to me Liza was doing this to keep him preoccupied. It didn't take us long to discover Liza was spending most of her stash on drugs.

"Yeah, that was AZ. He's bringing his toothless dancer here to the mansion," I say making Kal hop out of his chair.

"AZ's doing what?! That nigga got you whipped. KG, tell Joy what AZ did to us in Miami."

KG smirks and takes a Backwood out the pack to roll some weed. "I got my money, so I really don't care," he says cracking open the cigar, emptying the guts into the pack.

"Well, I care. I'll tell you exactly what he did to us!" Kal says, becoming very upset.

It turned out, at some point, Kal and KG were in Florida with AZ. Somewhere along the line, they thought they were in a pimping agreement with him. They expected AZ to share half the money he received from girls with them. Any real pimp knows that's ridiculous. There's only one leader in a pack of wolves. The problem is they brought Erin to Florida as part of the deal. When Kal and KG couldn't get any money from Erin, AZ took over. They, of course, felt jilted. Disappointed things aren't going their way, KG and Kal end up selling Erin to Big Will. Now, the two of them were upset with AZ.

"Taking that damn trip to Florida left me homeless. Me and my girl broke up after that," Kal snarls at me.

I look at him, jaws swelling with air. I could hardly hold back the laughter. *It's no wonder KG didn't tell me this foolish story.* I thought to myself.

"Kal, what AZ did sounds really bad. I'm only letting him come here because his mom is gravely ill. She's on her death bed. AZ wants to see her before she passes."

Even though I was telling the truth, neither bought my story. They looked at each other but said nothing. In retrospect, I felt awful. Allowing AZ to return was a stupid move on my part -- particularly after they warned me. It could mean blowing my entire deal with them. It was like holding a knife to my own throat.

"Fellas, I'm going to keep what you said under advisement. AZ will only be here for a short time," I say, trying to smooth things over with them.

Giving me the side-eye, they continue puffing and passing the blunt.

AZ arrives at the end of July on a beautiful Sunday morning. His truck comes roaring down the driveway blasting *Pop Champagne* by Jim Jones and Ron Browz. Hearing the loud music makes me run to the second-floor window and look outside. I see AZ behind the steering wheel with Shi seated on the passenger side. Excited, I shout out for Kal but receive no answer. He and Liza obviously slept through the noise. I ran downstairs to greet them myself. Before AZ's arrival, Kal decides he'll be cordial to them. He concludes that the mansion is big enough for everyone to live comfortably. Technically, I still lived around the corner at my other house. I only stayed at the mansion to keep an eye on the occupants and my investment.

I peeked through the glass window in the front door, patiently waiting for the truck to come to a full stop. Not knowing what to expect, I nervously walked out on the front porch. AZ steps from the Armada with a big grin on his face.

"Hi!" he says, walking over hugging me tightly.

Looking into AZ's face, I see the eyes of a stranger. *Who is this man I once shared my bed with?*

AZ looked the same but something about him was cold and oddly different. At this very moment, Shi steps out of the truck. The thin, frail girl is clothed in a white T-shirt and sweatpants. Her hair is rolled in a bun on top of her head, giving the appearance of an innocent child. Even without makeup, Shi is strikingly beautiful. AZ motions for her to come closer. I smile but feel a slight pang of jealousy.

"Karen, this is Shi. Shi, this is Karen," AZ says standing between us with a look of guilt.

Shi bashfully hides behind him. It's apparent she's uncomfortable meeting his ex-girlfriend for the first time. She smiles, covering her mouth so I won't see the four missing teeth.

"Don't worry about that. You're still very pretty," I say to her.

Glancing at AZ, he's very uneasy. He awkwardly walks to the truck and unloads their luggage.

"What up, boy boy! You finally made it!" Kal says, skipping down the front steps of the porch, smiling.

"Yeah man! I'm so glad to be out of that state," AZ drops the bags from his hand and gives Kal a big handshake hug.

"What's up, Shi?" Kal beams, happy to see them both.

"Hey, Kal," Shi says in a deep hoarse voice, not matching her small frame.

"AZ, let me help you with these," Kal says, picking up the two suitcases.

Together we walk inside to a small empty room on the second floor.

"I don't have any furniture yet," I say, opening the bedroom door for them to see.

AZ 's unbothered by it. He drops the luggage in the middle of the floor. "Shi. unpack these bags for us," he barks before walking out of the room behind Kal and me.

The three of us go downstairs into the kitchen.

"I know y'all got some smoke for me. I've been dying to puff since we left Florida," AZ says, feening for the weed.

"I got you. I'll be right back." Kal says, dashing off to his room. When AZ stares at me, my bottom lip quivers.

"So that's your new girl, huh?"

He takes a long deep breath before answering me.

"That's my dancer. She gets money. You need money for this place, right? Well, she gets it. And don't come at me with no square shit. I'm a daddy, nigga!" he snaps with no regard for my feelings.

Before I can drill him further, Kal returns, tossing a bag of smoke and a wrap on the kitchen counter.

"Roll up, my gee," Kal says to AZ.

Shi walks in, lovingly folding her arms around AZ's waist. He returns the public display of affection with a kiss on her forehead.

"Bae, why don't you and Karen go out on the deck? Let me smoke with my man, Kal," AZ says, ignoring my evil expression.

I keep my eyes glued on them, green with envy. *I can't believe this bastard called her bae in front of me.* Kal, anticipating some friction, glances at me. I'm cool as ice though.

Deciding to choose my battles wisely, I fight back tears and grab a beer out of the fridge. Refusing to let them see me sweat, I turn on my heels and head straight for the back door. Shi and I take seats on some folding chairs on the back deck. Neither having much to say, we look out into the horizon. Eventually, I start a conversation about her teeth.

"So, I hear you and AZ had a rough time in Florida," I say, leaning back in the chair, eyeing her closely.

"Ouch," Shi winces in pain, grabbing hold of her mouth.

I realize then she's reliving the horrible incident in her head. Waiting for her answer, I take a swig of the forty-ounce.

"I still can't believe the cops did this to me," Shi says, eyes watering.

"A cop did that to you!" I say as if I didn't know.

Shi was only ninety pounds soaking wet. I couldn't imagine what type of threat she posed to a gun-toting police officer.

"Yup, I still can't believe it myself. One minute, I'm in the strip club dancing on stage. The next minute, I'm on the floor in the manager's office, kicking and screaming for my life. The security guards dragged me in there and held me down accusing me of stealing some money. Before I knew what was happening, this big cop was pulling me to my feet. He told me to face the brick wall so he could handcuff me. Once subdued, he forcibly pushes the back of my head. He catches me off guard, slamming my face into the brick wall. The impact shatters my four front teeth making them crack and crumble in my mouth. All I could do was collapse to my knees and burst out in tears from the excruciating pain. Blood spews everywhere. The frightened pigs lift me to my feet, rushing me outside to a waiting police car. Everything after that is a blur. Now I'm uglyyyy!" she says, covering her mouth and crying."

Saddened by the spectacle, I forget about my jealousy and rush over to hug her frail little body. "That's not true, you're still very pretty," I say, squeezing her tightly. AZ steps through the sliding glass doors just in time to see us embrace.

"What's going on out here?" he asks, glaring at me intensely.

Kal comes out with Liza underneath his arm. They look at us with bloodshot eyes.

"Aww, don't cry," Liza says, interrupting the awkward moment.

Shi nervously chuckles, wiping away her tears.

"Hi, I'm Liza. You smoke?" she asks Shi, walking over and offering her the blunt.

"Thanks, Liza, I needed this." Shi takes the blunt, pulling hard on it.

AZ continues looking at us. I notice his overly protective stare and it reignites my jealousy.

That same night, AZ goes to Brentwood to visit his mom. Her illness is too far gone. It's the last time he will see her. She dies with him at her bedside. When he comes back to the mansion and tells us, I couldn't help thinking it's a sacrifice for the lifestyle he chose in the devil's playground. His return to New York is the end of many good things.

In the days to follow, I stayed at the mansion most nights to work on the situation with AZ and Shi. Three weeks had passed without them forking over any cash. They did the same thing that they did to Candy in Florida. Kal resented them living with us. He believed Liza was taking care of them because she was the only one working and paying rent. My constant arguments with AZ didn't change anything. One day Kal took matters into his own hands.

"All dressed up with nowhere to go," I said, teasing Shi when she walked into the kitchen looking fabulous.

Shi grins and leans over, peeking into the pot of spaghetti on the stove. "I'm going out with Angelo. No spaghetti for me tonight. We only eat Porterhouse steak," she says, winking at me while taking out a napkin and mirror to dab her flawless makeup.

I abruptly stop stirring the sauce.

"Isn't Angelo that crazy man who destroyed your apartment?"

Her expression of happiness quickly changes.

"You mean my cottage," she adds, proudly.

"Does AZ know you're going out with Angelo?" I ask, surprised that the man is even still around.

"What choice does AZ have? We need the money. I can't work with these missing teeth!" She opens her mouth wide, clenching her teeth together. "Besides, Angelo is going to pay to get my teeth fixed. AZ will enjoy having his eye candy again," she says to taunt me.

"That's if AZ don't knock out the rest of your teeth once he finds out about Angelo," I say, turning and continuing to stir the sauce.

Someone was laying on their horn in the driveway. Shi just shrugged her shoulders and strutted out of the front door to meet her date.

Liza entered the kitchen with her nose up sniffing the air.

"Something smells real good in here," she says, licking her lips.

"At least somebody appreciates good cooking," I smile at Liza, welcoming the conversation.

It was never as tense as the ones I shared with Shi. Liza was polite and pleasant though very sneaky. She had to be watched at all times.

"You want something to eat?" I ask, attempting to feed the only person who paid bills in the mansion. If anyone deserved a home-cooked meal, she did.

"No thank you. I'll grab something on my way to work. I don't have the luxury of sitting down for a meal. You enjoy it though!" she said sarcastically as she walked out the door.

The next morning, I awoke early and went downstairs to the kitchen for a beer. I surprised Kal who was sneaking out the front door with a small bag of clothes in his hand.

"Hey, boss man. Where are you going this early?" I ask, thinking nothing of the bag in his hand.

Kal's face flushes. "Who me?" he asks, ashamed.

"Yeah you!" I say, opening the refrigerator and taking out a cold can of Olde English.

Kal's blank expression camouflages his thoughts.

"Did Liza make one hundred fifty dollars last night?" I ask, chuckling at our inside joke.

"Yeah, you know she did." Kal laughs but doesn't hand over any money. "I'm on my way to the store. Do you want something?" he asks, walking out the door.

"Nah, I got everything I need right here," I say, tapping the can of beer.

I didn't want to seem needy by asking for the money. I figured I'd wait until he came back. Of course, Kal never returns to the mansion. And it only took AZ forty-eight hours to fill his shoes.

Shi was out on another date with Angelo, and I was at the other house when AZ made his move on Liza. The following afternoon Liza confessed her sin to me and Shi on the back deck.

"Guess what?" Liza says out of the blue, passing Shi the blunt.

We both stare at her waiting for her to say something.

"I had sex with AZ last night. Now he's my man, too," Liza blurts out with a quirky grin.

My head's on a swivel to catch Shi's reaction. You would've thought Liza had gut-punched her. Shi's whole body got tense. Her back stiffened and blood rushed from her face. It sucked the air out of her like a balloon. To me, it really didn't matter. I was starting to dislike the creep anyway. AZ wasn't the man I used to know anymore.

"Oh yeah?" Shi hisses through clenched teeth. "Yes, but I only did it to stay in the mansion. I don't really like AZ. My heart still belongs to Kal," Liza said cluelessly.

Shi looks out into the horizon without uttering a word. I was overjoyed to see her mental anguish. Unbeknownst to us, Shi was plotting to eliminate Liza.

Unlike Kal, AZ was serious about his gangster. He was a real pimp and expected all of Liza's money -- not some of it. He doesn't take long to figure out something is wrong when Liza hands him exactly one hundred and fifty dollars every night. I knew about Liza's little trick, but I didn't care. AZ wasn't giving me the money anyway. He and I were still having violent arguments over him not paying rent.

One morning in a blink of an eye everything came to a head. Liza played her little game on AZ until the shit finally hit the fan.

With Kal gone, Shi and AZ took over the master bedroom on the first floor. Liza and I occupied two bedrooms on the second floor.

I was fast asleep when suddenly awakened by loud, screeching screams. Jumping out of bed, I ran into the hallway in my bra and panties. I was confronted by Liza on the catwalk. She was screaming and crying with snot dangling from her nose.

"Somebody stole my damn money!" Liza yells, spitting nasty, disgusting snot in my face.

My hands went up to block it.

"Wait, what?!" I ask, trying to understand her through the tears.

"My money! It's all fucking gone!" Liza says hysterically.

By now her loud screams woke up AZ and Shi.

"What the fuck is going on up there?!" AZ barks, looking up at us from the living room floor. His silk boxers revealed a full erection.

"My money was stolen!" Liza screamed, placing blame on someone in the house.

AZ's face contorted in anger. I knew it was about to go down. I took off running to my room to get dressed.

"Bitch! What the fuck did you say?!" AZ, angrily yelled at her.

I rushed back into the hallway, a little too late. AZ was already upstairs tossing Liza's belongings over the bannister, calling her every type of bitch in the book. Shi, still downstairs, was throwing Liza's clothes out the front door.

"Nobody stole your money. You stupid bitch!" Shi yelled, hurling clothes into the driveway.

I knew Shi was waiting for this moment ever since Liza confessed to us. Having no success with stopping AZ, Liza ran downstairs to stop Shi.

AZ and I take off running behind her.

The tag team duo punches and kicks Liza around the living room like a puppet. The fight spilled out into the driveway. Exhausted, I tussle with the three of them trying to break it up. The rumbling continued until we were all out of breath. When it was all said and done, Shi and AZ went back into the house.

"Bitch! Don't you ever bring your raggedy ass back here again!" Shi yelled, slamming the door in Liza's face.

I was flabbergasted. My mouth hung open thinking, *These people are a different kind of stupid.* I couldn't believe the two dummies kicked out our only source of income. Liza was paying rent and buying groceries for everyone in the mansion. Both jobless, they needed her money.

"Girl, it's going to be okay. I'll find your money," I said, picking up Liza's clothes, and trying to convince her to come back inside.

"They can keep that little bit of change. I'm out of here!" Liza barks at me.

"I understand how you feel," I say, neatly packing her clothes in the suitcase.

Liza picks up the suitcase and proudly marches down the driveway, hearing nothing I have to say. I sadly watched as she waddled along, disappearing into the street. Inhaling deeply, I went back inside to face the idiots.

When I entered the kitchen, Shi was smoking a cigarette with her elbows planted on the counter. AZ was counting the money spread out in front of him on the table.

"What just happened out there?!" I yell at them.

They both ignored me. AZ continued counting the money.

"Did you take that girl's money, AZ?!"

Glancing up at me, eyes dark and sinister, separating the singles from the larger bills, he said, "I took a thousand dollars out that dumb bitch's purse while she was asleep. I'm a daddy nigga! She stole my money!"

Watching AZ count Liza's money, made me tremble with anger. "You stupid ass idiot! A pimp tells a girl the rules. They don't move like a thief!" I said, pissed at him for chasing Liza away.

He smirked. "Oh, you a pimp now!" he said, laughing out loud.

I stare at him in disbelief. *You're too stupid to realize we need Liza's money to pay these bills!*

"UGH!" I storm out of the kitchen, too furious to look at him anymore. "Rent is due, you asshole!" I yell on my way up the steps.

"You got it, big time!" AZ hollers after me.

After Liza left the mansion, I only had a few more days to come up with the rent money. I considered using money from my tenants in Coram. There was a family of four on the second floor and an exotic dancer named Leah living in the basement. Even with their money,

I hardly had enough to cover the rent for both houses. Desperate to pay the bills, I decide to work with AZ. Together we put the word out on the street. I was looking for members for the country club. Staying true to form to his pimp game, however, he remained in hot pursuit of a prostitute. Our conflicting agendas created a hot mess. When word got around town about the mansion, all the hood rats came crawling out.

"Cheeks, you need to clear your head, man," I heard AZ telling Mr. Cheeks as I came strolling down the steps in my slippers shuffling into the kitchen.

The sun was shining through the large living room windows. The back door was wide open. A smell of fresh morning dew filled the air. Wearing nothing but a long wife beater with panties underneath, I feel the cool breeze peaking my nipples. AZ has his cell phone on speaker resting on the table in front of him. He tilts his chair back, taking a long drag on the blunt. Exhaling big clouds of smoke in the room, his eyes stay trained on me. Walking slowly to the refrigerator, I take out a breakfast of champions and pop open the can of beer.

"I need to let it do what it do," Cheeks says over the speakerphone.

Hiding behind the refrigerator door, I bent my ear to eavesdrop on their conversation.

"We out here man. Just call if you need me," AZ says to Cheeks.

"Bing!" Cheeks replies, disconnecting the call.

After AZ stops talking, I walk over to him.

"I know you heard everything we said," he frowns, passing me the blunt.

"Yuck!" I cringe, holding it between my thumb and forefinger.

The blunt was saturated with spit.

"Not everything," I said, wrapping my lips around my fingertips, and taking a pull.

"I told Cheeks to come out here and stay with us," AZ says, making me choke on the smoke.

My expression is cold and guarded. *All I need is more people here who don't pay rent.*

"Is he coming?!" I ask, taking a sip of the beer to stop coughing.

AZ pokes out his thick lips.

"Cheeks is having problems with the wife. It's not working between them right now. I told him to come here and clear his mind." AZ's eyes dance in the back of his head, pondering the idea.

I frowned at him for inviting more people. I was especially upset because he wasn't even paying rent.

"Stop worrying, I see that look on your face. When Cheeks gets here, this place will be packed with chicks," he says to me.

I sucked my teeth and passed the blunt back to him thinking, *If I don't act fast, this fool will turn the country club into a whorehouse.*

Driving to the studio, I hoped KG was still on board with my plan. When I turned into the parking lot, the back door was wide open. I parked the car, got out and crept toward the open door. KG's back was turned, playing a beat on the keyboard.

"Boo!" I say, playfully entering the studio.

KG flinches, turning around to see who it is. "What's up, Karen Joyyy?" he says, laughing at me.

"What's up with you?" I say, flopping on the faux leather sofa.

"I'm good. Just working on some beats," he says, turning around playing another note on the keyboard.

"KG, I need some help. I have to get some paid members for this country club. I also really want to close this deal with Adriana. I have to get that budget to keep the mansion afloat. But first I have to be able to offer some options for her daughter's music career. That's where you come in. Are you still with me?"

KG lowers his eyes, turning his back to me. If it wasn't for music in the room, there would be dead silence. After a long pause, I hop off the sofa and go to face him.

"Look, Kay, I'm desperate!"

His eyes don't meet mine.

"Yeah, I know. I heard about Shi and AZ kicking Liza out. That girl was bringing a lot of money to the mansion. Her money could've held you down. I told you Shi and AZ ain't nothing but trouble," KG says, shaking his head, disappointed.

He and Kal both warned me not to mess with AZ. Now I was kicking myself in the butt. I felt like a fool standing here pleading my case. Convincing KG would be more difficult than I had anticipated.

"Here, light this blunt," KG hands me a half-smoked cigar.

I light it, take two pulls, and pass the blunt back to him. Then, I sit back on the sofa sulking. *Liza probably called Kal about the fight. I bet he's the one who told KG.* I popped open my can of beer and took two big gulps. KG played with the knobs on the track board. He listened to the beat over and over while toking on the weed. After a few minutes, KG clears his throat.

"Listen, I'm going to help you out," he says pointing a threatening finger at me.

Looking into KG's glassy eyes, I knew he meant business. "I need that money as much as you do! My monthly car note for that Benz is a thousand dollars. That bill is kicking my ass! How much money did you say that lady got again?" KG asks, passing me the roach.

I waive it away.

"She has a quarter of a million dollars for us. Let's get this money, KG!" I say excitedly, putting the can to my lips draining it empty.

"Okay, let's do it!" KG narrows his eyes, prepping me for the plan.

"This is how it's going down. You set up the meeting. Tell Adriana the budget needs to cover all costs. She has to pay for the tracks, engineering, studio time, and artist features."

I listen to KG intently, eager for the plan to come to fruition.

"Can you think of anything else?" he asks, licking his dry lips.

I shake my head confirming he's covered everything.

"I'll contact you with the date and time of her availability," I say, standing to leave. I was satisfied our plan was solid.

KG stood up to escort me out. He watched from the doorway, waiting until I got into the car.

"Karen, don't mess this up," he yells as a last-minute reminder.

"I got this, Kay," I say, slipping into the driver's seat.

Driving away, I see KG's happy smile in the rearview mirror. My heart skips a beat from the task at hand. I put the cell phone on speaker and dialed Adriana's number. I knew KG needed that money as much as I did. Chuck put the whole company in a bind when he embezzled money from Ruggett beats. Allegedly, he swindled a million dollars giving everyone cars but no money. He, however, purchased a home for his mom and took extravagant trips around the world.

Chuck used a shady car dealer to finance the brand-new cars. Luckily, AZ snatched the Nissan Armada. Dennis, the studio owner, got a Pontiac Solstice. Chuck drove a blue 750 BMW and KG sat pretty in a black CLS 500 Mercedes Benz -- though none of them paid any car notes. Now, the feds were hot on Chuck's trail.

All of the beer I drank at the studio was ready to come out. When Adriana didn't answer my phone call, I pushed the pedal to the metal. I sped all the way home thinking about AZ. He was the only one who stood by me when no one else did. When we first met, I was in over my head with bills. I was ready to give up and sell my home. AZ didn't let me. He gave me hope. He told me to be fearless and keep pushing for my dreams. Without his moral support, I might not have made it. AZ was a risk taker. He had the true makings of an entrepreneur. He might not make the best decisions to me, hence becoming a pimp. But who was I to knock another man's hustle? Adult entertainment was probably a logical option for him. Thinking about it, I was going to support AZ as he supported me. You win some and you lose some. KG would just have to understand my decision.

Hours after my meeting with KG, I stood in the kitchen washing dishes. AZ's truck came screeching into the mansion's driveway. Mr. Cheeks' song, *Lex, Coup, Beamers, and the Benz*, was blasting through the speakers. The mansion door swung open, and the two culprits walked in laughing.

"Hi, Cheeks!"

"Hey, Kay!"

Cheeks' oversized Dickie shirt barely covered his plaid boxers due to low, sagging pants. I smiled at him, surprised he was here.

Shi heard the voices and stuck her head into the living room. AZ quickly took off running behind her, like a lovesick puppy.

"Shi's here too?" Cheeks whispers to me when he was gone.

"Yeah, AZ bought his new girlfriend here. He can hardly stand to be away from her for more than five minutes," I say sarcastically.

"Hmmm. I want to be just like that nigga when I grow up," Cheeks chuckles. "You gotta pinch?" he asks, pinching two fingers together to illustrate a small amount of weed.

I smile, happy to oblige.

"Let me see what I can do for you, mister. There's some Heinekens in the fridge. Make yourself at home. Just don't touch my forty ounce of Olde E!" I yell, skipping up the steps.

"This place is banging! We gonna make it do what it do!" Cheeks shouts to me.

"It's okay!" I yell back.

I was happy Cheeks was here. At least now I might have some company. Shi and AZ stayed in their room all day like newlyweds. Most times it seemed like I was at the mansion alone. Returning to the living room, I hand Cheeks the small bag of weed.

He reaches inside taking a modest amount. "Ah bing," he says, showing gratification.

"You got woods?" I ask, not really wanting to share mine.

"I'm goody." He opens the top pocket of his shirt retrieving a pack of Backwoods. "I'm going out on this back deck and spark up," Cheeks says, pushing his long dreads over one shoulder.

"Okay, I'm going to the other house for the night. I have some business to handle over there. The family of four is giving me problems. Their social service checks stopped coming. I have some tricks for that ass though. Tell AZ, I left."

"No doubt!" Cheeks says, exiting the room.

After spending two days in Coram, I return to the mansion flustered. When I walk through the front door, Cheeks and AZ are in the living room entertaining two girls.

"Hey, Karen, this is Tee and her friend," AZ says, looking at me nervously.

"Oh!" I say, eyeing what might possibly be two underage girls. *You wasted no time bringing in new prospects.* I think to myself.

Tee was a cute young brown skin girl. She had on tight black spandex, revealing a round juicy butt. It was evident why AZ chose her. If old enough, she was perfect for his game. I didn't catch the friend's name, but she was homely,with no curves and was built like a stick.

The group played cards with a bottle of Jack Daniels on the table in front of them.

"Have a drink with us, Kay," Cheeks says, pulling out a chair for me.

I was hoping the girls were old enough to drink. Sitting quietly, I listened to the immature conversation at the table. I found out the girls, though barely legal, were in college. That didn't stop the old ass men though. AZ kicked his money game while Cheeks laughed and joked with the girls. In no time at all, Tee was infatuated with Cheeks. His subtle advances thrilled her. When it was time to retire for the evening, Cheeks invited the young girl to his room. Like most groupies, Tee accepts the offer. AZ propositions the friend, but she's not interested. She does, however, agree to stay.

With everyone in bed, the mansion is still enough to hear a pin drop. I couldn't sleep, disturbed by Tee's giggling. Eventually, she quiets down and begins to moan. The next day, Tee's up early delivering her bad news.

"Good morning!" I say, walking into the kitchen.

Tee and her friend stand arguing at the counter. I squeeze by them going to the refrigerator.

"Hi!" Tee says enthusiastically. The friend only grunts at me.

"Oh, okay. I see you two need some space," I say, taking a beer and bottle of ice out of the refrigerator.

They look at me strangely when I place the bottle of ice on my back.

"I have a painful herniated disc. My friends call me bottle butt," I say, giggling, before going into the living room.

"Are you crazy, Tee?!" the friend barks at her.

Opening the can of beer, I keep a close eye on them. If a fight ensued, I intended to stop it. I was not about to let them tear shit up.

"I want to try it. I can make a lot of money. I have a son to feed," Tee says stubbornly.

"You can't just drop out of college!" the friend says, becoming agitated with her.

"I'm not dropping out of college! I'm just not ready to go back yet!" Tee replies, stomping away and leaving the friend standing there.

The girl looks at me, rolling her eyes.

Both of them end up staying a few days longer. Every day the friend begs Tee to go back to college with her. At this point, Tee is really starting to like Cheeks. On this particular day, we're all in the living room having a good time. The girls erupt into an explosive argument, almost coming to blows. AZ, Cheeks, Shi, and I look on without interruption. Secretly, I wanted Tee to change her mind. Dropping out of college to become a stripper was undoubtedly a stupid idea to me. I was disappointed when the friend stormed out of the mansion without Tee. AZ glared after the girl with a menacing grin. He was elated to see her go. She had been interfering with his plan from the very beginning.

"I guess this means you'll be joining our team!" AZ says, hugging Tee.

The young girl stares at the front door, shaken and unsure. "I guess so," she says, sadly. "AZ, we better make this money. I'm giving up everything to do this!"

AZ raises his arms high above his head. "You see how we living. Need I say more," he grins knowing damn well he's broke.

The rest of us circle around to comfort Tee.

"You'll be okay. I'll teach you how to pole dance," Shi says reassuringly.

"Let ole girl go," Cheeks says, placing his arm around Tee.

"Everything will be fine," I say, passing her the blunt. *Actually, I wasn't so sure. The young girl was a sheep amongst wolves.*

"I'm okay," Tee says, looking very uncertain.

Days later, I awake in bed feeling very anxious. *Do these people think I'm a damn fool?! I don't know who to kick out first!*

These derelicts are pissing me off! It's been over a week, and no one has paid rent! They think this is a free for all. Questioning AZ, he only complains about it. Shi isn't working because of her teeth. Going out on dates with Angelo, she only returns with Porterhouse steaks and new clothing. Tee is still learning the game. Cheeks is chick bait. The little money AZ does receive only satisfies their food, liquor, and weed habits. The shit is really beginning to upset me.

Aggravated and confused, I reach for my cell phone to call KG. The phone connects immediately.

"Oh, you're woke now." KG says chuckling.

It was peculiar hearing the same music in the background that was playing in my kitchen.

"Where you at?" I say, slipping into my bathrobe at the end of the bed.

"Guess?" KG says snickering.

Listening closely, I heard AZ and Cheeks' voice. "I'm coming right down."

I hang up, excited that KG's in the mansion.

When I get downstairs, it's a happy-go-lucky scene. AZ and KG are sitting at the card table. Cheeks is in the kitchen frying two pieces of chicken for himself.

"Karen, I see you have one big happy family in here. Where's my room at?" KG says, ticking me off further.

"Well, KG, that all depends. Do you plan on paying any bills?!" I say, rolling my eyes at everyone in the room.

AZ angrily hops up walking away from the table.

KG squirms in his seat. "I'm only joking, Karen. I came by to talk to you about something. Let's go out on the back deck," he says quickly rising from the table.

Following KG out into the hot summer breeze, I listened to him conjure up a plot of twisted lies and deceit. His plan puts me right into gear. Afterward, I call Adriana. She agrees to meet with us the following week. Adraina expected to collect rent for the mansion. Our plan was to separate her from that quarter of a million dollars. After calling Adriana, I watch KG contact a few of his friends. One was a promoter named Fredro. The guy wanted to book a party at the mansion. They talked for a quick minute then KG reached out to another friend he called Raul. This man offered KG a female straggler who had nowhere to go. KG happily accepted the offer, agreeing to pick up the girl later that day. Satisfied we'd done our best, I rolled a blunt and sat back to review our strategy.

The day finally came when KG and I met with Adriana at the studio. The blonde, middle-aged Italian woman was always on point. In she walks looking and smelling fantastic. The gentleman with her I thought was an attorney. The woman was no fool and totally prepared for any bullshit I was serving. They were both nicely dressed in matching business attire. She wore a beige, low-cut blouse and a short skirt. He was a tall guy, equally sharp in a beige Brooks Brothers suit with wing-tip shoes. His vibrant features and crooked smile immediately caught my eye. Without speaking a word, he appeared young, gifted, and black. One look and I knew they were undefeated.

Though I was no slouch either.

"Hi, Adriana, glad you could make it," I say, springing up from the sofa, and inviting them in.

"Hello, Karen." Adriana purrs in her thick Italian accent. She used voluptuous curves to flirt and manipulate her target.

Wearing sneakers, I was a whole foot shorter than Adriana. Tilting on high heels, she leans over pecking my cheek.

"This is Isaiah, my finance guy. He brokers my mortgage deals. It's the reason I have so much money," Adriana gloats, introducing the handsome mystery guy.

"Hello," he says, smiling at me with his eyes.

"I'm glad everyone is on time. KG and I literally just got here to fire up the equipment. Have a seat. We can listen to some tracks he made," I say, pointing to the dusty, cracked leather sofa but neither accepts my offer.

They stand, glaring at its poor condition. I couldn't blame them. The sofa was only suitable for blunt-smoking guys wearing hoodies and jeans.

"Crank the system, KG." I say, rubbing my palms together.

KG presses a button and squeaky noise comes blaring through the speakers.

KG and I listen to the beat bobbing our heads. Adriana's disenchanted look tells me something's wrong. I notice her whisper to Isaiah. I immediately signal KG to cut the beat.

"So, what do you think about the music? I ask her.

Sighing as if dissatisfied, she starts, "Well, Karen." She lets my name roll slowly off her tongue. "The music is uh, how you say, sta-t-icy."

Adriana looks at Isaiah for confirmation. He nods in agreement. "Are we recording in this studio? The sound is not so good here!" she says, waving her hand at the equipment.

I gasp, looking at KG for answers. He drops his head, hanging me out to dry.

"Ah, of course not. This is our pre-production studio. We mix and master at our other establishment," I say quickly, as Kal walks in hearing me lie.

Kal, who frowns but says nothing, instead circles in like a vulture, introducing himself, "Hi, I'm Kal."

"Kal, this is Adriana and Isaiah." I say, rolling my eyes at him.

Adriana looks at him, flirtatiously batting her long eyelashes.

Isaiah, impatiently inhaling while tapping his briefcase, asks, "Is our business done here? I have to get back to the office."

"Yes, I believe it is," Adriana says, smiling at Kal. "Okay, Karen, I have to get this busy man back to the city. He's the reason I have so many houses."

As they turn to leave, Kal, to my dismay, intervenes. "Is this the Adriana who owns the mansion?" he asks, stopping them in their tracks.

"That's right! Silly me, I almost forgot the rent check," Adriana says to me.

My mouth drops open. *Damn you, Kal! She was about to leave without collecting the rent!*

"Isaiah is a notary, Karen. He can verify the signatures on the lease."

"Alright, Adriana, let's go in the other room," I say, glaring at Kal.

After we sign the lease, I write her a five thousand dollar rent check.

"Karen, get in touch with me when the other studio is ready," she says, leaving out the door with Isaiah.

Watching Adriana walk out with my last five thousand dollars makes me sick to my stomach.

"What other studio?" Kal snickers.

I look at him, sucking my teeth. "KG, I hope we didn't blow that deal," I say, plopping on the sofa.

Two weeks lapsed after that meeting with Adriana. I was in the mansion on the second floor when KG and Cheeks came in the front door. Looking over the catwalk, I saw them walk in with three rowdy females. Leading the way, a short, loud woman strutted fiercely across the living room floor, swinging her thick hips from side to side. The other two females lagged behind her like puppets on a string. Walking into the kitchen, she boldly snatches a bottle of Jack Daniels off the table. Cheeks takes off to his room while KG escorts the women to the basement. I wait a full hour before coming up with an excuse to spy on them.

Entering the basement, I caught a glimpse of the ladies playing cards at the poker table. Hundred-dollar bills were scattered on the table in front of them. The short chick watched me hurry through the room.

"Hello," I say, pretending to busy myself.

"Hi!" she says, flicking cards high into the air.

The cards land on the table in front of her. I notice she's wearing blue jeans and Manolo heels with a matching purse. Her wig and makeup are perfect. Clearly, she outshines her friends. Satisfied I've seen enough, I make my exit. Her piercing green eyes follow me up the steps while she barks orders at her friends.

On my way to the kitchen, I pass KG and Cheeks on the steps.

KG stops to speak with me.

"You met Rabyt and the other girls yet?" he asks. "Is Rabyt the flamboyant one with the money?" "Yeah, that's her," he says, chuckling.

"Rabyt works at a car dealership. Cheeks wants to buy a car. So, I took him to her job. We invited them back here hoping they'd join your country club." KG shrugs, continuing on his way, leaving me to ponder the idea.

Lingering on the steps, I overhear the conversation in the basement.

"Can I have my bottle of Jack Daniels back?" Cheeks asks Rabyt.

"You can get a cup and have a drink like everyone else. You're not going to just take this whole damn bottle away!" Rabyt snaps at him.

"Yo, KG. Who the hell is this girl?" Cheeks says, chuckling, though I knew he was serious.

"That's Rabyt! I don't know what else to tell you, man," KG says, laughing out loud.

Reaching the first-floor landing, I see Shi at the kitchen table chatting with Tee and two other girls.

"Hey, ladies," I say, pulling a chair out to sit with them.

"Hi, Karen." Tee says to me.

Shi grunts, folding her arms across her chest.

"Karen, these are my friends. They came out to visit me," Tee says, introducing the two black girls at the table with them.

"Hello," they say politely.

They appeared rough around the edges. They looked like two girls from the hood. I made myself comfortable, listening to them gab about nothing at all. Shi chimed in every now and then to annoy the girls with her sarcasm. Suddenly, out of nowhere, Shi called them dumb niggas.

Tee flashed me a look. I just stared in disbelief. What happened next, we both couldn't stop. The girls jump to their feet.

"What did you SAY?!" one of them barks at Shi.

Tee stands to protect Shi.

"Say it again!" The girl leans forward, narrowing her eyes.

"You heard me!" Shi says, head on a swivel, looking for the nearest exit.

Lunging forward, the girl screamed, "Bitch, I'll knock the rest of those snagged teeth out your mouth!"

Tee leaps to shield Shi.

"What's going on out there?!" AZ shouts from the bedroom.

The loud ruckus brings him running into the living room. He catches Shi dashing out the front door. One girl bolts out after her with me running behind them. Slim and fast, Shi sprints down the driveway like a deer. The road is slippery and wet when she reaches the street. The fat sloppy girl trots slowly behind her. Almost twice their age, I pace myself to catch up. Bent over and breathing heavily, the girl is a hundred yards down the road when I jog past her.

"That bitch better run. I'm a break her jaw when I catch her," she says to me.

Shi had easily taken flight without looking back. I doubted the girl would ever catch her--especially in this drizzling rain.

Keeping pace, I finally reach Shi a mile away. My heart was pounding rapidly in my chest. The run had pushed me to the limit.

"You okay, Shi?" I ask, uncontrollably panting to catch my breath.

Slightly hidden from the road, Shi was kneeling behind a large tree. Her eyes were wide with fear. Ignoring me, she continued looking down the road for the girl.

"Are you crazy? That girl is going to kill you!"

"Karen, go away and leave me alone. I can't stand this place or you people," she says, pissing me off.

"Alright then suit yourself." *I hope she whoops your evil ass!* I say to myself, turning around to leave.

Jogging back to the mansion, the rain beats heavily against my skull. AZ's truck came speeding by me with Tee and her friends inside.

I laughed to myself, thinking about Shi. That girl sure knew how to get rid of people. It's the same way she got rid of Liza. The mansion is quiet when I make it back. Hurrying upstairs, I get out of my wet clothes and jump into the shower. I'm only in the water a half an hour before people enter the house again.

Turning off the water, I hear girls giggling downstairs. *Sheesh, this place is like a zoo.* Toweling dry, I tiptoe to my room and dress quickly. I go downstairs where Cheeks is the center of attention. Mr. Cheeks was tossing back shots of liquor and choking on powerful weed. A *Lost Boyz* song played loudly from a small radio sitting on the living room floor. The girls wiggled their hips, laughing at his corny jokes. Everyone was having a good time until Tim surfaced and began pinching their butts. Tim is Mr. Cheeks' alter ego who comes out whenever Cheeks has had too much to drink. Tim says and does things Mr. Cheeks would never do.

Standing in the background by the refrigerator, I quietly watched Tim act like a fool. KG glanced over, surprised to see me there.

"Hey, Karen Joy! Where did everybody go? We just got back from the *Main House*. Rabyt bought us some drinks. Look at Cheeks; he's twisted!" KG laughs and points at him.

Shaking my head, I really didn't want to disclose any information in front of the girls. Rabyt, though, was all ears. Drama seemed to intrigue her.

"Yeah, what happened to everybody? We heard all the noise and came running upstairs, but everyone was gone," she says as her green eyes sparkle with excitement.

"Everything is good," I say to her.

Truth is, I really didn't know.

CHAPTER IV
DEAR DIARY

Dear Diary, it's July 9, 2010.

I was glad to be back in bed resting again. It was a crazy day, especially waking up to AZ having sex on my sofa. Looking back on time, I'd wasted many years in one toxic relationship after another. Between the Cop and AZ, I didn't think too highly about love anymore. The square life was far behind me. I only cared about chasing paper now.

When the telephone on the nightstand rang, the clock on the cable box read three-thirty in the morning. Tired and sleepy, I picked up the receiver to answer it.

"Who the fuck is this?!" Shi Boogie screams in my ear.

Inhaling deeply, I refrain from lashing out at her. Shi was always loud and belligerent when she was drunk. She and the rest of AZ's girls were at work. They've been at the strip club for several hours now and probably wanted to come home. The last time I saw AZ, he was running around the house with Suga. That's the new girl he's been trying to bag with his penis. After two years of pimping, AZ was still a square. He broke every rule in the game.

"Hey, Shi, it's me, Karen. What's up?" I say, trying to keep her cool.

When AZ met Shi two years ago, she was a nice exotic dancer. Now she's always rude and obnoxious to everyone. I couldn't blame her though. A few years with AZ would do that to any girl.

"Wwwhere's AZ at? Go get him now!" Shi slurs in a drunken stupor. "He's disrespecting me. I've been with him for years. All he doesss is mistreat me!" Shi whines, starting to cry uncontrollably. "I tell you what I am going to do to him! I'm calling the cops on his little bitch, Nina. See how he likes that!" Shi threatens, knowing Nina has an arrest warrant.

I could hardly hear her above the loud music playing in the club. Feeling exhausted, I was tempted to hang up on her. Instead, I put the phone down and hollered for AZ. When he doesn't answer, I return to the phone. Hearing my voice again, Shi angrily disconnects the call.

Crawling back in bed, I felt sorry for Shi. She was only acting that way because AZ was in the house with a new girl. Shi was very jealous when it came to AZ and other women. She plotted and schemed on ways to get rid of them. This was mainly AZ's fault. He broke the cardinal pimp rule by falling in love with a stripper. The same rule applied to drug dealers. Never get high on your own supply.

The next day I was looking out of my window when Shi hopped out of a cab. It was four o'clock in the afternoon. She never came home the night before. AZ was in the front yard mowing the lawn. Shi held her head high and marched straight past him into the house. AZ doesn't bother to stop her. He had spent most of the morning cleaning Shi's messy room. He swept up all of the tissue she used to dig in her nose after getting high. Shi usually threw the tissue on the floor instead of putting it in the waste basket.

AZ quietly follows behind Shi, scheming on the bag of money. I heard her stomp through the kitchen and snatch the truck keys off the table. The 1999 Ford Expedition was registered in her name because AZ didn't have a license. Whenever Shi got upset with him, she took the keys. I had my own car, so it really didn't matter to me.

Strolling into the kitchen, I heard Shi fussing to herself in her room. AZ was looking through the refrigerator pretending not to hear her. I could tell he was embarrassed though.

"First, I have to put up with this little prissy bitch, Nina. If that's not enough, last night he was laid up with some black bitch!"

Shi was racist, though humorously had a black pimp. Once I remember her telling me that all black people were poor and ignorant. I'm sure dealing with AZ hadn't changed her perspective much. *Wham! Bam!* We heard Shi slamming things around in her room.

"On top of everything, now this Spanish bitch won't go home!" she yells as Lexx enters the kitchen.

The hurt look on Lexx's face sends AZ into a rage.

He lunges forward, kicking Shi's bedroom door wide open.

Smack!

We hear him slap Shi before she falls to the floor.

"Bitch, say it again!" he yells, dragging Shi into the kitchen by her hair. "Say you want my money to go home again! This is Lexx's home! You get the fuck out!" AZ says, violently dragging her across the kitchen floor.

I can't just stand there and watch him physically abuse her. I run over and grab his hand, yelling, "Stop it, AZ!" Then, I strenuously struggle to yank her free.

"Please stop it, AZ!" Lexx says, trying to help me pry her loose.

Shi helplessly squirms on the floor holding onto her hair. AZ's grip is strong and firm. Finally, weary from tussling with the three of us, he releases Shi. Wildly looking around the room, he picks up a heavy metal kitchen chair. Shi scoots to the corner crouching in a ball to protect herself. AZ throws the chair at her with all of his might.

"Ouch!" Shi screams, using both hands to block the impact.

Just my luck the chair bounces off of her and cracks a kitchen cabinet.

"Damn, AZ! Who's going to pay for that shit?!" I yell at him.

Ignoring me, AZ drags Lexx out of the kitchen by the hand. Shi collapses on the floor, whimpering idle threats under her breath. I inspect the kitchen cabinet, then march to my room and slam the door.

AZ met Lexx a year earlier on the track in New Jersey. Her strict parents sent her to visit her grandmother for the summer. Lexx, however, got off the bus in Atlantic City and started turning tricks in hotel casinos. Luckily, the runaway befriended a seasoned hooker named Roxy who showed her the ropes. Roxy knew the innocent young girl was no match for the rough streets. Subsequently, Roxy, who was old friends with AZ, called him to get her. Whenever Roxy got tired of working the track in Atlantic City, she would come to Long Island and visit him. It was the closest place to home for her. AZ, however, viewed Roxy as a come-and-go girl, because she jumped from pimp to pimp. Every time Roxy left AZ, she beat him out of money. Therefore, every time Roxy returned, she came bearing gifts. Last time the gift was Lexx.

Shi was lying in a fetal position, crying on the kitchen floor when Roxy walked into the room.

"Is everything okay, Shi?" Roxy asks her.

"Leave me the hell alone!" Shi snaps, then jumps up and runs to her room.

"Roxy, don't bother her!" I yell from my bedroom.

Returning to the kitchen, I see Roxy at the table snacking on some leftover food.

"Hey, Karen, what's wrong with Shi?" she asks, flashing me a huge smile.

It saddened me to know Roxy was in her early twenties but looked much older. The streets had really taken a toll on her.

Roxy was a reformed addict who continued to relapse adding much age to her face.

"Shi and AZ got into a fight over Lexx," I say, sucking my teeth.

"Oh, I thought I heard someone fighting. That's why I came downstairs. Where's AZ now?"

"He's upstairs with Lexx," I say, rolling my eyes.

"I need him to give me some money to post on Backpage," Roxy says, frowning.

Backpage was a website girls were using to meet tricks online. AZ wasn't familiar with it yet, though he quickly acquired the knowledge from Roxy. It's another gift she brought along with her Oxycodone habit. The new technology leveled up his game, though the pill addiction spread through his team like a virus.

"What are you two talking about?" AZ says, entering the kitchen, eavesdropping on Roxy and me.

Her face lights up. "Hi, daddy! I was looking for you. I need some money for Backpage," she says, batting long eyelashes trying to look sexy for him. Even though Roxy worked hard, it was difficult for her to earn enough money for the addiction.

"Here, Yo!" AZ pulls out a wad of bills tossing a few across the table to Roxy.

She smiles, happy he's giving her enough to post as well as buy some Oxy pills.

"Where's Do Do bird?" AZ asks us, about Shi.

"I think she's in her room. Are you giving me some money too? I have bills to pay!" I say, sticking my hand out for the money.

AZ disregards my question and goes to Shi's room to check on her. When he returns, I jump up and block his path.

"What's wrong with you?" he asks, forgetting about my request.

"You heard what I said. I need some money to pay these bills! You should be giving me money every day," I snap, rolling my eyes at him.

"I ain't giving you no damn money every day! You must think you the pimp!" AZ sneers, angrily marching out of the room.

"Then you and these bitches are getting out of my house!" I yell after him.

"Put us out! We not going nowhere! I know how to squat!"

Bam!

AZ slams the bedroom door cutting off any further argument. Roxy looks at me bewildered.

"You hear this ignorant shit!" I say to her.

"Karen, I'm so sorry. I thought he was helping you with these bills. I'd love to pay you rent, but I give all of my money to him," she says, shaking her head.

"Look at this place, Roxy. It's a dump! I need new cabinets, floors, doors, a paint job and much more. He won't give me a dime. Sometimes, I think he's trying to pimp me too! I only allow him to stay here because of you girls. The last time I kicked him out, he took the girls to a garage, and they slept on car seats," I say, walking over to the sink, and turning on the water to wash the dishes.

Before Roxy showed up, AZ's girls rarely had sex for money. They only worked in strip clubs. That is everyone, except for Nina. AZ made her a porn star as soon as she arrived. He had big dreams for Nina Nelson. Her initial start in porn was very optimistic. The cute nineteen-year-old quickly became a hot sensation on the Miami scene. She was featured on many porn sites. She also appeared on covers of adult magazines and starred in a few low-budget porn flicks. It was a very lucrative opportunity for both of them, though after a few weeks they returned to New York. Nina got hooked on drugs, lost the opportunity, and ruined her career. Subsequently, she danced in seedy strip clubs for pennies in comparison.

It's shocking how many decent guys are actually perverted behind closed doors. Men of all professions are tricks. Lawyers, policemen, doctors, judges, and even husbands lurk on adult websites lusting for women. Prior to Backpage, AZ's girls were mostly working at strip clubs. It was less money but far safer than posting online. However, once AZ discovers Backpage, he milks the cash cow for all it's worth. He's thrilled with the capability of earning money through e-commerce. He makes Lexx, Roxy, Nina, and Reina post every day. Reina was a young black girl AZ bagged while living in Big Will's mansion. She came all the way from Atlanta to be with him.

"Roxy, are you done setting up those Backpage ads yet?!" AZ yells from upstairs.

Roxy sat at the kitchen table, typing quickly on her cell phone.

"I'm almost done, daddy. Just trying to find some good pictures that look l ike me!" she yells back to him.

"Karen, what do you think about these photos?" she asks, passing me her cell phone.

I dry my hands on the dishtowel and take the phone from her.

"Is this picture supposed to be you?" I ask, squinting for a better look.

"Yeah, why? Doesn't the girl look like me?

I wrinkle my brow, thinking to myself. *The girl in the picture was cute and petite. Roxy was an Amazon.*

"Not really. This girl looks short and thin," I say, trying not to hurt her feelings.

Roxy snatches the phone back and rolls her eyes at me.

"Well, what do you think about the profile pictures I made for the other girls?"

Leaning over her shoulder, I look at the phone again. "Yeah, these people look like them. Why don't you use their actual pictures?"

"Because of the cops, dummy! You don't want to post real photos for proof of solicitation!"

"Oh, that makes sense," I say, giggling at my ignorance.

AZ enters the kitchen in the middle of our conversation. "Roxy, hurry up," he scowls at her. "Tonight is Friday. I can make a lot of money on Backpage. Shi's not going with y'all. Don't make a page for her," he says dryly.

Roxy and I smirk at each other. Shi always managed to weasel out of work. AZ was lucky if she worked three days out of seven for him. Even then, Shi complained about getting her hair and nails done. Shi was a big headache, but AZ swore she was his bottom bitch. We all knew different. Shi had him wrapped around her little pinky.

"Lexx, Nina, Reina! Hurry up! We have to get to this hotel," AZ yells to the girls still getting dressed upstairs.

"I know daddy. My phone is ringing already. The customers are calling every minute!" Lexx yells back to him.

Nina and Lexx always had the most success on Backpage. Tricks usually preferred young, pretty white girls. They generally received more calls than Reina and Roxy.

On Backpage, girls were either paid for *in-calls* or out-calls. *Out-calls* meant they went to the customer. This could mean working at a customer's house, in his car, or wherever he wanted to receive service. AZ didn't deem this safe. He preferred in-calls, where customers came to the girls. AZ would book high-end hotels to attract affluent clientele. The money was much better, and it was less dangerous although still there were some disadvantages.

AZ finally got the girls to the hotel room. When the customers arrived, they saw Roxy was not the girl in the picture. Therefore, they immediately left. Reina ended up using her own pictures. The customers never even called her. She was a good-looking black girl but customers preferred light, bright, or damn near-white skin. Lexx and Nina, worked the entire night. The traffic drew so much suspicion, hotel staff had to kick them out for solicitation. AZ was so greedy he sent the girls right back the next day. This time hotel staff were waiting for them at the front desk.

"Hello, Ladies," the concierge says, recognizing Lexx from her picture.

Lexx shrugs him off, thinking he's trying to flirt with her.

"Hi, babe!" Nina smiles, handing him her license to book the room. The concierge doesn't take it. Instead, he leans over the counter looking in both directions.

"Listen, the police were just here showing me pictures of you," he whispers to Lexx. "They wanted to know if you were checked in this hotel tonight."

"Who me?" Lexx asks, eyes wide with fear.

The concierge nods at her. Nina, being young and dumb, disregards his warning.

"What that got to do with me?" she says, sucking her teeth, forcing the license over the counter to him.

Reluctantly taking the license and money, he gives Nina a room key.

"Lexx, don't worry. Those police are gone now," Nina says, walking down the hallway with her.

"I don't know Nina. Maybe we should go home," Lexx says, following her into the room.

Inside, Lexx ignores her ringing phone. Nina, however, answers the call -- business as usual. The first call, Nina screens accordingly.

"Hello, baby," she says in a sexy voice. Lexx sits on the bed, watching and listening.

"What's your nationality and occupation?" Nina asks the trick, as if he'll be honest. She winks at Lexx, giving him the hotel room number.

The customer arrives within fifteen minutes, knocking rapidly on the door. Nina quickly opens it for him.

"Hey, baby!" she says, happy to see the guy in the white collared shirt.

"Are you a cop?!" the guy barks at Nina.

"No, babe! Why do you ask?"Nina asks naively.

"Because I am!" The cop whips out his badge and several cops rush into the room behind him.

Lexx is in the bathroom when this happens. She quickly flushes her weed down the toilet bowl before they discover she's in there.

Fortunately for the girls, the cops have no cause for a big sting.

Nina never solicits the officer. He identifies himself before she accepts any money. Nina does, however, get popped when they search her purse and find some weed and a small bag of narcotics. The cops detain both girls advising them of a Craigslist killer on the loose.

They also question the girls about being pimped or forced into prostitution. The girls promptly deny these accusations. The cops allow Lexx to go home but take Nina into custody.

AZ bravely goes to bail Nina out. When he arrives at the precinct, police question him about their relationship. AZ tells them Nina is a friend. Therefore, the cops allow him to post bail. By law, they have to let her go anyway. Backpage was warning enough for them to quit and go back to the strip clubs. Nina never showed up for court to face her charges. A warrant was issued for her arrest.

At the strip clubs, it was still difficult for Roxy or Reina to make any money. Roxy convinced AZ to let her go back and forth to Atlantic City for work. She at least had one customer there. The guy was a pharmacist who supplied her pill habit. The pervert also paid Roxy five hundred dollars for dates. Her commute continued until, eventually, she didn't return. We worried about her and asked Lexx to call the pharmacist. He informed us Roxy wanted to stay in Atlantic City with him. AZ was cool with it. Roxy's pill habit was more trouble than she was worth. Days later, the trick grew tired of Roxy. When she called asking to return to New York, AZ told her to bring a stack with her. Roxy said okay but we never heard from her again. Reina did something similar. She conned a customer into buying her a plane ticket back to Georgia. She called once or twice to let us know she was doing poorly there. She received no sympathy from AZ.

CHAPTER V
DEAR DIARY

Dear Diary, it's July 28, 2012.

At three-thirty in the morning, I walked into the strip club to pick up Nina and Lexx from work. I ordered a drink at the bar while I waited for them to get dressed. Lexx's customer came over to keep me company. He was an older gentleman who talked too much. A stripper named Katt recognized me and began crossing the room. She was a beautiful, dark chocolate girl that used to be on the team. She was a superb pole dancer AZ scooped when Shi and Nina went to jail for a probation violation. He stole her and Suga from a pimp named DJ. At the time, AZ was lucky to bag them. Initially, Katt was loyal and well-mannered. Toward the end, she became a sneaky, conniving bitch.

"Hi, Karen." Katt kisses me on the cheek and sits on the stool next to me.

"Hey, Katt, how you doing tonight?"

"I'm fine, just got into some bullshit at the club last night. Did AZ tell you about it?"

He did, but I pretended not to know. "Nah, what happened?"

"I don't know exactly. I was in the bathroom when these three bitches started flexing. I gave my shoes and purse to Nina before they jumped me. I wasn't scared though. I held my own against them. Afterward, my boyfriend came in to help. He hit one girl upside the head with a beer bottle. The bouncer kicked them out after that."

Gasping, I act surprised. "Wow, Katt! I don't see a scratch on you. They didn't do much damage," I say to her amusement.

"Yeah, 'cause I held my own."

We burst out with laughter. Then the owner's son waves Katt back on stage.

"Karen, I have to go. We'll talk later," she says, putting her cigarette out in the ashtray.

Turning around to the wrinkled customer, I find Suga sitting on his stool.

"Where'd you come from?" I ask, startled by her presence.

Suga laughs, then kisses me on the cheek. She was a caramel color, small in the waist, and cute in the face girl.

"How you doing, Karen? I was in the bathroom putting on my makeup when they told me you were here. I came out to say hi. Look what that damn DJ did to me last night! See my swollen eye. He beat the shit out of me!"

Suga leans forward, but it's too dark to see her eye in the club.

"No, girl, you look fine to me," I said. But she continues to complain anyway.

"DJ broke my phone. I had pictures of me and my daughter on it. I was going to use that as evidence to get custody from him. Now, I have nothing. Karen, I really need somewhere to stay to get away from him."

Listening to Suga complain, I felt sorry for her. Suga and DJ had a baby girl together. It's one of the reasons Katt left him. I was a landlord, but the girls saw me as a house mom. They trusted my judgment and knew I could provide a safe environment for them. Looking in Suga's pitiful face, I dreaded her next question.

"Karen, can I come home with you tonight? I need a room

badly," Suga whispers to me.

Dropping my head, I'm unsure how to respond. I knew if Suga returned home with me, she'd only be falling into the hands of another pimp. I did, however, know AZ expected me to lure her in.

"Sure, Suga. You can come with me. Talk to AZ about your living arrangements when you get there."

I almost hated having to tell her this. AZ rarely recruited chicks. Somehow, they just ended up on his doorstep, begging to be pimped.

"Okay, I'll do that." Suga smiles at me hopping off the bar stool. *Another one bites the dust.* I think to myself watching her walk away. I called home before leaving the club that night to warn AZ about Suga. It was always drama wherever she was concerned.

Arriving at the house, Suga walks straight in looking for AZ. She finds him in the living room on the sofa.

"Hi, Boo!" Suga says to AZ.

He glares at her suspiciously. Suga leans over, seductively whispering something in AZ's ear. His lips curl at the corner and Suga opens her big purse, dumping a bag full of singles in his lap. By doing this, she submits to some pimping. Now, AZ owns Suga and everything she owns. Renting a room is definitely out of the question for her. Suga throws her bag over one shoulder and follows the girls upstairs to find somewhere to sleep. AZ now had Shi, Nina, Lexx, and Suga. He always said, "Chicks come and go." I never understood what he meant by that. I always thought new girls came to replace old ones. I never realized ol d girls would return.

The next day, coming out of my room, I couldn't find Suga. I went upstairs to Lexx's room where she was cuddled in a blanket watching TV. Trying to avoid trouble, she was hiding from Shi. Suga's face lit up when I walked into the room.

"What are you doing up here?" I ask.

"Oh, nothing. Just watching TV," Suga says, sitting up on the edge of the bed. "I ordered some Chinese food. Do you want some? Have a shrimp. It's real good," she says, handing me the bag of food.

"Thanks, I will."

Taking one bite, I spit out a handful. "Yuck! This shrimp is horrible," I say, grimacing at the nasty taste.

"You think so? I like it." Suga smiles at me, saturating hers with duck sauce.

"Why haven't you come downstairs yet?" I already know the answer to my question, but I ask anyway.

Suga frowns at me. "You know why. Shi is acting funny with me. She thinks I'm a fool for coming back here. She says AZ and DJ are both abusive."

"Girl, don't pay Shi no mind. She's jealous of everyone."

Suga removes the blanket and jumps off the bed wearing the same clothes she wore the night before.

"I should make myself at home, right," she says, brushing crumbs off the wrinkled dress.

It was nine o'clock in the evening. Suga and I were the only ones home. We went downstairs into the living room to finish our chat. Lexx and Nina were out on dates. AZ took Shi to the nail salon. I went to the kitchen to get Suga and me some beers out of the fridge.

Returning to the living room, I turned on the TV set. Suga was puffing a blunt AZ left in the ashtray. I didn't smoke anymore. I sat on the sofa, pulled my feet underneath me, and drank the beer.

"So, what you been up to since the last time I saw you?" I asked Suga, watching her pull hard on the blunt.

She always had some juicy gossip to share. Her tone always remained the same, though. It was bland and self-removed.

"Well, girl, you know I have a rough life," Suga says as a matter of fact. "They say, 'God never gives you more than you can bear. 'When I left your house, I didn't stay with DJ the last time. We don't get along. I went to Jersey to live with my aunt. That was a disaster. My aunt set me up with one of her good friends. She made me screw him for money. That's not the worst part. She had the nerve to watch us and play with herself. I cried the whole time. On top of everything else, she stole the money he gave me." Suga shakes her head, toking on the weed.

I stare at her in disbelief. Before I can say anything, AZ and Shi came through the door.

"Hi, daddy," I say, playing with him.

"What's up," AZ says, carrying two heavy bags over his shoulder.

Shi runs past us going straight to her room. I knew she was upset about Suga being in the living room, but I didn't care.

AZ went upstairs to Lexx's room to put up the brand-new stripper pole. A few minutes later he came back downstairs and placed a bottle of Patron on the kitchen table. It was for everyone to drink. He also put a bottle of Rose Moet in the fridge.

I opened the bottle of Patron and poured myself a big glass. Shi came rushing into the kitchen, snatching the bottle off the table. I frowned when she took it back to her room. I wondered why AZ tolerated her disrespect. If it wasn't for his other girls, he would've been broke messing with Shi.

I went to the kitchen cabinet, retrieved another glass, and marched right into Shi's room.

"Can I pour some Patron for Suga? It was her bottle of Old English you drank last night," I said, looking Shi dead in her eyes. She pauses before handing me the bottle.

"I thought that was your Old English. I didn't know it was hers. Otherwise, I wouldn't have drank it," she says, rolling her eyes at me.

"Yeah, right. I'm no fool. You would've drank it no matter whose beer it was," I said, turning on my heels, and exiting the room with the glass of Patron.

After AZ's done setting up the stripper pole in Lexx's room, he comes back downstairs into the living room.

"Can you take Shi to work?" he asks me rhetorically.

AZ had a one-track mind. He wanted the money back he just spent on Shi. It was eleven o'clock at night. The strip club closed at two o'clock in the morning. I didn't see the point in taking her, but I did it anyway. I asked Suga to join me for the ride. On our way out the door, Shi wanted some drugs. AZ told her he didn't have any.

When Suga and I returned an hour later, AZ handed her something wrapped in white cellophane paper. I couldn't see what was inside, but I figured it was drugs. I got our glasses of Patron out of the fridge, and we kicked back on the sofa. Some old episodes of

The Wire were playing on TV. Suga started snorting the white powder and it was like a truth serum for her.

"Karen, you see this mark on my arm," Suga says, pointing to a large keloid on her right arm.

"Yeah," I say, looking at the mark, shaped into a letter C. I never expected the story she was about to tell me.

"I ran away from this group home when I was twelve years old. I fell into the hands of bad company," Suga says, sniffing loudly. "One night, they brought me to this house and took me to the basement. They said I was going to be initiated into their gang."

I could tell by the look on Suga's face she was revisiting a dark place. I held my breath fearing what she would say next.

"The men were much older than me. It was too many for me to fight. They raped me one after another. I called out for help, but no one came."

Tears immediately filled my eyes for that twelve-year-old girl. Cringing, I became enraged by the story she was telling me.

Suga sat there, stiff as a board. As usual, she was self-removed from the conversation. It was as if she were talking about someone else.

"Karen, when they were done, this big fat bitch sat on me.

They used a red-hot hanger, shaped into the letter C, to brand me. The idiots didn't even clean the wound. They kept me kidnapped in that basement for days until someone finally had the nerve to report it to the police. I was rescued and taken back to the group home, just in time to save my arm. The infection got so bad doctors thought they had to amputate. This horrible scar is my reminder."

Suga circles the mark with her finger, staring blankly into space. Looking at her, I wanted to go back in time and save that little girl.

I wanted to stop those bad men from defiling and stealing her innocence. I could only imagine the damage it did to the child who was now a grown woman. I was all shaken up inside listening to her. The story hurt me to the core. All I could do was silently pray for Suga.

On August 3, 2012, it had been five days since Suga's return. Her horrible story stuck with me like a sword in my side. Every time I looked at Suga, I saw the twelve-year-old girl. I couldn't help but feel sorry for them both. In addition, Suga was treated very poorly at the club. Every night she was either teased, criticized, or robbed by her own teammates. Finally, AZ, who had enough, decided to go to work with Suga and resolve the issue. He was having trouble with the manifold in his Ford Expedition that day and drove my Maxima.

I was on a mission to renovate my house. Therefore, I used his truck for my local runs. Every time, AZ got mad at the girls, he destroyed my house.

Now the place was in shambles. Once he kicked a bathroom door and split it in two. Another time, he stuck his fist through one. I hung a picture over the hole to hide it from my guests.

Today, after returning home from Loews with two doors on the truck, I encounter Nina who comes flying down the steps and ambushes me.

"Karen, let me have the keys to the truck," she says when I

open the front door.

Staring into her dilated pupils, I was leery about giving up the keys.

"Nina, I have two doors on the truck. Let me unload them first," I say, trying to stall her.

"I just need to make a quick run. It's right around the corner. Pleaseeee give me the keys!" she begs, with her hand out.

Reluctantly, I hand over the keys.

"Come right back. I have more doors to get before the store closes," I say, watching her climb into the truck.

In my heart, I knew Nina was going to cop some drugs. I sat in my room over an hour, surfing the web, waiting for Nina. When the phone rings, it's her number on the caller Id. A lump forms in my throat.

"Hello!" I say, answering quickly.

"Karen, I'm being arrested! Come get the truck now! They are going to IMPOUND IT!"

Hearing the urgency in Nina's voice makes my heart skip a beat.

Beads of sweat form on my forehead.

"Where are you now?!"

"Come out the house, make three lefts. You'll see me!"

"Nina, put the keys under the front seat! Leave the doors unlocked! I'm coming!" I yell, before the line disconnects.

Jumping out of the chair, I grab my purse and bolt out of the front door. *This can't be happening to me. AZ's going to kill me when he finds out. I never should've given her those keys!*

The destination is only two blocks away. I run down the street at top speed. I'm out of shape and terribly winded. Panting heavily,

I have to slow down and catch my breath. I half walk and half jog the rest of the way. Turning the corner, I don't see Nina anywhere in sight. Crackheads are rummaging through the truck. A tall skinny guy jumps in and out, stealing whatever he can find. I see him stuff a pack of Newport cigarettes and a couple of CDs in his jacket pocket. The other fiends were standing nearby, posing as lookouts. It's a scene s out of *Bait Car*. I fear they will find the truck keys under the seat before my fat ass can get there.

"Aye, yo! Get away from that truck," I yell bravely down the street.

Still off in a distance, my presence isn't very intimidating. The tall man watches me jog toward him.

"Aye, yo, what?!" he yells back to me, continuing to take whatever he pleases from the truck.

Forgetting my whereabouts, my Trinidadian blood begins to boil. "Get the fuck away from my truck!" I scream, quickening the pace. Approaching without a weapon, I'm unsure if I pose any threat. I walk right up to the man, talking fast and furious.

"I know the white girl just got arrested! She called me to come get my truck!" I say forcefully.

The guy pokes his head out the truck window long enough to get a peek at me. Only 5'3", 155 pounds, I narrow my eyes, glaring at him intensely. He jumps out of the driver's seat and holds the door open for me. I guess it wasn't worth the trouble if the truck was really mine. Pushing him aside, I reach underneath the front seat, retrieving the truck keys. I climbed inside, breathing a heavy sigh of relief.

"Can I have this pack of cigarettes?" he asks, showing me the Newports he stole.

"Take them. I don't smoke!" I say, struggling with the ignition key.

The guy stands there, holding the door handle, staring at me strangely.

"Can I have your telephone number?" he asks stupidly.

I gawk at him unable to believe he has the audacity to take out a cell phone.

"No, you cannot! I don't buy drugs and I don't want your number!" I say, slamming the door in his face.

I can't get out of there fast enough. I almost tear his arm off, speeding away. *Lord, forgive me for getting involved in this mess.*

I'm a church-going woman. Please don't block my blessings. I'm in this world, not of this world.

The next afternoon, AZ and I spend half the day bailing Nina out. We arrive at the courthouse about an hour before the second call. Everyone is still out to lunch. We patiently sit in the hall waiting for the court officer to let us into the courtroom. As soon as he does, the arraignment proceedings begin. Nina and five male criminals are brought out in shackles. She quickly scans the room, finding our seats. The court officer clears his throat, telling her to sit down and face the bench. Eventually, they call Nina's government name. She rises to stand in front of the judge. One of the court officers stands behind her, preparing to take her back to jail at the judge's command.

The judge, glaring at Nina sternly over his specs, says, "I'm going to assign you a Legal Aid attorney due to your financial situation."

Earlier that day, one of the clerks called our house to interview AZ about Nina's financial status. AZ tells the clerk Nina's dirt poor and living on Social Services. He fails to mention she's a stripper, earning more money than the court officers. Nina kept her eyes on the floor refusing to look at the judge while he read her charges.

"The defendant has four charges, a five eleven. and three counts of possession. She also has three warrants," the judge speaks loudly enough for the whole courtroom to hear.

Embarrassed that everyone has heard her business and shuffling from foot to foot, Nina blushes.

"Your bail will be two hundred and fifty dollars each count, totaling one thousand dollars. Can you post bail?"

Nina looks at the judge and then puts her head down without answering him. She wasn't sure if AZ had the money or if he was even willing to pay it. On that note, AZ and I walk out of the courtroom. We head straight to the cashier window and pay Nina's bail. In Suffolk County, you're guilty until proven innocent and not the other way around. It's a money-grubbing, thirsty county. After posting her bail, we wait out front in the car.

It's hours before Nina is released. She exits the courthouse laughing and joking with a friend, instead of coming directly to the car. AZ watches as Nina stops to smoke a cigarette with the girl. Steam rises from the top of his head as he plays with his cell phone. In my peripheral, I see his leg shaking, trying to remain calm. I realize his patience is wearing thin. Nina hands the girl her cellular to make a phone call. When the girl is done, she hands the phone back. Nina tells her goodbye, then slowly walks over to the car , and slides in the backseat like nothing's wrong.

"Bitch! Don't you think I've waited here long enough? Then, your dumb ass has me wait even longer by talking to some bitch!"

AZ was raging mad. I was afraid some nearby cops would hear him yelling at her. Nina's jolly attitude quickly disappeared. She was embarrassed because her friend was still watching us.

"Don't you ever bring that shit into my house again!" AZ hisses through clenched teeth.

"What do you mean?!" Nina responds innocently.

This sends AZ's anger over the top. He spins around in the front seat to face Nina. I saw the pain in his eyes.

"I found all that shit you had stashed in your room. You know damn well what I'm talking about."

The night before, AZ showed me some cellophane bags he found in Nina's room. They had white powder in them. He had caught her once before with Oxy pills. She promised to kick the habit. Now the addiction seemed worse.

It devastated AZ to know Nina was still using. She was only twenty-one and once had such a bright future ahead of her. I remember Nina's budding career as a porn star. She was at the top of her game. Unfortunately, drugs ruined that for her. It was a shame seeing a beautiful, young girl kill herself. It also hurt, watching AZ berate her.

"What do you mean?!" Nina repeats, shocked to be exposed.

AZ can no longer hold his anger. Her denial enrages him.

"You stupid lying bitch! You know exactly what I mean!" AZ shouts, swinging his arm backward and slapping Nina so hard it leaves his handprint on her face. He hock spits on her, making me sick to my stomach.

"Eww," I exclaim and quickly jump out of the way, horrified the spit might get me.

Putting the car in gear, I whip out of the parking space, looking straight ahead. Nina softly whimpers, then gradually begins heavily sobbing in the back seat.

"You're lucky you took care of me when I was in jail. Otherwise, I would've left your stupid ass in there!" AZ says, voice trembling, full of emotion. He had been released from jail in December. He served two and half months for driving without a license. We rode all the way home in deafening silence. When AZ opened the front door, Suga and Lexx were at each other's throats.

They stood toe to toe, spitting profanity at each other. AZ was too tired to be bothered. He ignored them and went straight upstairs to Nina's room.

"You better get your bitch before I fuck her up!" Lexx says to AZ when he passes her.

Suga looks at him for approval.

AZ inhales, deeply. "Go ahead and fight. I don't know what else to tell y'all."

At this point, AZ's had enough. It's more drama than he can handle for one day.

He can't get the words out fast enough. Lexx swings first, hitting Suga square in the face. That's the straw that breaks the camel's back. Suga was older, stronger, and much bigger than poor little Lexx. She pushes Lexx so hard that the girl almost falls down the steps. Lexx bounces off the wall like a ball, right back into Suga's hands. AZ calmly walks down the steps away from the fight.

"Girls, stop it!" I yell, running up the stairs, and squeezing past him.

Reaching the second-floor landing, Suga's now tossing Lexx around like a ragdoll. She slams Lexx on her back, banging her head on the floor with loud thudding sounds. Holding firmly to each other's hair, it's hard for me to separate the two.

"Let go!" I scream, tussling with the bodies on the floor. Lexx is able to get some leverage to rip Suga's weave out. Nina stands in the doorway, watching us.

"Help me break this up!" I yell at her. Nina fumbles around not sure what to do.

"Grab Suga off of Lexx. I'll hold Lexx!" I say, exhausted from trying to do it all myself.

Nina joins in the scuffle and so does her little Yorkie. The dog hops around biting us like a pesky mosquito. He chews on my ankle and Suga's toes.

"Ouch! Ouch!" I cry out, trying to shake the dog off.

Finally breaking them apart, I sling Lexx into her room. She comes running back out swinging a Hennessy bottle. I step in front of her, grabbing it away. Lexx is so tired, it doesn't take much effort.

After the fight, my ankle was badly hurt. I limp to the corner of the room, retrieve a broom, and pop the dog over the head.

Nina grins at me. "Good boy, Louie," she says, bending over to pet him for defending her.

Once the fight is over, AZ returns upstairs to check on his damaged goods. He peeks into Lexx's room first.

"Are you okay?" he asks while she's nursing her wounds.

"Get the hell out of my face," Lexx screams at him.

"I thought you wanted to fight. Get the hell out my damn

house!" AZ yells back at her.

"You want me out your house? You want me out your house?!"

Lexx runs out the room, straight down the steps and out of the front door. I look through the blinds to see which direction she goes in. *Uh oh, here we go again.* I think to myself, dashing outside to follow her.

"Hey, wait up," I call out to Lexx.

Tears stream down her face when I catch up to her.

"Just leave me alone, Karen," she says, pouting like a little girl.

"Aww, I just want to make sure you're okay. It's been a rough day for all of us."

Knowing Lexx is upset, I try to pacify her. "Girl, communication isn't one of AZ's strongest points. If you get mad, he gets mad too. It only fuels his fire," I say, throwing my arm around her shoulder, falling in step.

"I'm never going back there, Karen. Suga is a troublemaker. She said that was her room because she was there first. She kept bothering me about it until I punched her in the face. AZ should've stopped the fight," she says, becoming more flustered thinking about it.

"Let me go get the car so we can take a ride," I say, hoping this will calm her nerves.

"Okay, Karen. Just take me somewhere to smoke my blunt.

You're the only friend I have," she says through teary eyes.

"Wait right here. I'll be back." I say, satisfied Lexx is calming down.

I run back to the house and get the car. Turning out of the driveway, I see Lexx at the end of the block. Nina's not far behind her. I drive up to Nina and stop to let her get in.

"Girl, the drama never ends in this house. Where the hell are you going?"

"I'm on my way to the store. AZ said I can't drive his truck anymore."

Nina, sulking, sits back in her seat. I drive a little farther and stop to pick Lexx up.

"Karen, I'm never going back to him. I'm leaving AZ today!" Lexx says, getting into the car.

I say nothing and let Nina deal with her.

"Pookie, is that a blunt in your hand? I just got out of jail. Can you please smoke with me?" Nina asks, selfishly changing the subject.

"Okay!" Lexx says, forgetting all about her anger for AZ.

Coming back from the store, I drop the girls off in the woods to smoke their blunt.

It was Wednesday, August 8, 2012. Time to make the donuts again.

AZ and Shi left early to take Lexx to work. Suga and Nina weren't ready to go yet. I thought it was stupid for AZ not to wait for them. The drive was forty-five minutes and when the cat's away, the mouse will definitely play. As soon as AZ leaves the driveway, Suga contacts her ex-pimp, DJ.

"Karen, look at this," she says, showing me a text message on her cell phone.

AZ finally bought Suga a new Android phone after DJ destroyed the old one. For two days, Suga secretly inboxed DJ on Facebook. Looking at the cell phone, I briefly read several messages left by him.

"I got to call DJ," Suga says to me with big puppy dog eyes.

My mouth drops open. *I guess you forgot that ass beating he gave you.* I watch Suga dial DJ's number and put the cell phone on speaker for me to listen.

"Hello, who is this?!" DJ eventually answers her call after several rings.

"Hi, bae!" Suga says, giggling.

"Where you at?!" DJ demands to know.

Leaning over Suga's shoulder, I listen closely.

"Why are you asking me that?" Suga says, in a low, sultry voice. She covers the mouthpiece whispering, "I already talked to DJ earlier today. He asked if I'm with that nigga, AZ, again. I hung up on him not knowing what to say."

"Where you at, Suga?! Stop playing games with me!" DJ barks, with a slight lisp.

His drilling continues until Suga, becoming extremely nervous, can only say, "Huh?"

I quickly intervene, whispering in her ear, "Tell him you're at a friend's house."

"I'm at Joy's house," Suga says, trembling.

"Well let me come get you!" DJ yells, trying to bully her.

"Tell him Joy doesn't want any drama at her house and you'll come to him," I say, which Suga repeats.

This seemingly calms DJ down. Afterward, they indulge in small talk about their child and their relationship.

"Will I live with you if I come home?" Suga asks him.

"You can't live with me anymore. You do dumb shit like running off!" DJ responds coldly, then catches himself. "I'm cleaning out another house. You can move in there by next month. I'm doing this for our family. I love you," he adds with no feeling at all. "Suga, it hurts every time we get back together, and you do dumb shit," he says sincerely.

Listening to them, I got the feeling he was more interested in her money.

Suga sighs. "You hit me, DJ. Why did that happen? Do you remember how bad you hurt me?"

"You did that to yourself," DJ responds harshly.

Suga turns to me with her hand over the mouthpiece. "He's so loveable. I have to go back to him and my daughter," she says, batting her fake eyes lashes.

I suck my teeth, disappointed in how easily he persuades her. Suga hops off the sofa and rushes up the stairs. She returns five minutes later carrying a large duffle bag over her shoulder. Still on the phone with DJ, she marches right out of the front door.

When AZ returned home, I was on the sofa in the living room watching TV. His slamming the front door startles me.

"Can you take Nina and Suga to work for me? I'm too tired to go right back," he says, walking into in the house.

I frown, not sure how to tell him Suga was gone.

"What's wrong with you?" he asks, eyeing me suspiciously. "Suga's not here, is she?!"

Nodding my head makes his nostrils flare. "Shit! Why didn't you call me?!" he asks, punching the palm of his hand.

"It's your fault for buying her a new phone," I say, placing the blame on him.

"I had to buy it. A bitch needs her phone for the customers!" AZ says, sitting on the sofa next to me. "I don't care about that damn girl! She's a come-and-go bitch. Plus, she causes too many problems with my main girls. She scratched Lexx's face. That's my money maker!"

AZ's head drops between his shoulders. He didn't want to admit it, but it was obvious he was hurt. Suga had a way of growing in your heart.

"I'm not like these corny pimps on Long Island. I don't follow their rules. I'm a daddy, not a gorilla pimp!" AZ begins listing the rules of the game.

"A pimp takes a girl's identification, her birth certificate, social security card, or anything she needs to escape his wrath. I'm not like that!" he says, inhaling deeply. "I might check her cell phone and go through the text messages. But that's it. I should've done that to Suga! I must be slipping," he says, shaking his head. "Some pimps kidnap girls and take them out of state to work. It's a felony to cross state lines and forcibly sex traffic. I'd never do that. I pimp by choice, not by force."

AZ pokes his chest out reveling in the moment.

His street knowledge was fascinating to me. He took pride in himself for emulating Big Will and Hugh Hefner, formerly of the Playboy brand. To me, AZ ran an establishment more like a transient house. He recruited runaways and displaced women, encouraging them to pursue better lives. Inspiring them to follow their dreams, he identified their strengths and weaknesses. AZ didn't ask for all of their money. He suggested they allow him to manage the money. He told the girls to give whatever they thought he deserved. AZ budgeted this amount for clothing, entertainment, transportation, food, and shelter. Unfortunately, most of the girls kept large sums for their drug habits.

I did my best to secure a place of residence for the girls. I supplied a clean, healthy environment whenever it was needed. I helped the girls learn basic skills for survival, like writing checks, cooking, cleaning, etc. I didn't mind providing this service if it could help save a life or keep them off the streets. At times it was difficult for me. AZ refused to pay rent. This caused constant bickering between us. He said that if he gave me any money, I was pimping him. I thought either AZ was very stupid, or he thought I was. Overall, I thanked the Lord for providing a roof over our heads.

The girls, on the other hand, loved AZ. Shi aspired to be a lawyer. Much like her, Lexx wanted to be a paralegal. They both had the brains to be whatever they wanted to be. He didn't force them to strip or prostitute. He only expected them to hustle and take care of themselves. They could've done this by working a regular job. He didn't judge, criticize, or demand much of them. To me, he was more of a gigolo than a pimp. Regrettably, the girls liked chasing fast money. In addition to this, AZ made them lazy. By doing this, he actually crushed their dreams instead of supporting them. There were no rules to follow. AZ allowed the girls to do anything they wanted. He took pride in spoiling them. Shi called living with him a rest haven for whores. AZ didn't condone a wild, chaotic lifestyle. This is where he differed from most other pimps. When he came across a real street whore, she usually returned to the streets. The atmosphere he provided was too boring for them. It was more like a normal household.

Other pimps operated much differently. They lived in hotels

or motels, hustling from state to state on a daily grind. Forcing women to prostitute and give up everything they earned, they threatened, beat, and tortured women. AZ was a nerd in comparison. Therefore, many pimps didn't respect his hustle.

Dear Diary, it's August 10, 2012.

It's been two days since Suga left us. She was back with DJ, and it was his duty to serve AZ. Meaning, it was customary for a pimp to inform his predecessor that the whore chose another pimp. If that didn't occur, a pimp will continue looking for his girl, suspecting she is dead or in jail. Both AZ and DJ had women working in the same strip club. It's inevitable they'll bump heads.

Stonehedge is empty when I drop Lexx off for work. The parking lot only has three cars in it. One car belonged to the owner's grandson, Cris. He drove the same white Maxima I had, except his had leather seats. Lexx spots his car in the cut as soon as we pulled in to park.

"Karen, Cris is here. That's his car over there. He is soooo sexy!" Lexx says, licking her lips.

She had been screwing around with Cris since the beginning of her employment at Stonehedge. His father, Bob, co-owner of the club, h ad recently died leaving the grandfather, Howie, as sole owner. Howie, who is too old to run the joint, allows his grandsons, Mick and Cris, to do it. The young men are so grateful that they hump every stripper in sight. Lexx, anxious to get inside, unbuckles her seat belt.

"You coming inside, Karen? I want you to meet Cris!" Lexx says excitedly.

I had other plans, but her enthusiasm convinced me.

"I guess I can have a drink or two," I say, not wanting to disappoint her.

Walking into the club, Lexx runs right over to Cris. The short, stocky, mildly attractive Italian was equally happy to see her. Taking a seat at the far end of the bar, I ordered myself a shot of Hennessy. I scanned the smoke-filled venue, resting my eyes on two patrons seated at the stage. The dancers with them immediately zoomed in on me figuring I was a customer. I recognized one girl named Champagne. I quickly turned my back to avoid any eye contact with her. Champagne worked for a pimp named Jay who once had a run-in with AZ. The two pimps fell out over Jay's other dancer named Hollywood.

One night at the club, Hollywood was talking greasy about AZ. Threatening to smack the taste out of her mouth, he tossed a drink in her face. Her pimp, Jay, was too much of a punk to do anything about it. He approached me to resolve the issue. I told him I would, but I never did. Hollywood's disappointment in her pimp ended up making her leave him. The incident still remains unresolved between our teams. Finishing my second drink and unnoticed by Lexx, I exited the bar. I drove home fast, anxious to finish renovating my kitchen. Maintaining the property value of my home was more important to me than having drinks at the club. Every house on the block looked better than mine on the outside. I could only imagine how they must have looked on the inside.

AZ went to pick Lexx up from work that night. All eyes were on him when he walked into the strip club. Men ogled the two bad bitches by his side. Shi and Nina were drop-dead gorgeous. The three of them took seats at the bar and AZ ordered their drinks. Laughing and talking, they enjoyed the atmosphere while waiting for Lexx to get off work. As fate would have it, minutes later, Suga walked in with DJ. AZ, squinting to focus, spotted them across the room. DJ's light skin and hairless face were easily recognizable. The well-built pimp strutted the floor in fine Italian leather, tightly hugging his chest and biceps. His spiffy appearance was a far cry from the other bummy pimps.

AZ turned his head pretending not to see them. He played on his cell phone, not paying much attention to his surroundings.

"What's up?" someone taps him on the shoulder, whispering in his ear.

AZ looks up, surprised to see DJ standing there. Patrons stare from every angle to catch a glimpse of the two pimps at odds. Feeling the tension in the air, the whole bar is on high alert. AZ's mind is foggy from the strong drinks. DJ has caught him off-guard.

"What's up?" AZ says smugly.

"You know what's up. That's my baby's mother. Don't let that shit happen again!" DJ scowls at him.

AZ's eyes grow narrow. He grips the glass tightly in his hand.

"What you talking about? You know I'm not turning no money away," AZ snarls back at him, ready for the standoff.

DJ chuckles, realizing his strong tactic isn't working. The slick pimp backs off, opting for another approach.

"I know that's right," he says grinning widely. "Like you, I'm a man who respects the dollar."

Eyeing him intently, AZ relaxes his posture.

"I let Suga sleep on my couch. I took good care of your bitch when no one else would."

AZ doesn't mention how he was busting Suga's ass wide open on that couch.

"I appreciate that. I just want you to know she's my baby's mother. I care for Suga. She's not like Katt and the other girls," DJ says in the wake of AZ once stealing both of his girls.

"You and me are acquaintances. We understand the guy code," he says, looking for some empathy.

"We are?" AZ says, eyes widening. "I thought we were enemies," he half-jokes

"Who told you that?" DJ asks seriously.

"Suga did." AZ glares at him, believing it's true.

DJ shrugs it off.

"Look, man. I need one of those houses you got," AZ says to lighten the mood and change the subject.

The two men knew each other from back in the day. AZ was aware of DJ inheriting many houses from his grandmother after she died. DJ smiles at AZ and pulls up a bar stool. He gets comfortable and calls the bartender to order himself a drink. Both current pimps, the fellas laugh and talk about how times have changed for them. Relieved that the tension is over, the whole bar exhales.

Sunday night, August 12, 2012, is no Sabbath day in the devil's playground. It's just another day for pimps and whores to get their money.

Shi stands at the stove cooking spaghetti and meatballs for everyone. AZ has me take Nina to the motel for her date.

It isn't long after, Nina returns throwing a few hundred-dollar bills on the table in front of him. Ignoring her, AZ continues playing his video game.

After finishing dinner, I lie down in my room. A little while after this, AZ comes into my room.

"Can you get Lexx from work tonight?" AZ asks me.

Looking at him, I desperately want to close my eyes and go back to sleep. Checking the clock on the cable box, it's one thirty in the morning. The bar closed at two o'clock. I only had about twenty minutes to make the forty-five-minute drive. If the bar closed before I got there, Lexx would be stranded in the street. Sucking my teeth, I got up and put on a pair of shorts and T-shirt. Brushing my hair into a ponytail, I stumbled out of the front door. Sleepy and tired, I got into the Maxima and found some soothing music on 107.5 WBLS to comfort me during the ride. I arrive at Stonehedge with two minutes to spare.

There's a car in my rearview mirror, burning rubber out of the parking lot. Looking over my shoulder, I catch sight of the driver. It was that lame-ass pimp, Jay. My senses began to tingle. *What's his big hurry?*

Glancing at the club door, I observe Lexx peeking through the glass looking for her ride. I flashed my headlights signaling for her to come outside. Usually, a bouncer escorted the girls out. Lexx was in too much of a hurry to wait for one. She ran outside without the protection.

"Damn, Karen, I lost my cell phone right before you got here. It has all my customer contacts in it. I was at the bar about to text AZ when I noticed it was missing. That was just before my last lap dance," Lexx says, sucking h er teeth and jumping into the passenger seat.

"Who was the last person around you?" I ask, trying to help her solve the puzzle. "Here, take my cell phone. Go back inside and call yourself. Maybe you'll hear the phone ringing," I say, handing Lexx my phone.

She gets out of the car and turns right back around.

"What's wrong?"

"Somebody got me," Lexx says, climbing back into the car. "Someone already turned the phone off. It's going straight to voice mail," she shrugs. "Forget that damn phone. I have a lock on it anyway. AZ will just have to buy me another one. Guess how much money I made tonight?" Lexx asks happily.

"How much?" I ask with little enthusiasm. It really didn't matter to me. I didn't see the money anyway.

"I made a stack tonight. That's good for a Sunday. I met this Jamaican guy who had the biggest package I ever saw. AZ ain't got shit on him." Lexx says, licking her lips.

"I know that's right. Them bitches are jealous of you. That's why they took your phone."

We burst out laughing while Lexx counts the money.

"So, who was in the bar at closing?" I say, remaining focused on her cell phone.

"No one but DJ and Suga. Jay, Hollywood, and Champagne were there too. I asked DJ if he saw the phone. He told me he hadn't," Lexx says as if she believed him.

"I do remember Jay coming over to me. He said his car was running outside and asked if I was ready to go. Then he leaned in close to my face, asking don't we look good together. That made me very nervous."

My eyes narrow listening to Lexx. Every pimp at that bar wanted her. AZ never talked to any of their girls. It was blatant disrespect for them to keep coming after her.

"I thought Jay was up to something. He was waiting outside in the parking lot when I got there. When he saw my car, he sped off. He probably was trying to kidnap you. I must've spoiled his plans. Most likely, Jay is the one who stole your phone. Without a phone, it would be impossible to call for help. In all probability, Jay wanted to retaliate for AZ making him lose Hollywood," I say to Lexx.

She nods her head and puts the money away.

As soon as we got home, Lexx told AZ the whole story. He was so mad he wanted to fight Jay.

"If that nigga ever says anything to you again, tell him your daddy is going to charge his ass!"

AZ hugs Lexx tightly, stroking her long, black, silky hair. She smiles at him with a false sense of security. AZ really couldn't charge Jay for talking to Lexx. Generally, it was the other way around. If a hooker talked to a pimp, she'd be charged. Technically, she was out of pocket for doing so.

It's August 17, 2012. AZ, Shi, and I are in the living room watching the Channel 12 news. AZ runs over to the set and turns up the volume.

"Is that Debbie on the TV?!" he says, eyes growing wide.

Debbie was a girl, who left AZ over a year ago. She was one of many come-and-go girls he acquired over time. Apparently, she had left AZ for a pimp who was selling drugs. The reporter alleges the pimp was involved in a lucrative heroin ring.

"Yup, that's her picture on the screen. Isn't that crazy!" Shi gasps, holding her hand over her mouth.

AZ grimaces. "Debbie is only twenty-one years old. It turns me off to see her addicted to that stuff. She was a pretty white girl when I had her. Now her life is ruined. She's going away for a very long time," AZ says, turning the channel.

The caller Id flashes my sister's name across the TV screen. I hurry to my room and pick up the landline.

"Hey, girl, I've been calling you all day." I say, curling up on my bed with the phone to my ear.

"Yeah, I know. I've been busy with these kids," she says, sounding very tired. "I even had to watch my grandkids today. Their mother went to visit her boyfriend in the hospital. It's been three weeks now and he's still paralyzed from that terrible motorcycle accident. It doesn't look good for him," she says, inhaling deeply.

I wince in the mirror on the dresser, listening to her talk.

"Things are hard for me. I have all these bills with little money. This damn light bill is five thousand dollars. I don't know how to pay it, Ugh," she groans, drifting into thought.

"Don't worry about those bills. God will make a way," I say, hoping to cheer her up.

"I want Barry to help me, but he's so needy himself. If he did what AZ does, he might have some money. I know he can do it. He's been using women all of his life," she says about her boyfriend.

I laugh, but she's not joking.

"Girl, pimping ain't easy. These girls are constantly jealous of one another. In addition to that, pimps always have to watch their backs in these streets," I say, trying to deter her from the idea.

"I know, but Barry can do it. I just don't think I can handle it. I have my kids here."

I subjectively listen to her.

"Sis, I wish AZ would get out of my house with these girls. Unfortunately, he won't leave. Most of his money goes to drugs and expensive food. AZ doesn't save or invest in anything essential. I'm displeased with this whole mess. Barry may have the same problems if he gets into the business."

"Isn't it illegal?" she asks rhetorically.

"It wasn't illegal for Hugh Hefner. The Playboy mansion was in business for years. That place was a known brothel. I can't see much difference in AZ doing it. Other than the fact Hefner paid taxes. Then again, when you're white, everything's right," I say, making us both laugh.

"Girl, bye! I got to get back to these kids."

"Call me later," I say, hanging up and enjoying the fact I made her laugh. I understood my sister was under immense pressure taking care of five kids and a lazy bum.

Dear diary, it's August 21, 2012. It's Nina's lucky day again. In the kitchen, she looks at a text on her cell phone. The customer wants to meet her at a nearby motel.

"Daddy, can I use the truck? I have a date!" Nina yells to AZ.

"The keys are on the kitchen table!" he yells back to her.

Listening to them, I couldn't understand why AZ didn't have someone drive Nina. Shi was home. Why couldn't she take Nina? If Shi worked two nights out of seven, she would complain about being miserable. It wasn't clear to me why she was so miserable. Shi lay around eating, smoking, and sniffing all day. To me, the least she could do was drive Nina to her dates. Besides, it was stupid to have Nina drive herself. Not only was Nina a crash test dummy, but she also had multiple charges for driving without a license. Somehow, AZ thinks tonight will be different.

After Nina gets dolled up, she stuffs a bag with illegal paraphernalia and walks out of the front door. The pretty young girl is a magnet for trouble.

Arriving at the motel, Nina turns into the driveway and parks the truck. The seedy establishment is poorly lit, surrounded by weeds and large bushes. Nina texts her customer, unaware of two suspicious characters observing her every move. The men sit lurking in a dark four-door sedan with the headlights turned off. Nina's customer responds to her text with his room number. Nina hops out of the truck and heads for the room.

In bed half asleep, I hear AZ in the living room arguing with someone over the phone. I get up, put on my slippers, and see what's happening.

"No! I don't have any damn money for you!" AZ screams loudly. "Where is all your fucking money?!" he barks at the person on the other end.

I lean over the sofa, whispering to Shi, "Who's AZ talking to?" Shi shrugs and continues watching the documentary on TV.

"You know these phones are monitored. Don't talk too much, idiot!" AZ yells at the person.

"Must be Nina," Shi says to me.

"Where the hell is Nina?" I ask, paranoid she's turned informant for the police.

"Evidently, she's been arrested again," Shi smirks.

"How did she get arrested?!" I ask with concern.

"Supposedly, she went out on a date. I think her ass went for some drugs again," Shi says, adding fuel to the fire.

"I don't know what I'm going to do! I don't have NO money! I'm hanging up now!" AZ says, slamming down the phone.

He knew Nina would be hysterical if he didn't bail her out. It still pissed him off to keep spending money on her. AZ grumbles under his breath, stomping up the steps. He comes back with a fist full of dollars and throws them on the glass table in front of us.

"Can you go bail that dummy out for me? She's at the fifth precinct," he says, directing the question to me.

"I don't even know how to get to the fifth precinct," I say, rolling my eyes at him. *Why me? Isn't that your job?!* "Why is Nina in jail anyway?" I ask, sucking my teeth.

AZ glares at me. "Just hurry and get dressed. They'll be shipping Nina to the fourth precinct with the other women if you don't get there soon."

I knew AZ didn't have a license and Shi definitely wasn't going. Shi wouldn't go if AZ was in jail. That is unless, of course, she was the only one free.

"Ugh, okay I'll go," I say reluctantly.

Once I was dressed, I returned to the living asking about Nina's charges again.

"Why did Nina get arrested?" I ask adamantly. *If it's a drug charge, I'm not going!*

"Nina said the detectives arrested her for not having a driver's license."

I breathe a sigh of relief hearing this.

"Alright, tell me how to get there," I say, holding my hand out for the bail money.

AZ gave very good driving directions. Sometimes better than a navigation system. He quickly tells me how to get there.

I leave out the door, hop into my car and take the twenty-minute drive to the police station. Parking out front, I immediately receive a phone call.

"Hello!" I answer, annoyed because I knew it was AZ calling me.

"Are you there yet? Nina called, crying about being shipped to another location."

If you're so concerned, you should be here. I think to myself, rolling my eyes at the cell phone. "Yeah, I'm here. I'm still outside parking the car.

I'll be in the station in a few minutes. I'll call you back when I know something."

I walk through the precinct doors into the lobby and stand directly in front of a tall desk. A Caucasian, slightly attractive sergeant, peers over the desk at me.

"Hello sir. I'm here to bail someone out," I say, being super polite.

He looks at the booty shorts I'm wearing and then at my face. "What's the perp's name?" he says, grinning widely.

I give him Nina's government name.

"Have a seat. Her paperwork will be processed in a minute."

I have to wait for a call from Albany to confirm her release. We want to make sure she has no outstanding warrants. She might've killed someone in another State," he says jokingly, before sitting back in his seat.

"Thank you," I say, retreating to a hard iron bench behind me.

The wait is almost forty-five minutes before he addresses me again. During this time, a woman comes in asking about her son's paperwork. It hadn't come through yet. She impatiently sucks her teeth and goes back outside to smoke a cigarette.

"Miss, we received the phone call from Albany. Her paperwork is ready. I'll just need some Identification from you and three hundred dollars for the bail."

Leaping to my feet, I hand the officer my identification card and the money. Sitting back on the bench, I'm confident I don't have any warrants. With time ticking away, I become very agitated.

"Miss, is this address good for you?" The officer asks holding up my identification card.

"Yes, that's fine," I say, anxious to get the process over with.

"Good. I'll just need your signature, and she'll be right out."

He motions for me to come to sign the bail receipt. I eagerly jump up, putting my Jane Hancock on the paper.

"It's freezing in here. Let her know I'll be outside," I say, quickly exiting the building.

It's not long before I see Nina through the precinct window. She's being escorted by a police officer down a long corridor into the lobby. I watch them release her property. Afterward, Nina walks out of the precinct doors with a big smile on her face. I definitely understood why she was so happy.

"What the hell happened this time?" I ask when Nina gets into the car.

"Ugh, I need a cigarette. I can't believe my bad luck," she says, fishing through her handbag. "When I got out the truck at the motel --" Nina stops talking and puts the cigarette in her mouth. "This scary car drives up and blocks me from walking to the customer's room," she says, lighting the cigarette and taking a long pull. "The car window rolls down and the passenger sticks his head out. 'Hey, you, come over here.' the man says to me. Karen, I was so scared, I didn't know what to do. It was dark out there. I thought about screaming."

"Why didn't you run for your life!" I ask her. "Because I thought they were cops," Nina says, inhaling the smoke.

"Who me? I ask, walking over to the car, playing it cool. 'Where you going?' the passenger asks me. To my room. I say, nervously. 'Oh yeah! You got a key?' he asks, doubtful. No, I'm meeting a friend there. I say to him. It's the wrong damn answer. The motel is known for solicitation. Both cops jump out and start interrogating me. 'Whose vehicle is this that you're driving?' the passenger barks at me. They approach me from both sides. It's my friend's truck. I say, anticipating they want to lock me up. 'You got a license?!' the driver asks. I handed him my state identification card. I knew I had several unpaid moving violations. The driver snatches my identification card. 'Stand right here while I run your information.' he says to me. Once they run my information through the computer, they frisk and arrest me on three counts. 'Hands against the car.' The driver cuffs and throws me into the back seat. They find some weed, wrappings, and a pack of cigarettes before taking me down to the police station."

I shake my head, unable to believe Nina's bad luck. "Girl, we have to go back to that motel and get the truck. I'm nervous about you driving again without a license."

"Forget the damn, Po Po!" Nina laughs at me and puts the cigarette butt out in the ashtray.

Arriving back at the motel, Nina is fearless. She could care less about those detectives. She jumps right into the truck, turns on the ignition, and drives out of the parking lot. I followed close behind in case her crazy ass was pulled over again.

August 24, 2012, the day starts off cool but ends up being a disaster.

I wake up late this day. I write out a check for the mortgage and rush to the mailbox before the carrier arrives.

Walking across the lawn, I hear Lexx's voice. When I reach the curb, she's down the block talking loud on her cell phone. Lexx smiles when she notices me watching her.

"Girl, that Puerto Rican blood is always boiling," I say, laughing at her.

Lexx hangs up the phone walking over to me. "Eta, I'm pissed," she says using the nickname we call each other.

"What's wrong?"

"I'm getting tired of his shit. You know what he did to me?" She was talking about AZ.

I put my finger to my lips. "Shush! The people across the street will hear you," I say, grabbing Lexx by the elbow and ushering her back toward the house.

Our neighbors were very nosy. Sometimes they sat across the street in lawn chairs just staring at our house.

"I don't know why AZ always does this to me. He treats me like a fool," Lexx pouts childishly. "He tells me he's coming to my room but never does. Why would he say it and not do it? When he says something, he should keep his word," she whines, stomping her feet.

"I always see him in Nina's room, hugged up with her. Is that what he wants? A drughead!" Lexx wonders, folding her arms across her chest. "I'm tired of sitting in my room alone looking at those four walls. It's the end of this shit for me!"

When Lexx takes a breather and finally lets me get a word in edgewise, "Let's go to the beach," I say quickly.

"Oh, Karen, for real! You always come through. Let's get out of this place," Lexx beams with excitement.

"I've been wanting to go to the beach all summer long. AZ never does anything but lay in between everybody's legs."

Looking at her, I understood exactly how she felt. There was a time I once felt like her. However, now I was numb to the situation. Nonetheless, the beach would be a refreshing change of scenery.

"Let's take Shi with us!" I say, walking into the house with Lexx.

"Shi! Hell no! She gets on my nerves,"Lexx reacts, immediately shutting the idea down.

I look at her, stupefied.

"I mean if you want her to go, I guess it's okay," Lexx says, switching her disposition. "I like Shi, but she's always doing dumb shit to me. Last night at the club she told some customers I sniff coke. She knows that's a lie! She's just trying to mess up my money. I brought home fourteen hundred dollars last night. I can't make that kind of money if the customers think I'm a drug head," Lexx explains, frowning at me.

I nod my head, agreeing with her.

"Okay. You and I will go," I say realizing Lexx is already very frustrated.

"Just you and me," she squeals with excitement. "I need some weed, though," she says, grinning wide. "Do you need some gas money? How much does the beach cost?" Lexx asks, skipping up the steps to get the money from AZ.

After she disappears, I go to my room to get dressed. I pull a blanket and some towels out of the closet. After that, I put on a one-piece bathing suit. Checking myself in the mirror, I looked like a beached whale. Quickly changing clothes, I put on some spandex shorts and a large t-shirt. Satisfied with this look, I slip on my flip-flops and return to the living room to wait for Lexx. In a few minutes, Lexx comes stomping down the steps. She's scantily dressed in a two-piece bathing suit with tiny white shorts. And her face is beet red.

"What's wrong now?!" I ask, knowing AZ was the problem.

Lexx throws everything in her hands on the couch and reveals, "He's up there laying with Nina again! She's not the money maker anymore. I AM!

I don't know why he spends so much time with Nina and Shi! They don't make any money! Brrrr..." Lexx blows wind through flapping lips as if she's freezing.

I watch the little girl have a temper tantrum, realizing she can't handle the game. *A grown-ass man should not take advantage of such a fragile mind.* I think to myself. I wait for Lexx's tantrum to subside.

"You ready to go now?" I ask, picking up my bag.

"Yeah, let's go to the beach. I'm done thinking about them!"

Lexx grabs her towel and purse off the couch and walks out of the front door with me.

On our way to the weed man, Lexx's phone rings. She looks at the screen and throws it on the car floor.

"Who's that?!" I gasp, shocked by her fiery temper.

"That's AZ. I'm not answering him!" Lexx says, folding her arms defiantly.

The phone rings again. This time I reach for it, concluding I must've taken Lexx without his permission.

"Give me the phone. I'll answer it," I say, rattled by her poor behavior.

"Hello, AZ."

"Oh, now you want to answer me," he says, sarcastically.

Checking the phone in my purse, I see there are two missed calls from him.

"You know I can't hear anything with the car radio playing. Lexx and I are on our way to the beach," I say to him calmly.

"Put her ass on this phone!" he says sharply.

I hand Lexx the phone. She listens for a few minutes, turning beet red. I can tell she's about to explode.

"Yeah, okay! I hear you! Are you done yet? I'm hanging up now!" Lexx says, then hands me the phone back before AZ's done with the conversation.

When I put the phone to my ear, AZ is yelling at the top of his lungs.

"I don't know what's wrong with that stupid bitch. I didn't do nothing to her!" he says, convincing me I'm dealing with two children.

The girl is giving you her money. It's obvious she wants to spend some quality time with you, dummy! I think to myself. I knew AZ didn't have a clue about women's feelings. To him, it was all business. I quietly listened until he was finished the rant. Hanging up, I turned around and smiled at Lexx. She was still fuming from their conversation.

"I want to go home!" Lexx says adamantly.

"You want to go back to the house?" I ask, whipping the car around.

"Not that house! I want to go home to Jersey! I'm tired of his shit!" Lexx says, putting her face down in the palm of her hands and begins to cry.

"What did he say to you?" I ask her.

"He said don't buy any weed. He already got some for me at home. He's confusing me," Lexx says in a cute Hispanic accent.

Inhaling deeply, I try to confront the problem. "If you don't want to go back to the house, let's just go get a dub. We can buy it from my friend, Ant live," I say, attempting to solve her little problem.

Actually, I just wanted to go to the beach and relax.

"Okay, cool. Let's do that," Lexx smiles, satisfied with my solution. I turn the music up and continue on our journey.

"Aye, that's my song," Lexx sings along with the record playing on the radio and forgets all about AZ.

On the ride to Mastic, I thought about Ant live. He was the person who helped me get the mansion. I hadn't seen my old friend in months.

Ant was standing in front of his car shop with some friends when we pulled up. I hardly recognized him. He had made quite a few changes to his appearance. Losing over twenty pounds unmasked a chiseled, muscular body. His freshly cut Caesar replaced nappy unkept braids. Ant's new look was quite appealing. I parked the car and hopped out to greet him. Lexx stayed in the passenger seat watching us.

"Hey, Ant, long time no see. How you doing?" I asked, grinning wide.

"Yeah, Kay, a lot has happened since the last time we spoke." Ant's eyes locked on Lexx as she slowly steps out of the car.

"Damn he sexy!" Lexx says out loud.

"You sexy, too!" Ant comments, blushing and licking his lips.

Lexx quickly walks over to us.

"Ant, this is Lexx. She wants to buy a dub of exotic," I say, watching them hug each other.

"We're on our way to the beach. You want to come?" I ask, knowing Ant would never leave his place of business. Especially, not when people came all day to buy weed and get their cars detailed.

"Nah, I'm good."

Ant turns around, jogging up some rickety steps to his loft to get the weed. He returns handing a small bag to Lexx. With a sly smirk, she hands him the money, then goes to the car for a grinder. Lexx walks back to us, flirtatiously batting her eyelashes at Ant.

"You want to smoke with me?" she asks him while grinding the weed.

"Sure, and I got something else for you too." Ant reaches into a bag on his workbench. "Want some weed brownies?" he asks us.

I had quit smoking and went back to church. It felt good to decline his offer. Lexx, however, took the brownie and ate a mouthful. We laughed and talked to Ant until he concluded his long break with us and said goodbye.

On our way to the beach, Lexx and I stopped for some food.

"Girl, give me a piece of that fried chicken," I said, driving through the cashier's booth at the beach.

"Is this piece okay?" Lexx asks, holding up a large leg for me.

"I'm starving; any piece will do," I say, snatching the chicken and shoving it in my mouth.

After locating a space in the crowded parking lot, we unloaded the car and took a long walk to the beach. At two o'clock in the afternoon, the waves were cold and choppy.

"It's too breezy to get in this water, Karen. My munchies are starting to kick in. Let's eat!" Lexx says, spreading out the blanket for us to sit down. I smile, watching her dig into the bucket of chicken.

"Eta, doesn't it feel good to get away from that house? See how relaxing it is by the water," I say to her.

"You're right, Eta. We need to do this more often. I hate staring at those four walls in my room. It's driving me crazy!" Lexx says, licking her fingertips.

Finishing the chicken, she stands up brushing the sand off of her shorts. "Come with me back to the car so I can smoke my weed."

"I'm still eating, Lexx. Plus, who'll watch the blanket? Here, take my keys and you go," I say, handing Lexx the keys to my car.

"Okay, I'll be right back," she says, running off into the sun. About thirty minutes passed. Lexx still hadn't returned yet.

I started to worry about her. I left the blanket on the beach and went to look for her. When I got to the parking space it was empty. I frantically looked around, convinced Lexx was *GONE!* My mind raced back to our last conversation. *Karen, I'm ready to go home. I'm tired of AZ's shit!* I remember Lexx saying to me. Panicking, I started making bad assumptions. The forty ounces of beer I drank on the beach was playing tricks on my mind. *Lexx took your car to JERSEY! You're sooo stupid for giving her your car keys! Call her now!* I fumbled around in my purse to get the cell phone. *Oh Gosh! You don't know her new number. What are you going to do now, stupid! Call AZ!*

Positioning the phone, I started dialing but couldn't see the numbers. The sun was reflecting off the screen. *Ugh, you can't see the numbers!*

Scared and upset, I couldn't think straight. Forgetting the blanket on the beach, I foolishly began the twenty-mile trek home. I was trotting quickly across the parking lot, ducking behind every vehicle, trying to shade my cellphone. A mile away on the bridge, I was able to see the screen clearly. I frantically dialed AZ's number. *Oh shit, it's his voicemail.*

"Lexx is gone! She stole my car! I'm walking down William Floyd parkway. Come and get me now!" I screamed frantically in my cellular.

Paranoia sets in. Half running, half walking down the highway in flip-flops, my feet blistered and burned. My hair blew wildly in the wind, making me look like a crazy woman to the passing cars. I dialed Shi's number in tears, repeating the same stupid message. I was two miles away from the beach when AZ returned my call. Hearing AZ's voice, I start talking fast and furious.

"Lexx is gone! She stole my car! Call her now!" I say to him, breathing heavily.

Feeling really dumb for giving Lexx my keys, I wait for AZ's tongue-lashing.

"What do you mean you gave Lexx your car keys?!" he screams at me. "Okay, let me call her!" he says, hanging up quickly.

It only takes AZ a minute to call me back. I nervously fumble with the phone to answer it.

"Lexx moved the car to smoke some weed. Go back to the beach. She's waiting for you," he says calmly.

My mouth drops open. All the blood drains from my face.

"You're always over reacting, and it makes me upset too!" AZ snaps before hanging up the phone.

I felt so foolish trudging back to the beach with swollen feet. I was so busy dialing everyone's number, I didn't stop to look for the car. Leaving the beach in such a hurry, I must've walked right past it.

When I got back to the beach, Lexx was laid out, sunbathing on the blanket. I breathed a heavy sigh of relief, wondering what she thought of me. I slowly walked over to face the music.

"Hey, homie!" Lexx yells to me.

I limped forward, head hanging low. I was too embarrassed to look at Lexx.

"I would never leave you. Why did you think that? You my homie. I wouldn't do that to you," Lexx says, eyes sad and red from smoking.

"AZ called me. He said, oh you stealing cars now?!" she smiles, but I feel awful for not trusting her.

My head drops between my shoulders.

"I'm sorry, Lexx. I went to look for you, but the car was gone. I panicked, thinking you left me."

"I can see how you might think that, especially after how I was talking today. But I'm no thief, Karen. I wouldn't take your car."

"I know, I know. I made a big mistake thinking that."

"It's all right, homie. At least we are communicating about it. That's all I ask from AZ."

We both laughed it off and spent the rest of the day enjoying the sun. Laying back on the blanket, I thought about my past life at the Mansion.

CHAPTER VI
TIGHTENING THE GAME

Coming down the steps after a short nap, I was just in time to see Rabyt plant a big juicy kiss on Cheeks' lips. They had spent most of the day in the mansion drinking together. Apparently, now they were well-acquainted. She was wasting no time getting her hooks into him. The drunken look on their faces revealed the sexual tension between them. I was glad Tee wasn't around to see it.

"I see everyone is getting along rather nicely," I said, entering the living room.

AZ and KG were busy talking on the speakerphone with Erin who was still living in Florida with Big Will. She stayed there after KG and Kal left her. AZ was making a feeble attempt to get her back.

"Is that you, Karen?" Erin asked, surprised to hear my voice in the background.

"Yeah, it's me." I said loudly.

"Hi, Karen!" she squealed, feigning excitement.

"Hey, Erin! It's good to hear your voice too. Are you still in Miami?" I asked out of curiosity.

"Yup, I have blonde hair now. And my body is super toned. I work out every day. You'd hardly recognize me. I look completely different."

I knew she was telling the truth. Big Will demanded nothing but the best from his high-priced whores.

"Sounds great! Hope to see you soon," I said, playing along knowing AZ was in hot pursuit of a prostitute.

"We are working on that now," Erin said before AZ rudely interrupted our conversation.

"Okay! Let me talk to her."

He took the cell phone off of speaker and walked out on the porch when it suddenly occurred to me why the phone was on speaker in the first place. AZ wanted to make Shi jealous. She had been playing him ever since they returned from Miami. He was becoming quite fed up with her nonsense. Not only was Shi pushing other girls away, but she was also still dating her ex-boyfriend, Angelo. AZ, more than likely, was using Erin to put an end to her shenanigans.

He returned to the living room looking very agitated. AZ was still very upset about the stunt Shi had pulled on Tee's friends. They were potential prospects for his stable.

"Where's Do Do bird?" he asks me and KG.

"I think Shi is in the bedroom on her cell phone," I say to him.

"Is she getting ready for work?!" he snarls, then sucks his teeth angrily storming off to find out for himself.

Minutes later, we heard a shouting match ensue between them. AZ was arguing with Shi about Angelo. Up until now, AZ allowed them to date because Angelo was her customer. But whenever Shi got mad at AZ, she threatened to leave him for Angelo. In order to control the situation, AZ had to dead that relationship. After speaking with Erin, he finally mustered the courage to do so.

Shi comes bolting into the living room, startling me and KG. "Come and get me NOW!" she screams into her cell phone.

AZ comes racing into the room after her. He grabs her by the hair, flinging her to the floor.

"Ahhh, stop it, AZ!" Shi yells, kicking and punching to fight him off.

KG and I are appalled. We just sit there helplessly watching them.

"Give me that damn phone!" AZ yells at her.

Shi puts up a struggle, but it's pointless. AZ successfully snatches the phone away from her. Rabyt and Cheeks come running into the room to see what's going on. By this time, AZ's acting like a crazy man.

"You talking shit about me to this white boy?!" AZ screams. "Angelo! Did this bitch tell you she's giving me all your money?! Did she tell you she is licking my balls every night?! The bitch is not telling you that, is she?! AZ hollers on the phone to Angelo.

KG blinks rapidly from all of the commotion. Entertained by it all, I snicker to myself. The thought of Shi licking AZ's balls probably made Angel want to throw up. She always told us that he didn't like black people.

Shi got up, running, and screaming, out of the front door. AZ continues his rant over the phone with Angelo. Rabyt and I follow Shi outside on the front porch where falling helplessly to the floor, she cries inconsolably, draws her knees up to her chest, and crouches into a ball. Rabyt and I rush to her aid, but she pushes us away. AZ comes running outside with us to hand her the phone. Hurt and embarrassed, she refuses to take it. AZ puts the phone on speaker and tosses it on the floor to her.

"Here, talk to your man!" he barks, satisfied he's ruined their relationship.

Angelo, hearing Shi crying in the background and wanting Shi to confirm the story, hollers through the phone, "Is that true?! Is it really true what he's telling me, Shi?!"

With tears streaming down her face, Shi whimpers barely above a whisper, "Yes, it's true. All of it's true."

Once Angelo receives his answer, we hear the phone click. Shi's beside herself with remorse, violently kicking and banging her fist on the porch.

"You've ruined my money! That's my best customer, asshole!" she screams loudly with hair sticking up like a peacock on top of her head from AZ pulling on it.

She squats with her arms wrapped around her knees, rocking back and forth like a psycho. Hearing her, AZ comes running back outside.

"Fuck your customer!" he yells, with strings of spit popping out his mouth. He's so angry, the veins protrude from the side of his neck.

Rabyt and I think he's about to hit her. Instead, he balls his fist and marches back into the house. I follow behind him, giggling.

"Now put her ass out!" I say, instigating the situation.

Later that night, I went to pick up Tee from work. By the time we returned to the mansion, everyone was asleep. Shi and AZ were locked in their bedroom as usual. I didn't mention anything to Tee about Cheeks. I figured she'd find out about his new boo soon enough.

The next morning, I lay in bed frustrated, thinking about the rent. Contemplating my next move, I watched rain drops bounce off the windowsill.

The money AZ's collecting from Shi and Tee still isn't enough to pay the bills. It's been two months since acquiring this mansion. I'm the only one paying rent with minimal help from anyone else. Hopefully, when Erin arrives from Miami that will change. If not, I'm prepared to leave this place. At this rate, how can I possibly afford to stay? Something has to give. Ugh! I'm thinking myself into a frenzy. It's best I go downstairs and let everyone know how I feel.

Happy laughter and chitter chatter come from the kitchen as I enter.

"Good morning! It's too early for all this damn noise," I say, smiling at Rabyt and KG.

Rabyt sat comfortably at the table with her shoes kicked off. It was early but she seemed dressed for a party. I assumed her tight-fitting dress and flawless makeup were for Mr. Cheeks.

"Rabyt wants to ask you a question," KG says to me.

"What's up, Rabyt? Speak your mind."

Yawning loudly, I reach for the eggs in the refrigerator. I crack two, placing them in the frying pan on the stove.

"Hi, Karen! I hope we didn't wake you," Rabyt says from beneath a big curly wig.

"No, this is my normal beer time," I say, removing the scrambled eggs from the frying pan.

"Karen, I told Rabyt we might have a room to rent," KG says, looking at me for approval.

"How much is a room in this beautiful mansion? The place is really nice," Rabyt says, piling the shit on thick.

I refrained from answering too quickly. I sat down, placing my plate and bottle of beer on the table. Rabyt squirmed with anticipation, waiting for me to speak. I was also eager but paused to carefully weigh my options. I wanted to avoid overcharging her yet, still, get enough to cover my costs. I knew Rabyt liked Mr. Cheeks. I just wasn't sure how much it was worth to her. I had to milk the cow for all it was worth.

"Currently, we only rent to dancers. They pay a fraction of their daily earnings to cover room and board," I say, gobbling a mouthful of eggs.

It's easily a lie. I couldn't get ten dollars from the girls.

"Is eight hundred dollars a month, too much?" I ask her, holding my breath, waiting for a response.

Rabyt's green eyes watch me closely. She looks over at KG, who nods his approval.

"Okay, I can handle that!" she says happily.

"Great!" I exhale, taking a big swig of the beer. "I'll even waive the security deposit if you move in by this weekend," I say, wanting her money right away.

"Shit! I can move in tonight!" Rabyt responds, opening her purse and peeling eight hundred dollars off the stack.

I'm blown away when she hands it to me.

"Ssssssssure, that's fine," I say, stuttering, as I take the money before she changes her mind. "Let me get you a receipt," I say, standing up and placing my plate in the sink.

"Hold it for me. I'm going home right now and start packing." Rabyt slips her feet into the six-inch stilettos underneath the table. "Tell Cheeks, I'll see him later."

She hugs KG and walks out, slamming the front door.

When Rabyt is gone, I leap into the air, skipping around with the money in my hand. I almost bump into AZ as he enters the room.

"What are you so excited about?" he asks me.

"Hmmm, KG just got me some rent money," I say, waving the bills in his face.

"Oh yeah! Where's my cut?" he says, scratching his chest and opening the refrigerator.

I roll my eyes so hard that they almost pop out my head.

"It was nothing. Rabyt wanted to move in," KG chuckles, rubbing his palms together. "I got another little surprise, too. My boy, Raul, has a girl for me. I'm going to check her out today," KG says, raising his eyebrows.

AZ frowns at us. "Does Rabyt work at the strip club? We don't need no square bitches living here. It'll only confuse things," he snarls on his way back to his room.

"Y'all better figure that Rabyt shit out!" he shouts, slamming his bedroom door.

KG and I completely ignore him and continue discussing our plans.

"Karen, I gotta get this money one way or another. Moving in here has ruined my relationship with my girl. I can't go back and live with her anymore. I also got that Mercedes Benz sitting outside. The payments are kicking my ass. Chuck calls every day about the car note. Me and AZ are ducking and dodging his calls."

KG stands to leave when we hear a loud knock at the door. Doubting it's for me, I look at him and throw my hands in the air. Most of the traffic was usually for him or AZ. I didn't know many people on Long Island. A majority of the years, I spent commuting back and forth to the city.

KG walks to the front door and opens it.

"What's up, Uni? Long time no see, man. How did you find me way out here?!" he asks the guy, giving him a pound.

"You know I got my ways," the guy says.

"When did you get out?" KG asks, bringing the ex-convict into the living room with us.

"Karen, guess who I found at the front door?" KG grins at the dark skin, medium-height, stocky guy standing before us. "This is my main man, Uni!" he says.

"Nice to meet you, Uni."

I shake the guy's sweaty palm. He squeezes my hand and kisses it. Appalled by his audacity, I frown, displeased with the criminal.

"Oh, you're quite the gentleman," I say, quickly snatching my hand away.

He grins, showing me a mouthful of gold teeth. Then he mumbles something inaudible.

"What you got good?" KG asks, eyeing the backpack in Uni's hand. "You know I ain't come all this way empty-handed. I always got something good," Uni grumbles, taking a six-pack of Coors Light out of his backpack. "You want one, miss lady?"

"Ugh. No, thank you. I drink Old English. Not toilet water!" I say, walking to the refrigerator to get my gasoline.

"I'll remember that next time," Uni says, winking at me. I flinch, unsure of what to think of this character.

"How about you, KG?" he asks, holding up the can of beer. "Nah, it's too early for me, homeboy."

Uni smirks at him. "I know what you like." He reaches back into the backpack, pulling out a big sack of weed.

KG's eyes light up. "Now you talking!"

Uni turns around, generously offering me some. "You smoke, miss lady?"

"Don't mind if I do," I say, walking back to the table and taking a seat next to the stranger.

"This is for you," he says, sliding what I estimate to be a half-ounce across the table for me. I smile, gladly accepting his gift.

"I got some Dutch Master cigars," he says, tossing two on the table for us.

KG opens one and empties the guts on the table.

"I don't like Dutch Masters. I have Backwoods," I say, real snippy and leave the table to go get them.

The sweet aroma of cannabis smoke fills the air, bringing all of the potheads out of their rooms. In no time at all, everyone is puffing and passing in the living room. Shi has her arms wrapped tightly around AZ's neck, keeping him hostage at the table. Tee whispers in Cheek's ear, making him grin while he smokes his blunt. In that moment, we all forgot about our worries. Uni has the perfect peace pipe to bring us together. AZ uses this opportunity to get into my good graces. He breaks free of Shi and walks across the room to me.

"I know you still want to start a country club. KG and I have this guy named Fredo coming to the mansion. He's a Latino party promoter. Fredo has some good ideas for this place. He can make it pop," AZ says, trying to strike up a conversation. "We also know a guy named H. He wants to shoot a video here for a rap artist named Mazaradi Fox." AZ pauses to see if I'm listening.

Fed up with the lies and daily arguments, I barely pay him any attention. To me, it all sounds like gibberish.

"Does this video guy have a budget?!" I snap, rolling my eyes at him. My curt demeanor tells him to leave me alone.

"Umm, Umm," AZ stutters with uncertainty. "Mazaradi just got out of jail. That's Fiddy's man. H will know if the label gave him a budget," he says, quickly walking away from me.

I decide to keep an open mind to what he says.

In the middle of the pow-wow, Rabyt walks through the front door dragging a big garbage bag in with her.

"Hi guys, I wasn't sure if y'all was home. The family cars are not outside," she says.

KG's and my car were parked by the garage. It's likely she didn't see them. But AZ's truck was parked directly in front of the house. Rabyt looks at Tee who's innocently leaning against Cheek's arm. Her cheerful smile immediately changes to an evil grimace. The dirty look makes Cheeks smartly wiggle free and go chat with Uni.

"Rabyt, my Armada is parked right out front!" AZ says, running outside to check.

"Oh shit! My truck is gone!" he shouts, running back inside. "KG, call that bitch ass nigga, Chuck! He probably got something to do with this!" AZ says, slamming the front door and storming to his room to get dressed.

KG quickly gets on his cell phone to make the call. We all stare at each other, baffled by the turn of events. Uni stands up to stretch his legs.

"Well, I guess the party is over," he says, gathering his bags. Cheeks watches Uni prepare to put the weed away.

"Yo, my man. You got some sticky-icky to sell?" Cheeks asks, pinching two fingers together, illustrating a small amount of weed.

"Yeah, no problem," Uni says, not bothering with the half of a pound on the table, and goes, instead, underneath into another bag of tricks.

By doing this, Uni misses a chance to see Shi stealing from him. She snatches as much weed as possible from the pound on the table. I narrow my eyes, thinking to myself, *Shi probably did take that money from those customers in Florida.*

Rabyt crosses the room to confront Tee. She's upset about what she saw when she came through the door. Uni comes from underneath the table with a small bag of weed.

"Here, this one is on me. Tell a friend to tell a friend. I got good weed!" he says to Cheeks.

"No doubt!" Cheeks says, grinning wide.

AZ enters the room fuming. If looks could kill, we'd all be dead. "KG, is that asshole on the phone?!"

"Yeah, this is Chuck," KG says, handing AZ the phone. The whole room pauses and falls silent.

"Where's my truck, asshole?!"

We can't hear what Chuck tells AZ, but it's definitely not good. AZ's bottom lip quivers. He tosses the phone back to KG and looks directly at me.

"Drive me to the studio!" he demands sharply.

Without a word, I run upstairs to get my purse and car keys.

Arriving at the studio, I turn into the parking lot. Before I can stop, AZ jumps out of the rolling car and charges through the back door of the studio. KG's tires come to a screeching halt behind mine. Six car doors fly open and slam shut. We all race inside to see the show. By the time I reach the doorway, I can barely see above the shoulders. Everyone in the studio has gathered around Chuck's room. AZ is foaming at the mouth, fist balled by his side. Chuck, whose eyes are bulging out of their sockets, is sitting in the chair.

"Where's my truck? You bitch ass nigga!" AZ stands over him, hollering in his face as specks of spit fly into Chuck's face. "Say that shit you said over the phone!" AZ fake head-butts, making Chuck flinch.

"I don't know what happened to your truck after me and Kal took it," Chuck stammers in fear.

It's the wrong answer. *Smack!* AZ's large hand slaps the color out of his face. It knocks Chuck clear out of the chair onto the floor. The crowd groans when blood drizzles from Chuck's mouth. He rolls around grunting and, grabbing the edge of the desk, pulls himself up. AZ pushes through the crowd, runs out of the room, and disappears down the hall. Trying to get out of there, we trip and fall over each other. No one wants to be around for the police.

Outside, six car doors open and close. Everyone's glad to be back in their seats. KG drives around to my passenger side where AZ is sitting.

"You alright man?" KG asks him.

AZ, still visibly shaken, nods. Shi rubs his shoulders from the backseat to calm his nerves. Witnessing AZ slap another man was very impressive to me. I had only seen him fight women before.

KG frowns, "Bro, this is too much drama for me. I'm going to Raul's house to check out that girl. I'll catch y'all back at the mansion," he says, speeding away, leaving us in his dust.

I quickly follow behind KG, driving as fast as I can.

"What happened in there?" I ask AZ.

Shi, Tee and Rabyt quietly listen in the backseat.

AZ inhales deeply. "That fool told me he took my truck because I wasn't paying the car note. He must think I'm a sucker! Nobody is paying their car note! Wait until I see that nigga, Kal. Chuck didn't even know where the mansion was until Kal showed him. Those creeps came late at night and stole my truck. I don't want to talk about it anymore! Grrrr..." AZ growls, shutting down.

Arriving back at the mansion, AZ immediately starts barking orders at us.

"I don't have a truck anymore! I need everybody to make some money tonight! Karen, you take these girls to work for me. Tee, you're going to Stonehedge, and Shi you're going with her! Rabyt, you get dressed, too. You're going to the Scene. It's a team effort," he says, eyes dark and vengeful.

Shi takes off running to her room in tears. Rabyt, runs to console her. Shi is opposed to working without her teeth. Angelo promised to buy her some dental implants , but AZ put an end to that.

Lacking any remorse, AZ shows no mercy. "What ya'll standing around for? Go get ready!" he says, angrily dismissing us.

Forty-five minutes later, everyone, except for Shi, is back in the living room. Rabyt and Tee practice dance moves in front of the fireplace. Tee gyrates her hips following Rabyt's instructions. AZ and I sit watching them.

"What's taking this Do Do bird so long?!" he sighs impatiently.

We all look at him but say nothing. It's been more than two hours waiting for Shi. He's convinced she's doing it on purpose.

"Shi, hurry the hell up! The club is going to close soon!" he yells, becoming frustrated.

After what seems like an eternity, Shi comes into the room pouting. She drags her feet across the floor in six-inch stilettos. Her makeup is flawlessly done. She smells and looks fantastic.

"There goes my girl. You look so pretty!" Rabyt says, rushing over to hug her.

AZ's eyes are cold as he scowls, "Karen, just take Tee and Shi to work. It's too late for Rabyt to apply for a job tonight."

We arrive at Stonehedge in record time. I speed the whole way there. Shi is extremely emotional when we walk into the strip club where T Pain's record, *Buy you a drink*, is playing on the jukebox. Shi stares at the customers with her hand over her mouth.

"You okay?" Tee asks her.

"Don't worry about Shi," I say to Tee.

"Okay, let me see if she can work tonight." Tee says as she heads in the direction of the bar looking around for the owner.

Shi nervously watches her walk away.

"Girl, relax. Everything is going to be fine," I say to boost her confidence.

"That's easy for you to say. You're not a toothless dancer," Shi snaps at me.

I ignore her nervous energy and concentrate on Tee, who's talking to the manager at the bar. When she's done, she waves for us to come over. The old man looks Shi up and down when we approach.

"Get dressed. You can audition," he says coldly.

Quickly escorting her to the bathroom, Tee grabs Shi by the arm.

A few minutes later, Shi comes out in a genie outfit with a silk scarf wrapped around her face. She hurries across the room and hops on stage. We can tell she feels instantly at home. In two graceful swings, she whips her legs around the metal pole, hanging upside down. Her fragile body loops in dizzying spins like a ballerina. The whole club is in awe. The enchanting dance is mesmerizing. Tee and I are amazed by her incredible talent. When she's done, the manager gives us a warm smile, agreeing to let her work for the night.

AZ borrows my car that night to pick them up. At four o'clock in the morning, I hear him bringing the girls home. Loud giggling tells me they made a lot of money at the club. Moments later, the mansion is quiet. I turn off the television and lay quietly in the dark.

Now I lay me down to sleep, I pray the Lord my soul to keep.

If I should die before I wake, I pray the Lord my soul to take.

The door cracks open, the hinges creak, and across the floor, his shadow creeps. A pimp inside for one last ride, I cry and cry, my feelings die.

The next morning word is on the street about AZ slapping Chuck at the studio. Shi, Rabyt, Uni and I listen to AZ telling the story. Local gossipers say Chuck rented AZ's truck to a guy named Mingo, a well-known gangster in the community. AZ calls him to confirm the rumor. Mingo tells AZ he's only test-driving the truck. No funds were exchanged, therefore no harm no foul. The two agree to meet so Mingo can return the Armada.

"Good morning! What's all this cackling about?" KG says, walking into the kitchen and interrupting us. The sexy blonde on his arm is wearing nothing but a wife beater and some panties.

"I bet it was a good morning," Rabyt says, staring at the young girl.

"Oh, this is Cherry. She's Raul's friend," KG says, gently guiding the girl in front of him.

My mouth pops open, surprised by KG's public display of affection.

"Welcome to the mansion," AZ says to Cherry who smiles with no shame in her game.

"Is Cherry staying with us?" AZ asks, sizing her up for his business.

"Yes, she is," KG answers for her.

Cherry nods at him with dreamy eyes.

"KG, I need a ride to the studio. I have to pick up my truck from Mingo," AZ says.

KG looks at Cherry for permission. "You gonna be all right until I get back?"

"Of course, she will," AZ says, passing him the blunt.

KG takes two pulls and hands it to Cherry who after taking two puffs passes it back to him. Afterward, they lock eyes like lovesick puppies. Watching them, my mouth pops open again.

"Those idiots were stupid enough to take my truck. Didn't they think I would find out? Chuck knows I'll slap fire out of him!" AZ says, shadowboxing around the room and displaying his talent.

"Everything good between you and Mingo?" KG asks with the blunt dangling between his lips.

"Y'all need my burner?" Uni mumbles, reaching into his bag.

Is he joking? I think to myself, rolling my eyes at him. It was bad enough Uni showed up every morning like clockwork with drugs. I only allowed that because it was free weed, a luxury we could not afford to turn down.

"Nah, Mingo's not like that! If he says he's bringing the truck back, that's what it is!" Rabyt says, twisting her neck and placing a hand on her hip.

Her defending Mingo surprises us all. We look at her, shocked by the outburst.

"Yeah, everything's cool. We chopped it up over the phone," AZ interjects.

"It's all good then. Let's go get your truck!" KG says excitedly.

Shi, hands AZ a cup of Hennessy along with two-hundred-dollar bills from her lap dance.

"Here's your drink, daddy!" she says to him. On-looking pimps, green with envy, stare at them.

"Thanks, bae! KG, you want a drink?" he asks, passing KG a few singles.

The whole team is at the strip club celebrating the return of the Armada. AZ and KG shoot pool in the back of the club, maintaining full view of their surroundings.

"Yeah, I'll take a drink. It doesn't look like Cherry will make any money tonight," KG sighs, watching her huff and puff on stage.

KG couldn't afford to buy Cherry a stripper outfit. Therefore, wearing some borrowed heels, she danced topless in a thong. The shoes were so big, it made her flop around on stage like a clumsy oaf. Her bruised knees were evidence of the pain she endured trying to table dance for her customer. Her heavy breathing to keep up with more skilled dancers was very embarrassing to KG. He grimaced, mortified by her performance. Cherry's only skill was having sex for money. It's an unforeseen problem KG doesn't anticipate before picking her up from Raul. It's not his only problem.

A dancer named Leah glared at KG from across the room. She was his longtime friend and confidant. Leah had been around for years and was not about to lose her position to Cherry.

"Karen! Who the hell is that girl KG brought to my club?!" Leah asks, angrily tapping me on the shoulder.

I spun around to face her.

"Oh, that's Cherry. She's a new girl that KG brought to the mansion."

Leah's eyes narrowed watching Cherry make a fool of herself on stage. "That girl got to go! KG is not about to embarrass me in my club!" she says, stomping her feet.

No longer listening to Leah, my eyes veer toward the door. Rabyt walks in with a light skin cutie.

"Who the hell is that?" I ask her.

"Who, Mingo? Ugh!" she grunts, following my glance.

"Oh, that's Mingo!" I say, intensely staring at the handsome guy gliding across the room.

Mingo's Kangol hat was twisted to the side. He was wearing a white collared shirt neatly tucked in silk slacks. His swagger was very different from the rest."Mingo is always in here. He never spends any money on us though. He only buys drinks for himself," Leah says, rolling her eyes at him.

Rabyt spots us at the bar and makes her way over. Mingo goes in the other direction. I watch closely as he reaches into his pants pocket waving to the bartender.

"Hey, girl! What time did you get here?" Rabyt asks, kissing me on the cheek.

"So, that's Mingo!" I say, watching him flirt with Kelz, the bartender.

"Yeah, girl. That's Mingo. I drove him here. We used to have a thing, but now that's over," Rabyt says, twisting her neck and popping her hip out.

"Where's everybody at?" she sighs, looking around the bar in search of Cheeks.

Five minutes earlier, he was sloppy drunk tongue kissing Tee. He left the bar just minutes before Rabyt arrived. She was lucky to miss him.

"The bar is closing soon. We're all going back to the mansion to hang out. Why don't you invite your friend?" I say, admiring Mingo from afar. I didn't care what AZ thought. Mingo was some fine eye candy. I couldn't take my eyes off of him.

"Girl, Mingo is mean as shit. You don't want no parts of him. He plays no games. And he will bust his gun at the drop of a dime. Leave his crazy ass right here!" Rabyt says, batting her long lashes.

A lump forms in my throat. *Rabyt was probably right. Mingo sounded like bad news. KG and AZ would never want his type around the girls. But damn he was fine!* I thought to myself.

We stay at the club until closing waiting for the girls to count their singles and pay tip out. Afterward, we hustle out into

the brisk night air and jump into AZ's Armada to head home. He drives so fast; we land at the mansion in under thirty minutes. Entering the house, he and KG, sit at the table in the living room to talk. The rest of us make beelines to our rooms.

I pretend to go to bed but linger on the catwalk to eavesdrop.

"Ahh, I'm not taking Cherry back to that strip club," KG sighs, leaning back in his chair.

AZ gathers the singles Tee and Shi left on the table in front of him.

"What are you going to do with her then?" AZ says, licking his fingertips and counting the money.

"It was torture watching her struggle for that chump change. Now, I see why Raul gave her to me," KG says, choking on the blunt.

AZ stacks the singles on the table. I quietly listen to the men, hoping AZ will say how much money the girls made. I knew if I asked, he'd only lie to me.

"If Cherry can't make any money, she's dead weight," AZ says, ignoring the hurt look on KG's face. "I got an idea, though. My man been calling me about his Brainfest," AZ says, toking loudly on the weed.

KG looks at him puzzled.

AZ leans in close, whispering, "You remember those underground parties I told you about."

"Yeah, I remember. What about them?" KG asks, eagerly siting up.

"I think we should take Cherry to one. The next Brainfest is in Queens. The girls make plenty of money!" AZ says excitedly. "The perverts come from all around, spending thousands of dollars to see freaky shit. The girls do everything. They sit on bottles, blow cigarette smoke out their ass cheeks and even get busy in the back room. Cherry will easily make thousands of dollars," AZ assures, laughing out loud, happy he thought of the idea.

"That's not a place for me, but you can take her. Cherry needs the money! I definitely can't feed her. I can hardly feed myself," KG says, shaking his head.

"Okay, it's settled then. I'll call my guy tomorrow and set it up!" They dap and shake on it.

After listening to them, I tiptoed down the hall to my room. I sat on the bed and a tear dropped from my eye. Besides being disgusted, I knew AZ's chicks would never go for something like that. Shi, especially, was too bourgeois. Sex, drugs, and illegal money were never my intention for the mansion.

Dear Lord, my poor country club is quickly taking a turn for the worst.

AZ's demonic activity is cursing the house.

God, you brought me to it. Please bring me through it.

Lying down, I dreaded closing my eyes. The red eyes and horns appeared to taunt me again. The devil wanted to kill, steal, and destroy my joy. To me, AZ unknowingly sacrificed his mom for this lifestyle. He was a pimp in training when she fell gravely ill. Hearing the news about her illness, he rushed home, but it was too late. I should've heeded the warning when my mom came to visit.

"Karen, get out of this place. Go back to your other house. I don't like it here!" my mom said after her tour of the mansion. I couldn't understand then, but now I know there was an evil presence here.

CHAPTER VII
DEAR DIARY

Dear Diary, it's September 8, 2012.

It's five days after Labor Day. The past few weeks have been very rough for AZ. He learns a hard lesson about doing business with family and friends. The one time he does make the mistake, it blows up in his face. A fascination with AZ's girls usually involved Lexx. She was young, outgoing, and always in need of attention.

This particular Saturday, she and I went out to celebrate the holiday. We attended a picnic at Gator's house. He was AZ's good friend. Arriving there, all eyes were on us. Lexx is a hot, sexy Latina. Men of all ages want a piece of the young girl. Strolling through the backyard, we spot Gator at a picnic table with some of his family and friends.

"Hi, Miss Parker," I said, approaching Gator and his mom.

"Hi, Karen. Glad you could make it," she says, smiling at me. "You remember my boyfriend and my two nephews, right?" She points to the three men sitting at the picnic table with her.

"Hello, everybody. This is Lexx," I say to them.

"I know Lexx," Gator says, giving her a quirky grin. "Y'all want some food?" he invites us to help ourselves.

"No, thank you," Lexx says, bashfully declining.

"I'll have some," I say, gawking at the large spread of soul food on the table.

I get a paper plate and dig in for healthy proportions, stacking it with barbecue chicken, fried chicken, a rib, potato salad, and macaroni and cheese.

After wolfing down my food, I listen to their small talk. The guys are pleased with Lexx. She looks very attractive in her tank top and cut-off booty shorts. They flirt with her, and she flirts right back. Eventually, they lure her away from the table to smoke some weed. I follow behind them to chaperone.

It's dark outside by the time they finished smoking and drinking. Lexx still wanted to go to work. Realizing the fellas are tricks, she smartly invited them to the strip club. The cousins agree to meet her there, but Gator insisted on coming with us. Stupidly, I allow him to come along for the ride. This is a huge mistake. AZ is furious when we stop at home first to change clothes. He makes this very apparent by loudly sucking his teeth when we walk through the door. The weed and alcohol had clearly taken their toll on us. Lexx was so drunk she couldn't go to work. We both stumbled to our rooms, leaving AZ to babysit Gator.

The next morning, AZ was up early blowing steam out his nostrils.

"Good morning, Peanut," I say, walking into the kitchen.

"It's not a good morning for me. I was up all night guarding the girls," AZ snarls, at me.

"Wait! What happened?"

AZ shakes his head. "Gator ran around the house all night, like a kid in the candy store. A few times I had to stop him from sneaking into the girls' bedrooms. His mission was to get some ass by any means necessary. I told him to go home but he refused. Eventually, he wore himself out and fell asleep on the couch. I kept one eye open until he got up and left this morning. Don't ever bring any guys here again! You remember what happened the last time!" AZ says with a stern look.

I nod in compliance. He was referring to a time we both regretted.

After Kal left the mansion, he got married. He and his wife started a lucrative publishing company around the corner from us. One day at the office they got into a heated argument. Kal suspected his wife was cheating on him. He thought he saw her car at the motel the night before. In a blind fury, Kal attempted to burn down the office with the staff still inside. There were over twenty employees watching when he poured lighter fluid throughout the office and ignited the carpet on fire. The poor frightened workers, running for their lives, escaped into the street. When the suicide and homicide attempt failed, Kal's crazy ass jumped in his car and came straight to our house.

"Yeah, that was a crazy day. Kal was OD mad," AZ says, taking a deep breath. "The horny little toad wanted to screw Lexx to get back at his wife. Against my better judgment, I allowed this. It was a big mistake letting him do it here. I told Kal he had an hour to handle his business. Too bad he didn't listen," AZ frowns, shaking his head with regret. "As soon as he went into Lexx's room, I started receiving phone calls from his wife. She had been looking all over town for him. The most logical place for her to check was our house. When I finally answered her call, Kal had been in the room for over an hour. 'AZ, have you seen Kal? I've been looking everywhere for him!' she said to me. Nah, I haven't seen him. I told her. I lie, to give him more time. At this point he was in the room too long. I was ready to shut shit down. Especially now that his wife was calling. 'Let me know if you hear from him. It's important!' she said, exasperated. Okay, I will. I said ending the call, running upstairs to warn Kal. Hey, man, your wife is calling for you. I yelled through the bedroom door. Without receiving an answer, I assumed Kal heard me. I left and went outside to walk the pit bulls. That's when you and Nina joined me on the front lawn," AZ finishes, sucking his teeth.

"Yeah, I remember! It was too late by then. Kal's wife drove by the house and noticed his Mercedes Benz parked in the driveway. She slammed on the brakes and backed up. All I could do at that point was hold my breath."

"Aww, man, she hopped out that Caddy truck with the quickness. She was in the middle of the lawn before I could react. I didn't know what to do next. So, I turned around running to warn Kal."

"AZ, that was a dumb-ass move. You left the front door wide open. She followed you right inside," I said, cracking up with laughter.

"I didn't know what else to do. She caught me by surprise. I didn't want to slam the door in her face," AZ sighs regretfully.

"Watching you and her, all I could do was freeze in my tracks. She went in the house right behind you, screaming Kal's name."

"I knew, she was right behind me. I literally leaped two steps at a time, yelling, 'Your wife is here!' I figured by then, he was done. I opened the bedroom door, rushed inside, and slammed it behind me. Kal was butt naked, which I didn't expect. Lexx was face down ass up with him hitting it from behind.

Seeing that was very traumatizing for me! At least he could've kept his clothes on," AZ says, bursting out with laughter. "Kal was knee-deep in with his wife standing right outside. I didn't expect her to start violently knocking on the bedroom door. Yo! Stop knocking on this fucking door! I said to her. By then, Kal was freaking out. This clown was so scared, he ran to the window and pushed out the air conditioner. He was willing to break a leg, jumping out a second-floor window," AZ says, grinning wide.

"I just remember hearing my expensive air conditioner hitting the ground. The loud thud made me run to the side of the house. When I looked up, Kal's whole body was hanging out the window with his legs dangling. 'Hey, who's that at the end of the driveway?' Kal asked, me.

"It's some people who came with your wife. I told him, not realizing his wife was standing right beside me. I was more embarrassed than she was. Kal was so surprised to see her, he quickly pulled himself back into the window. His wife sucked her teeth and stormed back to the Cadillac with her friends. They exchanged some words, got back into the truck, and sped away."

"Kal was a nervous wreck that day. He came out of Lexx's room shaking like a leaf. Apparently, he and Lexx drank a whole bottle of Hennessy and lost track of time. The poor guy was in no shape to drive. Mumbling something under his breath, Kal took off running out the house. That's when we heard his car recklessly peeling out the driveway," AZ says.

"I forgot to tell you. I saw Kal and his wife at the bank two weeks later. Seeing them together was somewhat awkward for me. Kal was bubbly as usual. 'Hey, Joy Joy!' he said, walking over to me. His wife nodded, barely spoke, and walked into the bank. The mood was very tense. Hi, Kal. I said, nervously smiling at him. He smiled back, then hugged me. 'You'll never guess what happened after I left your house that day. Speeding fast and reckless, I had a terrible car accident,' he said. WOW! Is everything okay? I asked him. 'Not really. The Benz wrapped around a utility pole a mile away from your house. The cops came, pulled me out, and arrested me for driving intoxicated. I'll catch up with you later, Joy Joy. Tell AZ hello for me,' he said, skipping away, disappearing into the bank."

Dear Diary, it's Monday, September 24, 2012.

It's only a few weeks after Labor Day and so much had happened since then. AZ incorporated a company to legitimize business with the girls by opening the ladies apparel store where he intended to sell stripper shoes, handbags, costume jewelry, makeup and much more. Everyone was very excited about the new business venture he called Pineapple Dreamz.

On this particular day, we all sat in the kitchen celebrating. though for us it was never drama-free.

"Hey, guys, look at this video. I took it at the club," Shi says, running around the table and showing us her iphone.

"Damn! When did that happen?" I ask, looking at a video of Suga passed out on the bathroom floor in the strip club.

"This was Thursday night!" Shi, giggles.

Nina stands to look at the video.

"That's messed up," she says, then sits back in her chair smoking the blunt.

Lexx scrambles around the table to watch it with us.

"Girls at the club said Suga left DJ again. Now that dumb bitch is living in motels with some strippers," Lexx scoffs.

"I just spoke to Suga Thursday night. Everything seemed fine to me," I say, sitting back and daydreaming about that night.

Suga was on stage when I arrived at the club Thursday night. She saw me come into the club and waved for me to come over.

"Hi, Karen!" Suga said, jumping off the stage and hugging me.

She whispered to her customer and dragged us both to the bar. The customer bought our drinks, then Suga ignored him after that.

"Karen, Shi did some foul shit to me last night at work," she said.

I let it go in one ear and out the other because she always complained.

"Suga, don't sweat the small things in life. Our team is doing big things these days," I said to her.

"Oh, really! Tell me more."

"We'll talk about it later," I said, finishing the drink, and leaving the club.

"Karen, Suga was carried out on a stretcher Thursday night," AZ chuckles, interrupting my daydreaming.

"Wait. What?! She never woke up!" I say, surprised.

"I don't know. But Shi has pictures of her being carried out by the paramedics. The cops came and everything. They say Katt stole her money while this was going on."

Shi stands up showing me more pictures of the incident. "Oh my gosh. I have to call Suga and see how she's doing!"

It was our last meeting of the day. AZ and I walked out of the Pineapple Dreamz store into the bright sunlight. I took out my cell phone to call Suga. The phone rang before I had a chance to dial the number.

"Hi, Suga! I was just about to call you," I said, answering the call.

"Hey, Karen!" Suga's voice is weak though surprisingly cheerful.

As usual, she begins complaining, "Karen, I fell out at the club Thursday night. People told me Shi videotaped it and put it on Youtube. They say she's even going to show it to my baby's father. Now I can't work at Stonehedge anymore and neither can she."

Not wanting to upset Suga further, I respond with a question. "How are you doing?"

"Oh, I'm doing all right. I'm just a little dizzy," she says enthusiastically, forgetting about her anger for Shi.

"Where are you now?" I ask, not sure if she's still in the hospital.

"I'm at a friend's house in Bayshore." She pauses before continuing, "I'm still feeling a little weak."

Her hesitation makes me uneasy about the conversation.

"Okay, Suga, call me when you're feeling better," I say, rushing her off the phone.

AZ turns up an eyebrow. "Who was that on the phone?" he asks curiously.

"That was Suga. She's out of the hospital. I told her to call me later."

"Really?!" he says, opening the car door to get inside.

AZ, who had other things on his mind, didn't give it too much thought. Five minutes later, my cell phone rings again. AZ looks at me. I show him the name on the caller Id.

Suga starts talking as soon as the line connects. "Karen, I'm at a friend's house in Bayshore. I'm worried about the dancers I live with at the hotel. They have nowhere to go. One of them is walking the streets with her eighteen-month-old daughter."

I inhaled deeply, listening to Suga. On the first call, she wasn't forthcoming. This time she sounded very desperate.

"Where are you exactly?" I asked, contemplating helping her.

Suga gave me her customer's address. I wrote it on a piece of paper.

"Okay, I got it," I said, hanging up the phone.

"What's up with Suga?" AZ sighs.

"She wants us to pick her up," I say, giving him puppy dog eyes.

"Did she say that?!"

"Well, not exactly. I think she does."

"Well call her back and find out!" AZ snaps impatiently.

I shot him a dirty look. Money was all that mattered to him. Whereas I was genuinely concerned about her health, he was just eager to get back on Suga's payroll.

"Alright, I will!" I bark back at him.

"Hello, Karen," Suga answers on the first ring.

"Hi, Suga. I'm in the area with AZ. Can we pick you up?"

"Okay, fine. I'll be ready," she says happily.

In fifteen minutes, AZ and I exit the ramp in Bayshore. We drive two blocks and park across the street from Suga's customer's house. I text Suga, letting her know we're outside. Within five minutes, she, without shoes or a coat, flies out of the house. Suga hops from foot to foot, looking up and down the street for our car. AZ was fuming when he saw her. It was chilly outside. The last thing he wanted was a sick girl on his hands.

"Drive over there and pick her ass up. Suga just got out of the hospital!" AZ grumbles.

"I am, I am."

Starting the car, I quickly spin a U-turn and pull up to the curb in front of Suga. AZ opens the back door for her. She jumps inside, pushing buttons on her cell phone.

"Hi, y'all. I died twice last night. They had to resuscitate me at the hospital," Suga says to us with the cell phone to her ear.

My mouth drops open. I turn around, facing her, to see if she's joking.

"Suga, that sounds crazy! What happened to you?!"

Lifting her shirt to show me the red paddle marks from the defibrillator, she says, "I had a little bit of this and a little bit of that. The doctors say I overdosed," she mumbles, holding her head down, embarrassed.

"How did you overdose? What exactly did you take?!" I ask, horrified by the news.

I knew Suga did coke. But plenty of people did that and didn't die.

Wrinkling her forehead, struggling to remember what happened, Suga says, "Nothing but the usual. I had a few drinks, some weed and a few bumps of coke that night. I think someone slipped something in my drink. I went to the bathroom, got dizzy, and passed out."

She looks at me, undisturbed by this.

"Hello, where you at?" Suga says to the person on the phone. She briefly talks to them, then quickly switches to the other line. "Where you at?" she asks, the other person. After addressing both calls, Suga hangs up the phone. "AZ, can we please go get these girls? They stay with me at the motel," she says to him.

"Where they at?" AZ asks, jumping at the opportunity.

I thought Suga still needed to rest but the mention of more girls excited AZ. His most recent scam involved a private house. In his mind, these girls would be perfect occupants.

"One girl is at the motel. The other girl is at work. I'll show you how to get there," Suga says, wincing in pain.

"Where's your coat and shoes?" AZ asks before we pull away from the curb.

"This is all I had at the hospital. The rest of my clothes are at the motel."

AZ shakes his head, motioning for me to drive off.

CHASE, I STOPPED HERE?

Listening to Suga's directions, I speed down the block and hop on the highway. In a few miles we exit the ramp in Amityville. I drove to a commercial area, made two right turns and stopped in front of an adult video shop.

AZ looks at Suga. "What is this place?" he asks her. "You never been here before? It's a peep show shop."

She looks at him oddly, then begins texting on her cell phone.

A pretty brown skin girl, with deep dimples, appears in the doorway. She's half naked from the waist up.

AZ perks right up.

"That's Toni!" Suga says, waving to the girl. Showing off, AZ turns the car stereo up real loud. The girl waves and disappears back inside.

She returns five minutes later and jumps into the back seat with Suga.

"Y'all, this is Toni. She's the girl I told you about." "Hello everybody!" Toni says cheerfully.

"Hi," I say, smiling at the young girl in my rear- view mirror.

"Hi, Toni," AZ grins bashfully.

Giving him the side eye, I knew he couldn't wait to get his hooks into her.

Our next stop was at a Dunkin Donuts. When we turned into the parking lot, I saw two shabby white women.

They were standing by some garbage bags with a little girl. Suga rolled her window down to speak with one.

"Is that our stuff?" Suga asked the woman holding the baby on her hip.

"Yeah! The motel kicked us out this morning. We couldn't pay the bill," the woman said.

"Okay, don't worry about it. Go inside the Dunkin Donuts and wait for me. I'll be right back," Suga said, rolling her window back up.

Driving away, I headed home listening to how things played out.

"What you doing with those girls and that kid?" AZ asks Suga. "It's something we need to talk about. Those girls work for me out of hotels," she says with a devilish grin."

AZ raises an eyebrow. "What about that baby?" he asks, waiting for an explanation.

Suga's face is stern and serious.

"Whoever doesn't have a date gets to babysit. I make a lot of money with these three girls."

In the rear-view mirror, I saw Toni frowning. She was unaware Suga was pimping her. Toni probably thought Suga was a caring friend.

"I need some help taking care of my girls until I get on my feet," Suga says, narrowing her eyes at him.

She knew asking a pimp for help was a sticky position to be in.

AZ slowly ran his tongue across his thick lips. His crafty brain was fast at work.

"Let's see what I can do for you," he says, pretending to comply with the plan. AZ knew Suga was scheming, but he was scheming too.

After we dropped Toni and Suga off at the house, AZ drove back to Dunkin Donuts. He interrogated the women, discovering they were sisters but only one turned tricks. AZ sympathetically got two hotel rooms. One room was for the little girl and the babysitter. The other room was to turn tricks and repay the debt.

AZ was smart enough to monitor his money. He had Lexx screen calls before sending customers to the room.

However, whenever customers arrived, the mother never answered the door. Supposedly, her bum ass fell asleep and missed all fifteen calls.

AZ believed she was playing him. Therefore, he sent Lexx to physically oversee the situation. This didn't sway the woman one bit.

At first, she pretended not to have any condoms. After that, she fell asleep again. The woman refused to earn any money for him that night. At checkout time, AZ realized he had wasted the money.

The women were not done with him yet. They called, asking for a ride to go cop some pills. Apparently, they had a drug habit. AZ was so angry, he told them to lose his number.

Overall, it wasn't a total loss for him. He still had Toni and Suga. The next morning, he took them to his new house in Brentwood. Parking out front, I listened to AZ talk on his cell phone.

"Gator, I'm at the address to that house you gave me. Are you sure everything is cool with this place? There's a padlock on the front door!" AZ said to Gator with much concern.

Finishing the call, he hung up aggravated. "What did Gator say?" I asked, leery about the house myself. I knew AZ made a shady deal with Gator's cousin for the house. She was a real estate agent who rented homes. AZ paid her five hundred dollars for this one. "Gator's on his way," AZ says, reaching over, turning off the ignition.

"Good. I want to unpack and get some sleep before work," Toni says restlessly in the backseat. She had already given AZ rent money for the house.

"Yeah, this house is real nice," Suga said, looking out the back window at it.

We waited over an hour before Gator turned the corner.

"Here he comes now!" AZ says, looking through his side mirror.

We all turned around to watch Gator peddle down the block on his bike.

At this point, we stepped out on the curb to stretch our legs. "Hey! What's up," Gator says, with a lazy drawl.

"What took you so long? I'm ready to get these girls inside. Toni has to work tonight."

AZ squints from the sun in his eyes. Gator nods hello to the girls.

"I had to pick up some tools and a door lock," Gator says, taking a bolt cutter from the backpack on his bike.

"Tools for what? Don't you have the key?" AZ snaps at him. "Who needs a key when you got these?" Gator grins and walks over to the front door with the bolt cutter.

I gasp, looking around to see if any neighbors are watching us. *It's broad daylight and these fools are breaking into someone's house.* I think to myself.

Once the pad lock was off Suga and Toni don't seem to mind.

They followed Gator into the house.

I went back to the car and sat inside. I was suspicious about the house.

AZ stayed outside with me, fumbling to change the lock. "Come your scary ass inside!" he yells once it's done.

I stared at him without moving.

The cops are going to lock your dumb ass up. I thought to myself. He waited for a minute then went inside without me.

I felt silly sitting outside alone, so I slowly got out and quickly ran inside.

The low ranch was newly renovated and very nice inside.

It had three bedrooms, two bathrooms and a finished basement. The place smelled of fresh paint and shallacked hardwood floors.

The girls danced around the empty house, delighted they had a new place to stay. Afterwards, they claimed their rooms and unpacked their bags.

Later that night, AZ drove Toni to work, leaving Suga in the house alone.

The next day, AZ returned with a flat screen TV and an X-box for their entertainment. Appreciating his hospitality, Toni went to work early to repay him. Suga, on the other hand, slept all day, claiming to be Toni's madam.

After AZ dropped off the TV, he traveled back to Coram, attending to more important matters. While he was there, he received a call from Suga.

"Hi, Daddy!" Suga's voice sings seductively over the speaker phone. "What's up?!" AZ says, being curt with her.

"I'm hungry and lonely," she purrs to entice him.

"I'm busy right now. I can't get over there. I'll send Karen with some food when she picks up Lexx from work. She'll make the stop on her way to the job," AZ says, sharply.

"Okay, daddy and send me some candy too," Suga adds stupidly.

AZ disconnects the call without answering her.

"I guess she hasn't learned her lesson from that overdose," I said to AZ, chuckling.

"Suga is crazy! Take this money and get her something to eat."

He tosses a twenty-dollar bill on the table for me. I was already running late for Lexx. I grabbed the money and rushed out the door.

I stopped at the corner deli and bought Suga and myself a hot plate of food. Getting back into the car, I sped down a side street then jumped on the highway.

Arriving in Brentwood, I knocked rapidly on the front door until Suga finally opened it.

"Hi, Karen!" she says, excited to see me. "Hey, Suga." I hand her the food and quickly turn to leave.

"Wait a minute! Where are you going?" she yells after me. "I'm in a hurry to pick up Lexx from work," I say, sucking my teeth, annoyed by the hold up.

"Let me come with you!" she says, slamming the front door, running to the car to hop in with me.

"Karen, I've been locked in that house all day," she says, digging in the bag of food. "Want some?" she asks, offering me a piece of chicken.

I knew it was a bad idea to take Suga with me. I drove away from the curb, shaking my head.

Lexx was standing outside when I turned into the Stonehedge parking lot. The frown on her face told me she was pissed.

Looking at the dashboard clock, I was two hours late. I drove up to her and stopped the car.

Lexx walked around to the passenger side and snatched open the car door. Her boldness startled Suga.

"Get in the back seat!" Lexx barks at her.

Suga narrows her eyes, clutching the bag of food on her lap. Obviously, Lexx is jealous because Suga is in the front seat.

It's a disaster waiting to happen.

Ignoring them both, I hopped out the car and went inside to talk with Shi.

"You got me fucked up!" I hear Suga say before the club door closes.

Lexx storms into the club behind me.

"Give me the keys to the truck!" she demands, holding her hand out.

Shi and I both look at her stupefied. We were not giving Lexx any keys. She could barely drive. Besides, the truck is Shi's only ride home.

"I'm going to black out in here!" Lexx screams at me, stomping her feet.

My mouth drops open.

On stage, Shi dances away from us, embarrassed.

I quickly turn and exit the club. Lexx follows me outside, continuing the argument. I ignore her, realizing she's new to the game.

"Give me your phone so I can call AZ!" Lexx huffs and puffs, holding her hand out.

Presuming her battery is dead, I hand Lexx my phone to make the call.

When AZ answers, she screams into the receiver, "I'm about to black out!" Then she quickly hangs up the phone.

Lexx knew AZ didn't tolerate her nonsense. That's why I couldn't understand her calling him.

Afterwards, Lexx hops into the back seat. She's still fuming about Suga being in the front seat.

Watching in the rearview mirror, I see the window go down and my food thrown out. This really pisses me off.

Lexx, I just bought that damn food from the deli! I think to myself, remaining calm. I just wanted to get everyone home in one piece.

When tossing the food doesn't work, Lexx starts an argument with Suga. "That's my seat, bitch." Lexx mumbles underneath her breath.

Suga isn't having it.

"Then move me bitch!" Suga barks back.

"I ain't that same little girl no more," Lexx growls at her.

"You look like that same little bitch to me!" Suga says, taunting her. It's all that's needed for a loud argument to ensue.

I intervene by turning the car stereo up so loud, they can barely hear each other speak.

Reaching Coram, the argument spills out the car into the house. "You a come-and-go bitch! Know your place!" Lexx growls at her. Suga balls her fist, ready to move in silence with violence.

They square up, ready to pop off.

"What the hell is all this noise about?!" AZ yells, racing down the steps into the living room. "Y'all better calm that shit down.

I'll whoop both y'all asses," he says, stepping in between them.

I was relieved when AZ came to break them up. It was too much drama for me to handle.

"Lexx, take your ass upstairs," AZ barks at her. She cautiously walks up the steps backwards, keeping her eye on Suga.

"Why are you here?! You're supposed to be at the house in Brentwood!" AZ scolds Suga.

"Lexx, started it. I just went for the ride," Suga says, avoiding eye contact.

"I don't care who started it. I don't want no fighting!" AZ barks, then goes upstairs to deal with Lexx.

Once the fight is resolved, I retire to my room.

"Can I have a blanket?" Suga yells from the living room.

Even though AZ had the house in Brentwood, Suga insisted on staying with us for the next few days.

One late afternoon, AZ was out shopping with his kids when the house phone rang.

"Hello," I said, answering the call.

"Yo!..YO!..The cops just broke down the door at that house in Brentwood!" AZ says, alarming me.

"The house in Brentwood!" I repeat, concerned. "Yes! And the broker said they found drugs inside!"

AZ's voice trembles with fear. My suspicions were now confirmed about the house being an illegal purchase.

I paced back and forth in the living room, thinking to myself, *If drugs were in that house, there might be some arrests.*

"I need you and Suga to go there and find out what's going on," the coward says to me.

Moving the phone away from my ear, I stare at it dumbfounded.

Are you crazy! It's amazing how brazen you are to do these crimes, but never ready to do the time.

Suga's asleep on the couch when I gently shake her arm. "Suga, wake up. Wake up!"

"Mmmm." Suga rolls over, moaning.

"Hey, Karen. What's up?" she says, peeking at me with one eye open.

"Let me tell you what's going on," I say, hanging up the phone on AZ.

Suga looks at me curiously.

"Girl, the cops are at that house in Brentwood." Her mouth pops open.

"What happened, Karen?!"

She yanks the blanket off and sits at attention.

"I don't know much else. We have to go find out."

Suga jumps up and goes to the bathroom. I wait on the couch for her to return. She comes back in five minutes, without washing her face or brushing her teeth.

"Are you ready?" she asks, with wrinkled clothes and a lopsided wig.

Suga didn't care about her appearance and neither did I.

"Ready, if you are," I say, not really wanting to go anyway. I feared it was a potential crime scene and we were walking into an ambush.

As usual, Suga complains the whole ride there. "Karen, I have several things of value in that house. I left seven hundred dollars in my pocketbook.

I have an iphone there. My customer gave me a blow-up mattress!" Suga goes on and on until we pull up in front of the house. "Girl, I understand. But we can't go inside right now," I say, looking at the padlock on the front door. Someone had replaced it, preventing our entry into the house.

Suga stares at the lock in disbelief.

"Oh shit, I can't get my stuff. Now what are we going to do?" she says calmly, though obviously very upset.

I was just relieved no cops were there waiting for us. "Hold on. Let me call AZ."

Dialing his number, I put the phone on speaker. Overall, I thought my efforts were futile.

Suga listens to the conversation when he answers the call. "AZ, we can't get into the house. It's been padlocked again." "What?! My damn X-box and flat screen are in that house. I'm five minutes away. I'll be right there!" AZ says, hanging up.

I felt better knowing he was on the way. The pressure was off me dealing with Suga. I only hoped he could actually do something.

Suga and I wait the five minutes it takes AZ's white truck to turn the corner. We permit him to park before bravely stepping out of the car.

"So, what's going on here?" he asks, then walks over to the house, peeking through the windows.

"Do you have a key to the side entrance?" I ask, cluelessly following behind him.

AZ's pissed when he sees the side door is also padlocked.

"I'm calling that damn broker!" he says, inhaling deeply.

The broker is very sympathetic speaking with AZ over the phone.

She admits to renting him a home that's already been sold.

AZ informs her his valuables are locked inside. She promises to arrange for him to pick them up the next day.

Dear diary, it's September 27, 2012.

The following day Suga and AZ are no longer interested in retrieving their confiscated property. Neither made an effort to meet with the broker.

Nina had court this day in Central Islip for all of her drug charges.

AZ asked me to take her because he wanted to stay home and lay up with the other girls.

I went with the intention of also meeting the broker afterwards.

Having an A-type personality, it bothered me to leave unfinished business.

Court isn't long for Nina. After she's done, the legal aid meets with us in the hallway. He advises her to enroll in a drug program before the next court date. He claims it'll help the defense. She nods, pretending to comply.

When we leave, we drive to the house in Brentwood to meet the broker.

Nina and I wait for an hour, but the broker never shows. Just my luck, exiting the driveway, I reverse into a sewage drain and get a slow leak in my tire. Now, I was mad we came.

I hadn't heard from Suga since dropping her off the night before at a retired pimp's house. Taking her there was very frustrating for me.

The conversation was exhausting. Suga never shut up the whole ride.

Suga puts on her lipstick in the mirror under the visor.

"I hope when we get to H house, he doesn't push up on me." *Suga says to me with a smirk.*

"You mean, he'll want some ass?" I ask, looking at her awkwardly.

She nods, at me.

"*Suga, of course he wants some ass. Isn't that what every man wants?*"

She chuckles, smearing on too much lipstick.

"*Shit, he'll be a pimp turning into a trick. Because I'll want some money if that's the case.*"

We burst out laughing. She and I, both knew it was a lie.

Being jobless, homeless and moving from place to place, Suga would be lucky if H, even gave her a bump of coke for that ass.

After some thought, Suga decides to tell me her rules to the game. "*Karen, when I'm with a man, I take full control of the situation. I don't let him run me. If he spends a hundred dollars, I make him sit in a chair or sit on the bed. I get on top of him, not the other way around. See what I'm saying.*"

She looks at me to see if I get her drift. I listen with no emotion. "*It's nasty to let them hit it from behind. Their balls slam up against your ass.*" *She chuckles, leaning over to nudge me.*

I slightly nod as if comprehending.

"*It's also nasty, if you lie on your back and let him get on top. If that happens, he can have his way with you. I mean maybe for a thousand dollars, I'll let him climb on top. But for a hundred, I'm on top!*"

Suga inhales deeply.

"*I don't like black men. They're too cheap. White men spend more money but they're big freaks,*" *she says, as an afterthought.*

"*I have one customer who's a teacher. He hardly ever wants any sex. He just wants to be humiliated. He likes to be abused. I tie him up, spit on him and slap the shit out of him.*

I have another one, who likes it in the ass with a dildo. Katt, says this about one of her customers. He might be the same guy."

Suga goes on with her stories, until I drop her off at H's
house, wearing the same smelly clothes Shi gave her three days
ago.
    It was a tight fitting dress with spandex shorts underneath.
Shi gave her the outfit to work at the hotel. Unfortunately,
Suga never received any calls from the Backpage ad.
    AZ welcomed her decision to leave and go with another
pimp. Giving her drugs, food and rides all day became more
trouble than she was worth.

I dropped Nina off at the house and drove around the corner on my rim to repair my tire. While there, I received a call to come sign the lease for our Pineapple Dreamz store. I made an appointment for AZ and me to meet with the landlord the following Friday.

After the mechanic fixed my tire, I drove back to Brentwood, hopeful the broker might be there by now.

Arriving at the house, I parked on a side street to watch cars coming in every direction.

It was four o'clock when a U-Haul truck drove up and a man jumped out. He was about five feet tall and looked Iranian. He couldn't see my car hidden behind the large bushes on the corner.

"Hello! Are you the agent for this house? I'm supposed to meet them at this address," I say politely, approaching him.

The man frowns at me though remains cordial.

"No, I'm the owner of this property. I just bought this house from the agent," he replies calmly.

"Oh, there must be some misunderstanding. My friend is renting this place. Her belongings were mistakenly locked inside," I smile, pointing to the padlock on the front door.

The man becomes hostile.

"Yeah! Someone broke the other pad lock off and moved in without permission!"

He's looks around uncomfortable, suspecting I'm not alone.
"I don't know anything about that, sir. I just came here to pick

up my friend's belongings. She had court today and couldn't make it herself," I lie, hoping the man will just open the front door and let me inside. Instead, he nervously pulls out his cellphone.

"The agent told me someone broke into my house and if they return, I should call the cops to have them arrested," he says, hitting the buttons on the phone.

"Oh no! I don't want any trouble," I say nervously backing away from him.

"I'll send my friend to deal with this herself. What's your name, sir?" I ask, quickly walking away.

"My name is Mr. Con Artist," he sarcastically yells after me. Turning the corner, I jump in my vehicle and speed away.

I drive in the opposite direction so the gentleman can't see my license plate number. Scared to death, I think the man is calling the cops on me.

On the way home, Suga calls me repeatedly. After her third time calling, I decide to answer.

"Karen, did AZ get into that house yet?!" Suga asks, very irate.

She was still unaware of the scam. AZ only told her the house was sold and the realtor forgot to update the computer.

"No, dear. Not yet."

"Karen, I don't have any clothes to wear. I don't understand why I have a lease but can't go inside. I'm going to that damn house and burn it down!" Suga says, threatening me.

I snicker to myself, though it's not very funny. "Karen, why isn't AZ answering my calls?"

"I don't know but AZ is meeting with the agent today," I say, trying to fix his mess.

"Oh, alright then," Suga calms down, realizing she has no other choice.

"I'll give you a call if anything changes," I say, hanging up on her quickly.

Dear diary, it's September 28, 2012.

Rolling over with my eyes still closed, I hear AZ walk into the room. He crawls into bed with me and turns on the television set. The smell of strong weed hits the air.

I hear Shi coughing in the next room.

Slowly opening my eyes, the cable box reads two o'clock in the afternoon.

AZ puts the blunt out and lays on his back.

"I have to order some pizza for the girls," he says, then passes out asleep, too tired to make the call.

I sit up to watch the documentary he turned on.

It's a biopic about the Harlem drug dealer, Alpo. AZ begins to snore so loud it forces me to hold his mouth closed.

He wakes up, reaching for the phone to order the pizza. Afterwards, he goes into the kitchen, returning with some cold chicken.

I give him the side eye when a piece falls off the plate hitting my blanket. AZ knows I can't stand when he eats on the bed.

He looks at the grease spot, then looks at me, pretending to lick it up. I can't help but laugh at his silly gesture. AZ grins and makes a better attempt to clean it up.

"Yo, Lexx got robbed last night. It was one of her regular customers," he says, as a matter of fact.

Listening to him, I remain calm because he does. "The guy didn't get any money though. I taught Lexx very well," he says, ending the story.

I knew not to question him further. If I wanted more details, I had to ask Lexx.

Lexx was in the living room talking to Nina when I walked in. "Hey, what happened to you last night? I want to put that creep in my diary," I say, interrupting their conversation. "Oh, you mean the customer? Okay, I got you, my gee." Lexx smiles, happy to oblige.

"Let me light my cigarette," she says, running upstairs to get a lighter.

When Lexx returns, we go out on the porch to talk.

"So, let me tell you what happened, Karen. It was my regular, but he bugged out last night." Lexx's eyes twinkle with the excitement of danger.

"What did he look like?" I ask, wanting to know his nationality. Lexx points to her forearm.

"He's a white guy in his forties with tattoos. He was drinking all night, but I didn't think he was drunk."

Lexx bounces around the porch, happy to tell her story. "I left work an hour before closing to do a date with him.

Our deal was four hundred for the hour. He only gave me two hundred before I left with him.

On our way to his house, we stopped at another bar. He started arguing with some girl there. I didn't like him involving me in his drama. Plus, it was wasting my time.

Finally, we got to his house. I sat on the couch for a while, but nothing happened. I told him to take me home. His time was up. He asked for the money back. I got mad because my time is money. You know how I get, Karen."

Lexx frowns at me.

"I wasn't giving him no money back, so we started arguing. I got up to walk out before it came to blows. On my way out the door, he grabs my work bag, thinking there's money in it. I let him have the bag and ran out the door. There was only twenty singles in it. My cell phone and the rest of the money was on me. I was mad as hell though. I wanted to call AZ, but I didn't want to start any trouble. I went to the nearest gas station and called a cab to take me home."

After the story, I gave Lexx a long hug. I was glad to hear how she handled the awful situation.

Meeting men at the strip club was a dangerous game. Even though it was her third time on a date with him, there was no guarantee with perverts.

My cellphone rang in the middle of hugging Lexx.

It was Suga on the caller Id. I ignored it, wanting some peace for the day.

Dear Diary, it's September 30, 2012.

"Shi! Where are you?!" I heard AZ yelling, when I walked into the kitchen. He was talking to her on the landline. Shi had been out all night on a date. Whenever Shi went on dates, she didn't return home for days. She said men thought of her as their girlfriend. Therefore, she gave them that experience.

AZ hated the idea. He was very jealous when it came to Shi. Therefore, he rarely allowed her to go on dates.

"Hurry your ass home!" he says, snatching the truck keys off the table. "Here, you talk to her. I'm going out with my kids. I'll be back later."

AZ hands me the phone and storms out the front door.

I was also upset with Shi. It had been forty-eight hours, and she still wasn't back yet with my car.

"Shi, when are you coming home? I have something to do today!

Gator called, saying he spoke with his cousin. She told him we can go back to the house in Brentwood and get our belongings!" I barked at her.

"I'm on my way," Shi said, abruptly hanging up on me.

Two hours went by, Shi still wasn't home yet. I called her again.

This time, she offered some lame excuse about being late. I waited a little while longer before calling repeatedly.

When Shi doesn't answer my calls anymore, I become very irate.

I start sending her nasty text messages.

Shi, if you don't bring my damn car back, I'm reporting it stolen!

After receiving these messages, Shi comes home right away.

"Honey, I'm home!" she teases, walking in the front door. I fly out of my room, meeting her in the kitchen.

"Hi, Karen. You want some food? It's Porterhouse steak! Nothing but the best."

Shi grins at me, placing the bag of food on the table.

I was more upset with her than I was hungry.

"Shi, I have somewhere to go!" I say, rolling my eyes, holding my hand out for the keys.

"Where's AZ?" Shi asks, with a smug look, then tosses the keys on the table.

AZ's truck comes roaring into the driveway.

"That should be him now," I say, angrily snatching my keys off the table.

AZ was sitting in his truck when I walked outside.

"I see Do Do bird is back," he says, frowning at me. "Yeah, Shi just got here!" I say, still annoyed with her. "Where are you going?" he asks, stepping out the truck. "To meet with the agent for your Xbox!"

"Oh, okay. I'll go with you," AZ says, getting into the car with me. We rode about twenty minutes from Coram to Brentwood.

Getting off the highway, AZ suddenly falls ill. "Ouch!" he says, holding his jaw.

"What's wrong with you?" I ask, coasting down the street, giving him the side eye.

"It's my tooth. Can you knock on the door when we get there?" he asks, pretending to be in excruciating pain.

I look at him suspiciously.

You know damn well nothing's wrong with your tooth, punk ass!

"I guess so. Somebody got to do it," I say, sarcastically, rolling my eyes at him.

When we arrive at the house, I get out the car and walk across the lawn, knocking lightly on the front door. I hear some kids giggling inside of the house.

A little boy, about ten years old, pulls back a sheet hanging over the window.

"Wait a minute," he says, peeking out at me.

I look back at AZ, who's no longer holding his jaw.

Within minutes, the little boy opens the front door. I step aside, allowing him to walk past me. He motions for me to follow him. We walk to a garage where he raises the door.

Once AZ spots his X box and flat screen tv, he gets excited and steps out the car to help me. He and I remove everything on the floor without incident.

Driving home on the highway, I breathe a heavy sigh of relief. In my peripheral, AZ digs feverishly through Suga's bags. "Ain't nothing in here but an iPhone and forty bucks. There's nothing of any real value in her bags," AZ says, shaking his head.

Even so, I know he has no intention of returning it to Suga.

Dear Diary, it's October 6, 2012.

Today, AZ and I finally meet with the landlord to sign our lease and get the keys to the Pineapple Dreamz store.

Driving home after the meeting, AZ accepts a call from Toni. We hadn't heard from her since losing the house in Brentwood.

"Hi, AZ!" Toni says, sounding upbeat. AZ's cell wasn't on speaker, but I could still hear her very clearly.

"What's up?" he says. AZ reclines the car seat, holding the cellphone tightly to his ear. Toni sniffles, loudly. I suspected she was getting high.

"AZ, I've been living in these streets. Suga, told me we can't get back into that house anymore."

"Ugh, let me call you back," AZ grunts, hanging up on her. "What did Toni want?" I ask out of curiosity.

"What do you think? She needs a place to stay," AZ says, with a smirk.

"Then, why did you hang up on her?" I ask naively.

"To make her sweat. We haven't heard from Toni in weeks. I don't need her. She needs me!" he says, poking his chest out proudly.

By night fall, AZ sends me to Amityville to pick Toni up.

On my way there with Lexx, I receive a call from her. "Hi, Karen," Toni whispers when I answer.

"Hey, Toni, I'm in route to get you now," I say, thinking I'm running late.

"I'm not at work. I'm at the Cloverland housing complex in Amityville. Meet me here," she says oddly.

Lexx and I exchange glances. Toni didn't sound like her regular upbeat self. "Okay, I'm on my way," I say, hanging up the phone.

"What was that all about?" Lexx frowns, turning the radio back up. "I'm not sure," I say, shaking my head.

"Well, you can drop me off right here. My date lives in that house on the corner, " she says, pointing to a large brick house at the end of the block.

"Are you going to be okay?" I ask, pulling to the curb, thinking about the trouble Lexx had with her last date. She waves her hand at me and hops out the car skipping down the street. Once she's inside of the house, I write down the address.

Arriving at Cloverland, the complex is dark and gloomy.

It's dimly lit by broken streetlamps. I call Toni's cell phone but receive no answer. Preparing to leave, I get a text from her.

Karen, meet me around back, behind building number seven.

Driving through the winding parking lot, it's pitch black.

I can barely see the numbers on the buildings. Stopping at building number seven, I turn my headlights off but keep the car running.

It's spooky out here! Toni, you better hurry up. I think to myself. After some time, I call Toni again.

She answers the phone breathing heavily.

"Karen, I'm only a few minutes away. Don't leave me!" she says, sounding in distress.

"Hurry up! I'm scared out here. This parking lot is dark," I say, hanging up the phone.

I squint to see two silhouettes rounding the building.

One person is smaller than the other. I can't tell their gender, but they are tussling hard. The smaller one is putting up a valiant fight. The larger person is pulling and pushing the little one like a ragdoll. Both head in my direction, stopping right in front of the car.

I quickly roll up the windows and lock the doors.

The fight is now directly in front of my windshield, but it's too dark to see their faces.

"Stop it! Leave me alone!" Toni yells loudly.

I gasp, hearing Toni's voice and partially roll down the window.

"Toni, is that you?!" I ask, fearing she's being attacked.

Toni runs from her assailant and attempts to open my front passenger door.

"Yeah, Karen! It's me!" she says, struggling with the locked door. "You not going nowhere," the attacker barks, running to the back door, pulling on the handle.

Frightened by this, I keep both doors locked.

"She has the doors locked on you." the guy says, pushing Toni away from my car.

"Leave me alone! Get off of me!" Toni yells as he drags her farther away from the car.

People begin turning on the lights and looking out their apartment windows. Unnerved, I grab my cell phone to call AZ.

He quickly picks up.

"Yo, AZ! Toni's in trouble! She's fighting with some dude. He won't let her get in the car with me!" I say, staring out the car window to see if he's hurting Toni.

"Karen, help me!" Toni screams for me.

My mother did not raise no fool. I am not getting out this car, Toni. I think to myself.

Ignoring her cries for help, I continue talking with AZ. "Can you hear her screaming?!" I ask him.

"Who is the guy? Is he a daddy nigga?!" AZ asks, thinking it's Toni's pimp.

"I don't know who he is! I don't know what's going on!" I say, watching Toni push the guy off of her.

"What do you want? MONEY?!" Toni yells, then opens her purse, tossing some bills in his face.

"Here's sixty dollars! Take that and leave me alone!" Toni screams, making me think she's being robbed.

"Are you going to leave her?" AZ asks me.

"No! I'm going to stay to see what happens to her!" I say, bravely hanging up the phone.

A car speeds past me screeching to a halt.

The passenger door swings open.

Toni's assailant tries to shove her inside.

Thinking quickly, I immediately spring into action. Driving fast, I pull up beside the car.

"I don't know who you guys are! But it looks like she's being abducted to me. I'm calling the cops!" I say, courageously holding the cell phone to my ear.

The driver turns to his friend.

I can't hear what they say, but they release Toni. She runs to my car and jumps in the passenger side. .Her assailant looks over the other car roof at me.

"I'm her man!" he says sharply.

Toni yells out the window at him, "If you want money, all you have to do is ask! I have things to do out east! I don't stop your hustle! Why you stopping mine?!"

Her man quickly runs to my open window, spooking me.

I prepare to drive away but see a pair of pink heels in his hand. "I'm so sorry about all of this," he says, calmly handing them to me. Apparently, the shoes fell out of Toni's workbag during the struggle.

"Sorry we had to meet under these circumstances," I say, carefully removing the shoes from his hand.

Driving off, I give Toni the shoes in my lap.

I don't exhale until the fellas disappear in my rearview mirror. "I'm so fucking embarrassed you had to see that," Toni says, twisting her wig around to the front. "He can go anywhere he wants. Soon as I want to go somewhere, he acts crazy.

He's younger than me. I snatched him up when he was only seventeen. I take care of him now."

How can you take care of him, and you can't even take care of yourself? I think, chuckling to myself.

Toni and I drove to a nearby liquor store where she bought a bottle of vodka. We drank it in the parking lot waiting for Lexx to finish her date. I quietly listened to her vent. Hearing her talk, I surmised Toni was much smarter than Suga.

After I picked Lexx up from her date, we all went back to my house. Walking in the front door, Toni received a call. She was skeptical about answering it.

"What y'all want now?" Toni says, putting the phone on speaker for us to hear.

"Your man just got arrested!" the guy on the other end says excitedly.

Toni's mouth drops open.

"What happened to him?! I just left y'all!"

"I know! We got into a car accident leaving the complex. When the cops came, your man blew up on them. They put the nigga under arrest."

Toni takes a deep breath.

"Damn! Call me with his bail amount." "Okay, I got you!"

Toni waits for hours then days, but that call never comes.

She stays with us for the next couple of weeks.

We take her to and from work. The ride is forty-five minutes each way. Toni never offers us any money for our hospitality. She was even too cheap to pay for the gas.

In the interim, she had nerve to invite her girlfriend, Jazz, to our house.

The girl stayed for two days. When the friend left, we plotted on getting rid of Toni.

AZ was up early drinking coffee in the kitchen. "Did you wake Toni for work yet? he asks, when I walk into the room.

"No, 'cause I'm not driving her cheap ass to work!" I say, sucking my teeth, opening the refrigerator.

"Don't worry. I got a trick for that ass today. It will be her last free ride," AZ grins deviously.

After I take Toni to work, AZ and I handle some business for the Pineapple Dreamz store. We buy paint and some other supplies to decorate. On our way home, his phone rings continuously.

"Who's that calling you?" I ask him.

"That's Toni calling. It's time for her to get off of work," he smirks, sending the call to voicemail.

The phone rings again. AZ looks at it, inhaling deeply. "Toni?" I ask him. He nods, rolling his eyes.

"Do you want me to talk to her?"

"I wish you would. I want nothing to do with this girl anymore," AZ says, staring out the car window.

Arriving home, I stomp through the kitchen and go straight to the landline. AZ and I wait for Toni to pick up the call.

"Hello!" she answers, perky. AZ presses his ear against the phone listening with me.

"What do you want, Miss Karen?"

To make this easier, I hoped Toni was upset with us for not picking her up from work today.

"I know dropping me off and picking me up was too good to be true. People do it for a while, then all of a sudden, they stop," Toni says to me.

They stop because your ass is cheap. I think to myself, listening to her speak. What she says next surprises us both.

"That's alright. I got a ride anyway. I'm upstairs in Lexx's room," Toni snickers.

AZ's bottom lip hits the floor. We stare at each other in disbelief.

"She's here in Lexx's room," I whisper to him, covering the mouthpiece. AZ's face twists in anger.

"You better go handle that. I don't want Toni here anymore! Last night she got some drugs from me and didn't pay for them.

I took the money when she went to sleep. She woke up asking about it. When I told her I took the money for the drugs, she tried to beef with me," AZ snorts.

"This girl's been eating, sleeping, smoking, sniffing and getting rides for free. I want her out of my house right now!" he snaps, storming away, leaving me to deal with his headache.

I gingerly go up the steps to Lexx's room.

"Hi, homie," Lexx says, when I walk in the door.

She and Toni were relaxing across the bed watching TV. Toni smiles at me, wickedly. I sit on the edge of the bed preparing my speech.

"Hey, Toni, we need to talk," I say in a non-confrontational manner. Toni sits up to listen.

"We'll help you get a place but, in the meantime, you have to start paying for food and rent," I say, looking at her sternly.

"Oh, okay. Is that it, Karen? That's all you have to say to me," Toni smiles and lays back on the bed.

Two days passed with us driving Toni to and from work again.

She got paid daily though still refused to give us any money. She did, however, continue buying weed, drugs and alcohol.

We became totally fed up with her nonsense.

Early Saturday morning, Toni bangs loudly on my bedroom door for her daily ride to work. Hung over from drinking at the club all night, I roll over groggy and look at the clock. It's ten thirty in the morning.

Hearing me stir around inside, Toni screams my name through the bedroom door, "Karen, please take me to work!"

I suck my teeth and roll my eyes.

Toni, I'm sick of taking your conniving ass to work!

I thought to myself.

"Okay, I'll be right out!" I say, quickly jumping up because she's already late.

Opening the bedroom door, Toni impatiently exhales, placing her hand on her hip.

"Excuse me!" I say, blinking rapidly, surprised she's blocking the doorway.

Going to the bathroom to wash my face, I hear Toni in the living room harrassing Lexx. It was her daily routine to beg Lexx for free weed in the morning. I rushed out of the bathroom to rescue her.

"Lexx, you wanna ride with me to take Toni to work?"

"Sure, let's go," she said, all bright-eyed and bushy-tailed.

We all walked out the front door and got into my car. Leaving the driveway, we didn't get very far.

"I sent my boss a text telling him I was going to be late. He told me not to come in at all. Damn, I had two customers coming today. I was counting on those four hundred dollars. This screws me up!" Toni pouts, slumping in the back seat.

I smile, thinking now she understands how it feels to play with other people's money.

I never saw anything like her job. Inside was set up like an adult video shop. Customers came to rent porn from a wall display of tapes. The strangest part was the girls walking around in lingerie propositioning customers while they shopped. If customers got hot and horny, it was Toni's job to turn that fantasy into a reality. There was no liquor or pole dancing. The action took place in a VIP room.

This is how she earned her money.

Still dizzy from the alcohol, I was relieved not to make the long drive.

"So, now what?" I ask, determined not to take Toni back to my house.

Her body stiffens, knowing it's the end of the road for her. "Just take me to my friend's house around the corner," she says, head hanging low. "But first take me to get some weed and a roll up," she mumbles, underneath her breath.

Swinging the car around, irritated by her final request, I thought to myself, *Sure, anything to get rid of you!*

Stopping in front of Toni's friend's house, she says, "I'm not coming back tonight."

I look at her stunned, thinking, *You better not!* But instead, I say, "Yay!" Making everyone in the car laugh out loud.

"Stop playing, Karen. I'm only going for a few days.

I'll be back soon. Next time answer my calls. Otherwise, I'll just show up on your doorstep again," Toni jokes, getting out the car. I knew her crazy ass was serious.

When Lexx and I returned home, I told everyone in the house not to open the door for Toni.

CHAPTER VIII
CHERRY IN THE MANSION

Today was the big day. AZ strutted around the mansion poking his chest out. He darted in and out of the girl's rooms, rushing them as they dolled up for the infamous Brainfest.

Even though the event was for Cherry, somehow AZ convinced Tee and Shi to go too. Rabyt and I patiently waited for everyone in the living room.

"Hurry up! I promised the host a truck full of hoes to open the show. We better be on time! If we're late it's going to make me look bad," AZ yells throughout the mansion.

"I don't know why you promised that! I don't care nothing about no damn Brainfest!" Shi hollered back from her room.

Rabyt and I sat on the couch giggling, listening to her complain.

She always had a smart mouth.

"Because I did! That's why! Now hurry your ass up before I drag you out here!" AZ barks, showing power.

This only made Shi take longer.

AZ's eyes are dark with emotion speeding down the highway.

He curses the whole way there because we are late for the Brainfest. "This stupid bitch always fucks up my money!" he says out loud to no one in particular.

Shi sits in the back seat rolling her eyes at him.

The rest of us quietly listen to the radio.

I gaze out the window counting rain drops, watching trees turn into the concrete jungle. Exiting the ramp, I realize we are closing in on our destination.

Are we really going to an illegal sex party? Will the men grab on me?

Can AZ protect all of us?! I think to myself.

Driving like a mad man, AZ turns on the block and stops in front of a barber shop. He spins around, placing his arm across the seat.

"Remember, we are here to get this money. There's nothing to be afraid of. We are in and out!" he says, glaring at us.

Everyone except Shi obediently hops out the truck. She remains in the back seat with her arms folded across her chest. Rabyt notices she isn't moving.

"You coming, girl?" Rabyt says, trying to coax her out of the vehicle. Shi ignores her and continues staring out of the window.

"Come on, Rabyt. Forget that stupid bitch!" AZ hisses over his shoulder, keeping in step with the rest of us.

He was clean from head to toe in a new jean suit and bright white Nike sneakers. The rest of us matched his sexy.

Filing into the barbershop behind AZ, I didn't know what to expect. The butterflies in my stomach made me nauseous. One of the barbers stopped cutting hair to look at us, then pointed his clippers toward the back of the shop. We walked past thirsty customers who gawked at us like we were fresh meat to eat. It was obvious some would join the party after their cuts.

In the back of the shop, a greasy bald guy waited our arrival.

He licked beefy black lips when he saw us coming. "We're VIP guests." AZ told him.

I suspected the guy was the owner. He reached down, opening a metal door on the floor.

We carefully walked down the steep rickety steps into a pitch-black cellar. At first, I could hardly see anyone in the room.

"It's crazy dark in here," Rabyt whispered in my ear.

It took a few seconds for my eyes to adjust. The tiny place was lit by one red light bulb, dangling from the ceiling, over a chair in the corner. We tripped and stumbled over stretched out feet, heading in that direction.

Hearing sexual moans and groans, I clung tightly to AZ's arm. I feared touching someone would imply I was a working girl. Cherry, Tee and Rabyt followed close behind us.

Reaching the corner, AZ sat on the chair with me climbing on his lap like a scared little child. Cherry, Tee and Rabyt stood next to us.

We watched fully nude women performing erotic tricks in the center of the floor. Some females straddled men in chairs, skillfully maneuvering to hide lewd sex acts.

Others secretly dipped into a back room to fornicate. "Everybody alright?" AZ grins at us sadistically. We all cheerfully nod, but it's traumatizing for us.

Everyone seemed extremely uncomfortable, except for Cherry. "Anybody want a drink?" AZ asks, observing a guy serving drinks across the room behind a makeshift bar.

"I'll take a double shot of Hennessy. If that will help," I say nervously.

"I'll have a beer. I don't want to get too drunk in this spot," Rabyt says, leering at the people in the room.

"And you two?" AZ asks Cherry and Tee. He wanted them loose enough to earn some money.

"I don't like this place. I'm ready to go," Tee says, eyes wide with fear. The college girl was way out of her element.

"None for me. I'm just ready to get busy," Cherry giggles. "Okay, I'll be right back," AZ says, crossing the room with me tagging on his heels.

When we came back, Cherry was gone.

I gulped the double shot of Hennessy, trying to relax.

"Where is Cherry?" AZ asked Rabyt, handing her the beer.

She sucked her teeth, pointing to a curtain hanging over a doorway. "It doesn't take a snow bunny long to get a customer in here.

Some negro whispered in Cherry's ear and slid her into that room over there," Rabyt said.

AZ looked at Tee, who shrugged, confirming the story.

Smiling, he sat back in the chair waiting for the results.

When Cherry was taking too long, AZ became impatient.

He checked his watch every five minutes, looking at that doorway. "I think something is wrong. It's been over an hour.

Normally, it only takes fifteen minutes per customer. Y'all go back there and check on Cherry," he said to me and Rabyt.

By this time, I was drowning in Hennessy and brave enough to go anywhere.

"Come on, girl. Let's go see what's going on!" I said, leading the way.

There's only one bodyguard blocking the entrance when we get there. He politely steps aside letting us through. Men weren't allowed back there unless they were customers. Apparently, women were free to roam.

Rabyt and I went inside looking around.

We couldn't see or hear anyone. The large room was separated into sections by hanging curtains.

Turning to leave, we heard Cherry whooping and hollering in orgasmic ecstasy. She was so loud it was embarrassing for us. You would've thought she was the only one in the room. Everyone else was relatively quiet handling their business. Rabyt and I rushed from the room, covering our mouths giggling.

"Yo! Cherry is in there screaming like she's falling in love with the guy," Rabyt says, reporting back to AZ.

We all laugh out loud.

"Oh, okay. Cherry's making her money. Let's give her a little more time," AZ says, standing up to go get more drinks for us.

Minutes later, Cherry emerges from the room with her customer.

The guy runs by us laughing and stops at the bar whispering to a friend, and they both burst out in laughter.

AZ is nearby eavesdropping on their conversation.

When AZ returns with our drinks, he is pissed.

"Let's get out of this dump! These clowns are not spending any money! I overheard some punk telling his man that he didn't give some dumb bitch any money for her services.

Let's go home now!" AZ storms away with us happy to follow.

It's dark outside when we crawl back into the Armada.

Shi is fast asleep across the back seat. We were in the barbershop three long hours. AZ's content, believing at least Cherry made some money. "So, Cherry! How much cash we got?" AZ pops the question as soon as her fat ass plops on the leather seat. Cherry's mouth pops open, staring at him blankly.

"I didn't make any money. I didn't have sex," she says, squirming awkwardly under his X-ray vision.

"But we came back there and heard you screaming.

Right, Karen?" Rabyt says to me.

I nod, dumbfounded by Cherry's answer.

Shi sits up in the back seat, rubbing her eyes.

"Yes, that's because he was fingering and eating me out.

We didn't do anything else. I promise! He said if he only ate me out that didn't count as sex!"

Cherry's eyes roll in the back of her head, reminiscing in the moment.

AZ puts two and two together about the conversation he overheard at the bar. He now realizes the men were talking about Cherry. He can't believe she's that stupid.

"ARE YOU CRAZY?! I can never show my face here again!" AZ screams, banging his fist on the dashboard.

He swiftly spins the steering wheel, quickly leaving the curb. The SUV pops into gear and speeds down the block.

Without seat belts on, his erratic driving tosses everyone around the truck.

Cherry stares at him, discovering her mistake. Rabyt and Tee cling to each other holding on for dear life. Shi snickers in the back seat, happy not to be a part of the problem. The liquor had me squeamish. I sat back, quietly giggling to myself. Riding home in silence, passing gloomy tenement buildings under bright city lights, we all feared upsetting AZ. I was more disappointed than he was because we still had no rent!

An hour later, the Armada pulled into the mansion driveway.

The doors flew open, and everyone hopped out and went in the house. Anything said might have sent AZ into a rage.

KG was on the sofa with a pillow propped underneath his arm watching TV. He smiled when we came through the door.

"How'd it go?!" he asks, jumping up, turning off the TV. The girls rush past him without uttering a word. AZ shakes his head, disappointed.

"Let me roll something first. You're gonna need it once you hear this bullshit," he says.

KG looks at him strangely.

"Why? What happened? What's wrong with Cherry?

She looks upset," he says, handing AZ a blunt already rolled. The three of us take seats at the kitchen table waiting for AZ to tell the story.

"Cherry is damaged goods. You won't believe what her crazy ass did at the Brainfest. I'm too embarrassed to ever show my face there again," AZ says to him.

KG's eyes widen with concern, patiently waiting for him to explain.

AZ lights the blunt and takes a long pull.

"First of all, Shi never got out of the truck. That was strike one.

Once we were inside, the girls acted so stupid it made me look like a lame ass pimp. I had to remind everyone why we were there in the first place. Cherry, though, was all for the game.

She went right to work in the back room." KG sits forward, hanging on every word.

AZ pauses, taking another toke of the blunt. He exhales slowly, letting circles of smoke float through the air.

He sits back in the seat allowing the weed to overcome him.

KG squirms, anxiously waiting for the punchline.

AZ narrows his eyes, poetically dragging out the story. "The girls say hanging curtains separate rooms.

Bodyguards sweep cash with ragged brooms. One on one Cherry has fun.

Moaning and groaning until she cums. I expect money when she's done.

Later I find there is none!" AZ stops rapping.

At this point, we expect KG to say something.

When he doesn't, AZ takes another pull on the blunt and continues.

"I ask Cherry, where is the money? That's when things get funny. She said,

'I didn't have sex.' He used his fingers first and his tongue next." AZ ends his story and places the roach in the ashtray. He then bursts out in laughter like a mad man.

It scares KG and me. We flinch, joining him in laughter until the room falls silent. Minutes pass with the three of us just sitting there.

"So, you think Cherry is lying?" KG asks, rhetorically. "Let me go find out what this crazy girl did," he stands to leave, backing out of the room with us watching him.

"KG got to get rid of that girl," AZ says when he's out of earshot.

I leave the table mumbling underneath my breath, "Yes, he does. There are enough people staying here for free. I can't afford this bullshit."

"Shut up! I heard that. You're gonna get your damn rent money!" AZ hollers after me.

Turning around, I see him rolling another blunt.

That's where all the damn money is going!

The next morning I'm too upset to get out of bed. I lay frustrated, head resting on the pillow. I let my cell phone ring and go straight to voicemail.

The situation I dreaded was finally here. Adraina was coming from Jersey to collect the rent money. Judging from the last time she called, I expected her within the hour.

Refusing to check her message, I sat up yawning and stretched for my pocketbook on the nightstand.

I eased the money out the side pocket and counted it slowly. "Shoot! It's only two thousand dollars here! Adriana, is expecting five stacks!" I said out loud to myself.

This whole month, I haven't collected any rent from these ingrates. Getting money from them is almost impossible.

Shi barely works. AZ bought her a gold grill but her customers don't like the teeth. After Rabyt discovers she is living amongst dead beats, she stops paying rent too. Cheeks has a starving artist named Shamal living with us. Neither contributes financially. The little money Tee earns mostly goes to her son.

AZ spends his money on food and weed. KG has Cherry, but she's dead weight. This whole burden lies solely on me.

I can't get the country club off the ground with people who don't share my vision. In addition, they're running the house into the ground.

The driveway is always overflowing with garbage because the men are too lazy to take it out. No one seems to care but me.

The mansion is just a party spot for them. I'm beginning to think I'm in over my head.

With a deep sigh, I gather the money scattered on the bed and scribble a few words on a notepad. Satisfied with what I've written, I get dressed feeling more confident about meeting Adriana.

Going downstairs, I was shocked entering the kitchen. The heavy smell of weed and liquor danced through the air. The residents scampered around doing their normal nothing. The whole place was in disarray. In addition to the usual derelicts, there were other people sitting around smelling up the place.

KG was at the table with Kal, Uni, and his brother Shaq.

His brother's girlfriend was there too.

"No, No, No!" I yelled, slamming the notepad on the kitchen countertop. "Whatever is going on in here has to stop! I need this place clear in a matter of minutes!"

I knew Adriana was only a few miles away. I couldn't let her witness this spectacle. I wanted the illusion of running a country club not a trap house.

"What's wrong?!" KG asked, alarmed by my outburst. "You have to open these windows and air this place out.

My people are on their way!" I said, panicking.

I didn't necessarily want them to know Adriana was coming. I just wanted them to get the hell out of there!

"KG, please ask your company to leave and come back later!" I smiled at him, trying to compose myself.

"Sure, okay." KG quickly escorts his company out the front door.

Once they are gone, I holler through the mansion, "People, stay in your rooms and out of sight! Adriana is on her way. She's under the impression I'm running a country club -- not renting rooms."

All of this is done in not a minute too soon.

Adriana's Nissan Rogue enters the front driveway as KG's guests exit out the back. I'm lucky she doesn't see them. I stand on the front porch, arms folded, nervously watching everything unfold.

Adriana pulls up and stops right in front of me.

She jumps out smiling and hugs me.

"Hi, Karen," she says in her thick accent.

Inhaling her sweet perfume, I wish she hadn't come. "Hey, Adriana! I'm so glad you could make it," I say, squinting from the sun above her head. "Meet my daughter, Mary."

The pretty young girl climbs out the SUV and stands beside her mother.

"Hello," I say, not really paying the daughter much attention. My frown focuses on the fleet of cars returning up the driveway.

This can't be possible. These idiots are not coming back!

"Who's that, Karen?" Adriana asks, puzzled by the car procession.

"Oh! That's KG's friends." I say, rolling my eyes, pissed that the vultures are returning.

"Let's go in the house," I say, guiding Adriana by the arm.

"Hold on, Karen." she says, yanking free of my grasp to wait for the cars to pull up.

KG appears in the doorway, blinking rapidly.

His friends, drive up and hop out, ready to meet her.

KG and I briefly make the introductions, then whisk Adriana and her daughter into the house. The group remains in the driveway waiting for her to come back outside.

In the house Adriana starts off the conversation. "So, what's going on here, Karen?" she asks, with a huge grin on her face.

I wasn't really sure if she was on to me.

"Adriana, I've been working on developing a business plan for the country club." I flip open the notepad revealing my illegible notes to her. She looks at the paper. I smile, confident she can't read it.

"This plan will bring the income needed to stabilize our overhead.

In addition, it focuses on your daughter's music project." I smile at the daughter, knowing the child is a soft spot in her heart.

Suddenly, Rabyt appears out of nowhere being nosy like everyone else. She was scantily dressed in pom pom shorts. Adriana observes the robust body float across the floor.

"Oh, I also have some models staying here. Would you like to meet one?" I say, referring to Rabyt.

Adriana gasps and looks at me turning her nose up. "That's a model?! She's a little too big, Karen."

Her reaction motivates some quick thinking on my part. "Shi! Can you come in here for a minute?!

I scream, loudly. Shi enters the room in a hot negligee, looking like America's next top model. It pleases me that she strolls in without an attitude.

"Adriana this is Shi," I say, introducing them.

Shi was a natural beauty. It made me proud to put her on display.

"Nice to meet you!" Adriana says, shaking her hand. It's obvious she's taken back by her stunning look.

After Shi leaves the room, Cheeks unexpectedly walks in brandishing a blunt in his hand. Thinking fast again, I stop him before he lights it.

"Adriana, this is Grammy award winning artist Mr. Cheeks. He's one of the celebrities shooting a video here. If you're lucky, he'll do a feature on a song for your daughter."

I wink at Cheeks, hoping he'll play along.

Adriana looks at him suspiciously.

"Oh, really? That's very interesting. My daughter would love that.

Maybe we can do some business in the future," she says, glaring at Cheeks.

"No doubt! Karen will hook it up!" he says, easily charming her, disappearing on the back deck to light his blunt.

Relaxing a bit, I feel it's an easy sell from here.

"Adriana, I have something for you. It's only half of the rent, but I'll make up the difference next time," I say, handing her a check for two stacks. "Okay, Karen!"

She accepts the short money to avoid blowing her daughter's music deal. We talk a little more, then they leave.

KG's guests are still in the driveway when they walk out of the house. Watching through the window, I see Kal approach her. She stops to talk with him before getting into the SUV.

When they drive away, the unruly bunch marches right back into the house to resume their activities. Kal spots me by the window in the living room and comes over to talk.

"Did everything go alright with Adriana?" he asks, interrupting my train of thought.

Turning around, I notice his nervous energy. "Yeah, everything's fine," I say, careful not to disclose much to him. Kal had already betrayed me once. "I'm just asking because she mentioned something about her daughter's music," he pauses, waiting for a response. "Oh, yeah?" I reply, nonchalantly.

"KG doesn't have the equipment she needs. I suggested taking her to my man, Special. He works with Busta Rhymes," Kal says, sparking my attention.

I bite my tongue to avoid lashing out at him.

Is this clown really shifting the budget to another team?!

I stare at him, wondering what's in it for him.

"I'm going to set up a meeting for her. Is that okay?" he asks, making my temper boil.

Knowing Kal, the meeting was already set. It gave me little time to strategize. Staying ahead of the game would be chess not checkers. With little choice in the matter,

I had to accept his offer or be excluded all together. "Sure, let me know the time and place. I'll be there."

I smile at him, but it's hard with the dagger he had stuck in my back. Watching him slither back across the room in baggy pants two sizes too big, my attention diverts to KG.

Cherry opened the front door. KG kissed her goodbye ,then closed it behind her. It was peculiar to see KG act that way. Cherry brought something out of him I never saw before. When

Cherry left, I went over to talk with KG. I needed someone to talk to that I could trust.

"Hey, KG!" I said, making him jump. Like most Pisces, he had a habit of daydreaming.

"Huh?" KG says, without moving his eyes away from the window. Looking outside with him, I saw nothing.

"KG!" I repeated to get his attention.

"Yup," he says, slowly taking his eyes off the window. "Where is Cherry going?" I asked, figuring I'd start the conversation about her to get his interest.

"I don't know. I just saw her get into a car with some strange looking men. I don't like people knowing we're out here in the cut. I got my protection just in case," he says, patting his hip, suggesting he's got heat.

I dismiss what he says, planning to revisit it later.

Right now, I had bigger issues to address.

"KG, I gave Adriana two thousand dollars. Next time, I won't be so lucky. On top of everything, Kal is infiltrating our plans. He's setting up a meeting for her at another studio," I say, hopelessly babbling.

"Calm down, the worst is over. Adriana is gone. It'll give us more time to come up with a better plan. Don't worry about Kal. He's a small fish in a big pond.

My man H is bringing the rapper Mazaradi Fox here.

They want to use the mansion to film a music video. Fox just got out of a jail. Word on the street, he has a big budget from Fiddy cent.

In the meantime, I got this Puerto Rican kid named Fredo coming to promote the event. We'll get plenty of money from the party."

Eyeing KG, I questioned how much of this was true.

It certainly sounded good.

"Everything will work out," he chuckles confidently. "I guess so. Whatever will be, will be. The future's not ours to see.

Do you think Cherry will be alright?" I ask, changing the subject back to her.

"I hope so. She feels bad about the Brainfest.

She thinks I'm disappointed. I told her I wasn't but all she could talk about was making it up to me.

She left today, promising to bring back thousands of dollars. I just want her to be safe."

KG sighs, looking out the window in despair.

Watching him, I felt bad. KG really cared about Cherry. The rest of us knew she was a wild girl. She used to sneak out at night to be with Uni. He was renting a room at my other house.

Uni was really good with managing the tenants over there.

He also took in any girls that we kicked out of the mansion. Tee was one of those girls. She became disenchanted with giving up her money after losing Cheeks to Rabyt.

A few days went by before we heard anything about Cherry.

We were all in the living room watching the news when her picture popped up.

"Hush, everybody!" KG said, giving the newscaster his full attention. We all stopped what we were doing to listen too.

The news was about an alleged violent crime.

At first, I didn't know who it was about. The reporter used Cherry's government name.

Apparently, she and her accomplices botched a home invasion. Luckily, the police were tipped off beforehand. They were able to ambush the crew while they did a drive-by to case the place. The gang was caught with an arsenal of loaded weapons in the trunk of their vehicle. Fortunately, the home invasion was unsuccessful, and nobody got hurt.

Hearing the news, KG's body goes limp.

He slumps on the sofa looking dumbfounded. Listening to the chitter chatter in the room, he can stand no more. KG slips out the front door and goes to visit Cherry at the county jail.

A couple of hours later, KG returns to the mansion.

Everyone is still in the living room smoking, drinking, and discussing the incident.

He walks through the front door, angrily tossing his keys on the kitchen counter.

"I just got back from that jail. Y'all won't believe this jackass did," KG fumes.

Rabyt, sitting on the kitchen counter, was the first to react.

Her and Cherry had grown extremely close over time. "What happened, KG? You good, my nigga!" Rabyt said, eyes wide with concern.

I walked to the refrigerator to get my third beer.

Uni was at the table with Shi and AZ, who was rolling a blunt. Cheeks came in off the back deck. We all quietly listened while KG talked.

"Yeah, Rabyt, I'm good. I just can't believe this crazy girl. Somebody pass me a blunt."

AZ handed KG the blunt he had just finished rolling.

KG lit it and inhaled deeply.

"I don't know where to begin," he says, choking on the smoke. "Cherry was planning a home invasion for weeks with some girl in jail! How stupid is that?!" he says, head sinking between his shoulders.

Uni pours him a cup of liquor. KG grabs the cup and takes a big gulp.

"I knew it! I told Cherry not to go!" Rabyt says hopping off the kitchen counter.

We all look at her, surprised.

"You knew she was going to do a home invasion?!" KG asks her. "I knew she was talking about it. I didn't think she would actually do it!" Rabyt replied in her defense.

AZ bursts out in laughter. "Cherry was planning a robbery with a girl in jail. What a dummy!" he says, slapping his knee, laughing even louder.

"Oh, WOW!" Shi giggles, covering her mouth to hide the gold grill.

"Yup! Cherry planned the whole thing with her friend in jail," KG sighs in frustration. "Karen, you remember when Cherry left with those guys?"

"Uh huh," I say, not really sure where he's going with this. "Well, that's the day she went to do the home invasion. The worst part is the entire plan was recorded by the police!" KG swallows the whole cup of liquor, wincing from the burning sensation.

"She's a different kind of stupid. Not the brightest candle on the cake," I say, taking a sip of the beer.

"Not only that, but Cherry's also being charged as the ring leader. She's facing over fifteen years in prison!" KG shakes his head, banging a fist on the table. We all gasp, saddened by the news. A cold sweat drips down my back.

"Fifteen years!" Rabyt says, eyes revealing deep anguish.

The room falls silent.

The rest of the evening KG sat at the table drinking liquor to drown in his sorrow. We all tiptoed past him with pity.

CHAPTER IX
DEAR DIARY

Dear Diary, it's October 17, 2012.

AZ and I worked hard putting the finishing touches on the Pineapple Dreamz store. We were trying to rush for the grand opening. AZ found some neighborhood fiends to paint the store hot pink.

He then hung cheap inventory and shabby ornaments on the walls. When it was all said and done, I thought the place looked very tacky. I didn't tell him because he was very proud of himself.

Also, because I knew his main objective was in the basement.

For weeks, he and KG banged around downstairs, replicating the inside of a fancy gentlemen's club. KG built a long stage and a lap dance room for the strippers. AZ surrounded the basement with intimate lighting for a seductive setting.

Lastly, he bought a wooden bar off of Craigslist filling it with liquor. With everything complete, AZ was ready to rake in the dough.

I had to admit, it was great seeing Pineapple Dreamz come to fruition.

Our unofficial grand opening was a simple celebration for family and friends. The event wasn't meant to generate income. AZ opened the store on Halloween and invited everyone we knew in the neighborhood. Our friends laughed, danced, ate hearty and drank heavily.

The next day we were open for business. We sold lingerie, stripper apparel and other accessories. But it was all a cover for the basement. Actually, his goal was to lure customers to the strip club. A few weeks would lapse before AZ felt it was safe to do so.

One by one, AZ plotted on trustworthy strippers to work at his underground establishment. The first girl he seeked out was Toni. He knew she was staying in Amityville with some close friends.

AZ called Toni one day when we were cleaning the basement. KG and I quietly listened while AZ macked Toni over the phone.

"What's up, girl? What you mean who is this? It's your daddy!" AZ said, winking at us when she answered the call. "You got your apartment yet?" he asked, knowing she was homeless.

After attentively listening to her, AZ propositioned Toni to come stay with him. She accepted his offer walking right into another one of his traps.

Two days later, we arrived in Amityville to pick Toni up.

Turning on the block, we saw her waiting on the sidewalk with her bags. AZ quickly pulled to the curb where she was standing.

"Hey y'all! Long time no see," Toni said, hopping into the car with us.

It really was good to see her again. Especially after so much time had passed. Wherever she was staying, I figured she'd worn out her welcome by now.

"Hi, Toni. How have you been?" I asked, turning around hugging her cold body. The skimpy jacket and flimsy dress were hardly enough to keep her warm in these nippy temperatures.

"Hey, Toni," AZ said with a sly smirk. Toni smiled with deep dimples, handing him a hundred-dollar bill. AZ looked at it strangely.

It seemed they had already discussed an exchange of cash.

Though as usual, Toni was probably acting funny with his money. Obviously, needing her for the strip club, AZ didn't complain.

He put the money in his pocket and drove away from the curb. "You got a little something for me?" Toni asked, plucking her nostril. AZ glared at her in the rearview mirror. Ignoring her plea for drugs, he pressed hard on the gas pedal.

Toni laughed at him.

"Well, you can't blame a girl for trying," she said, curling up in the back seat to warm herself.

I looked at her thinking, *everyone has a trick up their sleeve in this grimy game.*

A half hour later, we dropped Toni off at AZ's house in Brentwood.

She was so tired when we got there, she didn't question him about the location. AZ grabbed her bags off the back seat and walked her inside.

I waited the few minutes it took him to return.

AZ got back in the car, inhaling deeply.

"One down, one to go," he said, referring to Suga.

He also intended to put Suga in that house. He didn't call her right away because she was always trouble. He planned to let Toni live there by herself for a few weeks.

Stupidly, Toni remained in contact with Suga without disclosing her whereabouts. Toni kept up the charades until it blew up in her face.

On this particular day, AZ had me drive him to Brentwood to confront Toni. As usual, she was acting funny with his money.

AZ sat with his legs wide, straddling a mattress on the floor. Toni sat opposite him. He passed her the blunt and reached for his cellphone to make a call.

"Hello! What you doing?" he asked the person on the other end.

Toni and I didn't pay his conversation much attention. We were too busy peeking out the window at the nosy neighbors.

AZ put the cellphone on speaker so we could hear.

"Oh, nothing. I'm at the Hollywood motel working Backpage. What are you doing?" Suga asked him, voice soft and sultry.

Toni's mouth popped open.

AZ smirked at her. It was just the reaction he was looking for.

He wanted to make Toni feel jealous.

"Suga, I told you I was going to call back," he said, leering at Toni.

"Oh, yes! You mean about your strip club. I can't wait to see it!" Suga said, becoming excited. Her eagerness prompts AZ to seize the opportunity.

"I also got a new house for you to live in. You don't have to stay in motels anymore."

"Really, AZ! That sounds great! I got this white girl living with me named Vanilla. I stole her from H. She has two kids, though,"

AZ snickered because Suga swore she was a pimp.

"I don't want no kids living at this house. Matter of fact,

Toni is already living there," he said, knowing Suga would eventually find out anyway.

"What?! That bitch Toni is already at the house! She's been playing me all along by not telling me this. Y'all are my people, not hers! I'm going to punch that bitch in her face!" Suga says.

Toni's eyes grew narrow, listening to Suga talk about her.

AZ placed a finger over his lips, silencing her during Suga's rant.

"Look Suga, forget I even called you! I don't need no drama at this house! I just thought you might need a place to stay!" he said, becoming fed up with her nonsense.

"But, but, but!" she stutters. Suga was so upset she couldn't think straight. "I don't need nothing from your ass, AZ. I'm good!" she finally screamed, hanging up the phone on him.

AZ, frowns at us.

"That went well," he says, putting the cellphone down to reach for the clip in Toni's hand.

"There's no more weed or beer. It's time for me to go," he says, looking at me.

I pick up my shoulder bag preparing to leave.

AZ, however, doesn't budge from his seat. Embarrassed, I assume the remark is meant for me.

"Oh, okay. I'll check y'all later," I say, opening the front door, quickly exiting.

As soon as I got home, Suga called my phone. "Hi Suga!" I said, picking up.

"Karen, I'm so frustrated with AZ. He told me y'all got another house and Toni is living there. Now, he won't answer my calls. He's letting them go straight to voice mail.

I need to verify the story. Can you be quiet while I call Toni on three-way?"

Before I can give consent, Suga begins dialing the number. "Hello!" Toni answers jovially.

"Are you at that house in Brentwood with my people and not telling me?!" Suga barks at her.

"Yup, I am. You could be here too, but you're disloyal. You should've waited for them, like I did. Instead, you ran from place to place," Toni says, teasing Suga.

"What you mean? Those are my people! Not yours! I put you onto them. I been talking to you for weeks.

You never once mentioned being there and you know I'm on these streets!" Suga says angrily.

Toni giggles and hangs up on her.

Suga is so pissed she calls us right back on three-way.

This time Toni is even more obnoxious.

"Suga, what do you want?! AZ is my man now.

We are smoking and chilling at our new house. Stop disturbing us!" she laughs, hanging up again.

"Karen! Do you hear this bullshit?!" "Yeah, Suga. I hear it."

"Karen, come pick me up! I need you to take me over there so I can kick her ass!" Suga says, hyperventilating. I pause, not really wanting to get involved.

"Suga, don't let Toni get under your skin," I say, feeling slightly amused.

"Nah, Karen, it's no problem. I just want to beat her fucking face in. Are you going to take me or not?"

"Suga, you know I can't do that."

"Thanks, anyway!" she says, hanging up abruptly.

Determined to seek vengeance, Suga sends AZ sexy photos all night long. She also calls him from different numbers until he eventually answers her. AZ's loyalty lies with the money. It all came down to who was giving him the most. Therefore, a few days later, he let Suga move in with Toni.

Their first encounter was a little rocky. Toni tried to flex on Suga when she walked through the door. Being the bigger person, Suga ignored her idle threats.

Ultimately, Suga felt triumphant for being able to move in.

Overall, AZ was very content with the arrangement.

Now he had Shi, Nina, Lexx, Suga, and Toni working for him. It was more than enough girls to open his establishment.

The very next day, that's exactly what he did.

Opening day at the strip club was very hectic.

AZ sorted out every little detail, making sure everything was perfect. He stressed handing out invitations to all the customers who came in the lingerie store that day.

When nightfall came, he was extremely excited.

"Hey, bae. It's nine o'clock. What time are we closing the lingerie store?" he asked, sweating profusely, running up and down the steps to the basement.

Watching him struggle with the heavy box of liquor made me smile.

"I'm just waiting for the barbershop next door to close. They still have a few customers I can advertise to," I said.

AZ raises his eyebrow.

"Hmmm, good idea!" he says, on his way down the steps to stock the bar with liquor. Forgetting something else, he's back upstairs in two minutes.

"I'm hiring a security guard to cover the back door. I want the girls to be safe tonight," he scratches his head, then picks up the store telephone.

"Everything will be fine. You're doing a great job," I say, stepping from behind the counter, giving him a big hug and kiss.

Checking my wristwatch, it's eleven o'clock at night.

It was almost time to lock up and head out back with the handsome security guard. The strip club had been open for two hours, but there were no customers downstairs yet.

The girls restlessly waited for them while AZ sat behind the bar ready to serve.

He had Suga at the hotel working Backpage to secure another source of income in case things didn't go well at the strip club.

Overall, he was confident it would. I also planned on making some money tonight. I was charging patrons at the door.

While I stood chatting with the security guard, a car rolled up and parked a few feet away from us. I got excited, thinking it was a car full of thirsty men.

I become discouraged when Asha and her two friends stepped out of the car. I forgot that AZ invited extra girls to work at the strip club tonight.

"Hey, ladies. Right this way. The party is over here," I whispered to them.

"Hi, Karen. Is that you?" Asha squints to see me partially hidden behind the back door.

"Shush! Yeah, girl, it's me," I said, laughing at her.

Asha rushed over, hugging, and kissing me on the cheek.

"I wasn't sure if we should come in the front or the back door.

These are my friends. You remember Pollax, right?" Asha slurs, already having too much to drink.

I frowned, disappointed in her.

"Yeah, yeah. Let's hurry inside before someone sees us," I said, rudely pulling her inside.

Asha tripped over the door saddle.

"Oh, okay, Karen. Where can we get dressed?" she asks, once we were inside of the small foyer.

I noticed the girls had on makeup but still needed to change clothes. Lacking a dressing room, I had to do some quick thinking.

"Follow me, ladies." I said, leading them through a side door into our storage room.

"You can change in here. When you're done, leave your bags," I smiled politely.

"In here?!" Asha looked around the small space, crowded with inventory.

I was embarrassed to not have a more befitting dressing room for them. The one stall bathroom was also too small for three people.

"Yes, in here! Don't worry about your bags.

I'll come back later and lock the door when you're done." "No problem," Asha relents then drops her bags on the floor to get undressed.

"I hope a lot of customers come tonight. We left our jobs to be here," she says, winking at me.

"That's right! Cause, I got four kids to feed!" Her friend Pollax snaps with a snotty attitude. She was a sexy dark skin girl but not as cute as Asha.

"Honey, we have a club full of people coming tonight!" I said, nervously backing out the door. It was a bold face lie. Actually, I wasn't sure if anyone was coming. I only hoped the guys next door from the barbershop would show up.

Returning to my post, I heard a female giggling. Pushing the back door open, I found Shi outside.

She was holding a drink in one hand and a few bills in the other.

"Hey, Karen," she says, swaying unsteady on her heels, flirtatiously leaning up against the security guard. I couldn't blame her. The handsome red bone was full of muscles. He reminded me of Rock, the actor.

"What a surprise seeing you here, Shi," I said, making the Rock blush.

"Is that for me?" I asked, pointing to the money in her hand. "It certainly is, Joy Joy." Only she and Kal called me that.

It was a term of endearment she adopted from him.

Shi handed me the money. I quickly counted it, determining six men were downstairs. Looking up, I saw more men coming.

I was happy, thinking Asha and her friends would be very satisfied. "Shi, since you're doing so well, hold it down for me.

I'm going downstairs to check on AZ," I said, convinced this would please her.

"You know I got you. Go, do what you do," she smiled, flirtatiously brushing against the Rock again. He was wearing a wedding band but didn't seem to mind.

"We got this," he said, grinning wide at Shi.

"I bet you do," I said walking away, leaving the two alone. Opening the metal door, I bumped into Asha and her two friends, exiting the storage room.

KAREN JOY

"WOW! You girls look fffantastic!" I stuttered, looking up at Asha. She was towering over me in six-inch stilettos with her hair twisted in a bun. Though pencil thin, her body was shapely and very sexy. I was blown away by her appearance.

"Thanks, babe," Asha puckered, blew me a kiss, then strutted down stairs in her sadomasochist leather outfit.

I suspected it was an outfit she wore regularly at the strip club.

Her two friends were also dressed nicely but nothing compared to Asha. I couldn't stop staring at her.

Arriving downstairs, Asha went right to work on some lonely guy sitting in the corner. I recognized him from the barbershop next door.

He was a regular who sold music to their customers. I headed to the bar with Asha's friends following behind me.

"Hey, bae. Everything okay?" I asked AZ.

"Yeah, everything's good," he said, watching Asha's friends hop on two bar stools.

"Can you pour us pretty ladies a drink?" one of them asked him. "If you pay for it!" AZ snarled, returning his gaze to the patrons in the room. He was focused on money being exchanged between the clients and his girls.

Nina was swinging back and forth around the pole, mesmerizing men in her hot pink outfit. She stopped temporarily to collect tips being tossed on stage and stuck them in a garter belt, bound tightly around her thigh. Toni was uninterested in pole dancing.

Her objective was to get men into the lap dance room. She was grinding on every man in a chair, whispering seductively in their ears. Her deep dimples and caramel skin were very alluring to them.

Lexx played bar girl. She took drink orders while simultaneously entertaining a friendly fireman.

"Well! Are you buying something or not?" AZ snapped at the girls.

224

"Are you serious? We came here to help you!" the snotty one replied.

AZ knew exactly how to handle unruly strippers. She was no match for his fury.

"Does it look like I need your help?! You should be asking the customers for drinks. Not over here tricking me. I'm not the mark! You lucky I don't charge you a house fee to work tonight!" AZ said sharply.

The girl just stared at him, blinking rapidly. Before she could say anything else stupid, AZ dipped two cups into a fruit bowl.

"Here take this!" he said, sucking his teeth.

The girls took the drinks, slid off the bar stools and walked their asses across the room.

"Thank you!" he hollered, after them.

An hour later, the basement was crowded with men.

I saw Rabyt walk in with her girlfriend, TuTu. They always came to party with us. I nodded when they saw me sitting at the bar.

TuTu's booty was so big it bumped into every man on the dance floor. Rabyt casually flirted with the men. She wouldn't have sex for money, but she sure would screw them for free. Like many women, Rabyt looked for love in all the wrong places.

"I'm thirsty. Can you pleasssse pour me a drink?" I asked, joking with AZ.

He frowns at me.

"Pour your own troubles. I might need you to serve these drinks anyway. I have to concentrate on this lap dance room." His forehead wrinkles, thinking about it.

Reaching behind the bar, I got the bottle of Hennessy and poured myself a big drink. AZ grinned at me and flashed two hundred-dollar bills.

"This party just got started and Nina already had two lap dances," he said.

"Oh, yeah. Check this out," I said, showing him the money I received from Shi.

"Where did that come from?" he asked, eyes wide with greed. "It's money I collected at the door."

Winking at him, I stuffed the bills back into my purse.

"We're collecting money at the door, too?!" he asked, surprised he hadn't thought of it.

"Yup! And I gotta get back upstairs to check on my stash with Shi. This place is filling up quickly.

"Oh, that's where Shi is. No wonder I haven't seen her on the floor with the other girls."

"Rabyt is here. Maybe she'll work the bar for you," I said, tossing back two more shots of Henny, then pouring a drink to take to Shi.

Asha approaches us with her customer.

"Y'all want a drink?" AZ asks them, reaching for two cups.

"Nope! How much is that lap dance roommm?" Asha slurs, rocking back and forth, rubbing the bulge in her customer's pants. The man grins, squeezing her hand tightly.

"Oh, that's why you're here," AZ says, eyes sparkling with excitement.

I knew AZ didn't have a set price for the room.

He would charge whatever he could get from the sucker. If Asha wasn't careful, he would keep her share too, like he does his girls.

"I'm going to check on Shi," I said, slipping away from them.

On my way up the steps, I could see a line forming at the back door. The Rock was running a meddle detector up and down one man's pant leg. I arrived just in time to see Shi collecting his money. She took a twenty-dollar bill from the man but didn't give him any change.

Knowing it only cost ten dollars, I looked at her strangely. She shot me a look to be quiet.

Stepping aside, we allowed the man to go downstairs.

The Rock and Shi continued checking and charging the men until the line was finished.

"Hey! How's it going up here?" I whispered to her. "See for yourself," she said, opening her shoulder bag.

Looking inside, there was a bunch of crumpled ten- and twenty-dollar bills.

"For me? You shouldn't have."

I grinned, reaching inside to retrieve the money.

Shi simultaneously took the cup of liquor out my hand. "For me? You shouldn't have." she mocked, drinking two big gulps, emptying the cup.

"What are you charging at the door?" I asked, counting the money.

"Whatever they give me. And I don't give back any change!" Shi giggled, turning to go downstairs.

"Where are you going?" I asked, not sure I had nerve to do what she was doing.

Shi had an uncanny ability to get money from men. At the strip club, I once saw her toss back any tip less than ten dollars. She was a beast at the game.

She taught Nina and Lexx how to play.

"I'll be right back. I'm going to check on daddy and get another drink. I like Patron not Hennessy." She flipped her long black hair over one shoulder and walked down the steps. I turned to the Rock.

"Well, it's just you and me!" I said, smiling at him.

"What's going on downstairs? Is everyone having a good time?" "Yes, they are! Men seem to like half-naked women," I said, teasing. His face flushed, embarrassed for asking.

I laughed, realizing why Shi wanted to keep him company. His personality made him easy to joke with.

In no time at all the place was overcrowded. We had as many people outside as we had inside.

The patrons ran up and down the steps, going in and out to smoke. It was the type of activity that drew police attention. Standing outside tipsy with everyone else, that's exactly what happened. An unmarked police car crept down the parking lot with the headlights turned off. Seeing it, I became paranoid thinking they were robbers.

It was too late to react once they were upon us.

The passenger window rolled down.

"Hey, what's going on out here?" the officer asked the Rock.

"Hello, Officer," I said intervening because the Rock was clearly shaken by their presence.

"This is my store. We're just having a little celebration for the grand opening."

The officer looked at me suspiciously. It was two o'clock in the morning. As far as he was concerned all stores in the strip mall should've been closed.

In my peripheral, the Rock was pushing drunk patrons through the metal door. He slammed it shut, leaving me to fend for myself.

"Isn't it a little late?" his partner asked, watching the crowd disappear.

"Yes, and we were just about to shut it down before you came," I said politely, backing away from them. I tapped lightly on the back door, but the Rock wouldn't open it.

"Okay, so you won't be here when we come back around," the driver said, slowly coasting away.

When they were gone, I knocked rapidly on the door.

This time, the Rock slowly opened it for me and cautiously peeked outside.

"I wasn't sure if that was you or the cops knocking. This party is illegal. We should shut it down!" he says, nervously stepping outside with me.

"Just relax. I'm going downstairs to tell AZ what happened. Keep the door closed until I get back," I said, rushing off.

When I got downstairs, AZ was at the bar, laughing and drinking with Rabyt and her friend. I walked over, grabbing him by the arm.

"Hey, let me have a word with you!" I said, pulling him aside.

Sensing something was wrong, without hesitation he emptied the cash box.

"Rabyt, hold the bar down for me," he said, leaving her in charge with a few bills for change.

I dragged him into the stairwell away from the loud music so we could talk.

"What's up?!" he asked, seeing my concern.

"The police just came here. It's illegal for us to be doing this!

We have to SHUT IT DOWN!" I frantically screamed, afraid the police would return with a Swat team.

"Are you crazy?! Forget the damn Po Po! I'm not shutting shit down!

I'm getting every last dollar out these niggas' pockets. Here, take this money and send security home."

AZ handed me two hundred dollar bills.

"Don't let nobody else come downstairs!" he said with a take charge attitude, storming away with a crazed look in his eye.

I heard the dj lower the music.

"From now on, everybody smoke inside!" AZ said, voice roaring above the noise.

Upstairs, the Rock was waiting for me. The scared look on his face told me he was very frightened.

"Is AZ shutting the party down?" he asked, nervously.

I lowered my eyes, handing him the money AZ gave me.

"I'm a licensed security guard. I don't want any trouble with police. I have to go!"

He took the money, peeked outside then slipped his burly body through the cracked door.

I slammed it behind him and went back downstairs to the party.

After the Rock left, the knocking upstairs continued.

We ignored it, fearing it might be a police raid.

AZ wouldn't allow anyone to come or go until the party ended.

When it was over, we all made out pretty well.

I pocketed a few hundred dollars. AZ took in a few thousand. Asha, stayed in the lap dance room until she drained the poor customer dry. It was rumored, he even went deep sea diving on her.

Dear Diary, it's January 30th, 2013.

A gloomy, cloudy sky hovered overhead.

The temperature outside was unseasonably warm.

I was bored to death at the Pineapple Dreamz store.

Business had become extremely slow since our grand opening three months ago. It was mainly because the inventory stunk.

The customers either came to complain or make friendly conversation.

AZ didn't open the strip club downstairs anymore due to constant police surveillance. Now, being at the store everyday was quite frustrating for me.

Rrrrinnnggg! Hearing the store phone ring excited me.

I quickly picked up, eager to talk to someone. "You better get over here RIGHT NOW!

This bitch is tearing your HOUSE UP!" AZ screamed when I answered the call.

"What bitch? Who are you talking about?!" I asked, jumping to my feet, frantically searching for my car keys. "Suga, is wilding over here! I had to drag her ass out the house and body slam her on the front porch! Now she's outside breaking your windows!

Come get this bitch before I put hands on her!" AZ said, breathing heavy.

"Oh, hell NO!"

Running outside with the store phone still in my hand,

I jumped in my car and sped down the block like a mad woman.

Suga and Toni, got kicked out of that house in Brentwood after the basement parties ended. Gator had found that house abandoned when the owner died. Subsequently, he sold it to AZ.

The neighbors became suspicious once Suga and Toni moved in. Whenever the cops came to investigate, Toni presented a fake lease. This went on until police had the utility company turn off all the lights. In the interim, everyone was kicked out.

After that, Toni was pissed. It's yet another house she's evicted from.

She disappears for good this time. Somehow, Suga managed to move in with us.

I got to my house in a nanosecond with the tires screeching to a halt in the driveway. Suga was pacing back and forth on the porch, yelling at the top of her lungs like a crazy woman. Jumping out the car with my heart pounding hard in my chest, I ran to the porch, ready to pounce.

Suga was shocked when she saw me coming.

"Karen, I'm so glad you're here," she said calmly, as if nothing was wrong.

Her misleading demeanor relaxed me. I glanced around at the droplets of blood and broken pieces of glass on the floor. "What's going on, Suga?" I asked, narrowing my eyes.

Walking the full length of the porch, I gasped seeing the shattered window pane. Even though the inner glass was intact, I was still very upset.

"You have to go!" I hissed through clenched teeth, firmly grabbing her arm.

Suga wiggled free, backing away holding a piece of glass to her neck.

"No, Karen! AZ pulled a gun on me! I'm not going anywhere!" she screamed, threatening to cut her throat.

I wanted to grab her again but thought twice about the broken glass in her hand.

"If you don't get off my damn porch, I'm calling the cops!" I screamed back at her.

"Call 'em! I'll tell them, AZ hit me. He dragged me out that house and pulled a gun on me!" she yelled through fake tears.

Looking at her, it was a scene I wanted to avoid.

Surely, my nosy neighbors were watching out of their windows. If I didn't move fast, they'd call the police and complicate matters more.

"Listen you're mad, he's mad and I'm certainly upset about my broken window. Why don't you leave until cooler heads prevail?" I said, faking empathy.

Suga looked down, pretending to nurse a bloody wound on her hand. She seemed ready to comply before AZ opened the front door and tossed her bag of clothes on the lawn.

"That bitch got to go! She's disrespectful in front of my other girls. Look at these cuts on my face! That bitch is finished!" he shouted, angrily slamming the door.

Suga frowned and slumped to a seated position on the porch. "I don't have anywhere else to go," she said sobbing heavily. "Ugh!" I groaned in frustration thinking, *First you're leaving, now you're crying. I don't care! You can't stay here!*

"Let's get you on your feet," I said, helping Suga stand up. "I'll drive you anywhere you want to go."

I picked up the bag of clothes and handed it to her.

"I have no money," she said, with big crocodile tears running down her cheeks.

You should've thought of that before you started a big fight, asshole. I thought to myself.

"We'll figure something out," I said, helping her over to my car. When I opened the trunk, a cop car pulled into the yard.

This snitch bitch ran to it and sung like a canary.

"Officer! Officer! There's a man inside who pulled a gun on me!" she said, pointing to my house.

The two cops jumped out, running past us with their hands on their holsters.

"Who lives here?!" one cop asked Suga.

"I do, Officer! There's no one inside. As you can see, we were just leaving," I said innocently, eyes wide with fear. He looked at Suga who said nothing.

"This girl says there's a man inside with a gun! We need to investigate," the cop angrily insisted.

"There's no need for that. I just came out of the house.

No men are inside. We're leaving right now!" I said, looking at Suga sternly.

The officer sighed and flipped open his notebook. "Okay, we'll take a report and be on our way," he agreed reluctantly.

After convincing them, to my dismay, Gator opened the front door. The cop dropped his book and pounced on him like a tiger.

"Whoa!" Gator said while the officers pushed him to the ground. They slammed him face down and began frisking for a gun.

Minutes later, another cop car pulled into the yard.

Two more officers jumped out.

"Where's the gun?" they yelled at Gator.

"What gun? I didn't do anything. Ugh!" he groaned, struggling with the cop's knee in his back.

"Stay down! Don't move!" the officer said, making Gator remain face down on the porch.

The arriving cops offered assistance. "What's the problem here?" they asked.

"This young lady claims she was threatened by a man with a gun. We have an alleged gunman but no gun.

We need to go in that house and check for one," said the officer kneeling on Gator's back.

Suga never told them Gator was not the perpetrator.

Deemed a liar, I had to open the front door and allow them inside to check for a gun. Gator, Suga and I stayed on the porch with the first officers.

The other two cops went inside to search. Finding nothing, they returned empty handed.

"You have a lot of steps and rooms in that house. But we didn't find any guns," the officer said, exiting the house.

"I told you that. Now, please remove this menace from my property!" I said, glaring at Suga.

Gator stood up, brushing his clothes off.

"Yeah, get her ass out of here," he said, looking distraught. I walked over to the car, opened the trunk, and threw

Suga's bag on the lawn just like AZ did. The police took her away without further incident.

Gator and I went inside where AZ was waiting for us in the kitchen.

"Where did you hide?" Gator asked him, giggling. "I was in the basement between the drywall and itchy insulation," AZ frowns, scratching his arms.

"What the hell happened?!" I asked, upset about my broken window.

AZ huffs and puffs through wide nostrils.

"Suga can never come back here again. She's a crackhead!

All I did was try to help her," he said, shaking his head. "That's true. I remember when you brought her to our store.

She had on a dingy sweat suit and told us she was pregnant again."

"That's right! I gave the bitch some clothes and a place to stay.

Grrr, look how she repays me. She came here tonight, saw Gator's friend, and went crazy!"

AZ points to the woman sitting at the kitchen table.

"Suga claimed she knew this girl from the street.

She tried to pimp her right in front of us." The girl nods at AZ, agreeing with him.

"Suga, wanted this girl to leave with her. When she refused, Suga became violent. That's when I stepped in. The crazy bitch started fighting me!" AZ said, balling up his fist.

"I hope you learned your lesson. Don't ever let Suga come back here again!" I said, walking out of the kitchen, very upset about my broken window.

CHAPTER X
MANSION WOES

When Cherry is locked up everything and everyone is back to normal except for KG. Somehow, he felt guilty about her being in jail. I attempted to keep him busy with the upcoming party.

This particular day started off like most others. We were hustling to pay rent for the mansion. KG and I were in the sunroom at the computer with Fredro. He was the party promoter developing the Myspace page for our event.

AZ rushed in the room interrupting us.

"Karen, take Shi to work for me!" he demanded with no regard for what I was doing.

"Can't you see I'm busy working on this party!" I snapped at him.

Fredro stopped and looked at him. "Hey, AZ! What's up man?" he asked.

"I'm good," AZ said, giving him a pound but keeping his eye on me.

"Oh, so you not gonna take her for me? You know I hit a deer last week. The truck still runs but the dent might get me pulled over," he said, continuing to stare at the back of my head.

AZ always used not having a license as an excuse whenever it was convenient for him. I lingered in my seat ignoring him and kept watching Fredro upload the flyer.

"Karen, we got this," KG said to me. In his experience, AZ and I fought like pitbulls.

"Okay, KG. I'll be back as soon as I'm done."

I didn't want the situation to escalate so I got up from my chair smiling on the outside but steaming on the inside.

We arrived at Stonehedge nine o'clock on the dot. Opening the club door, Shi stopped in the entryway and stared at the people.

"There's more girls in here than customers. I hate this filthy ass club!" she snarled, letting her gold fangs show.

"This is where you work. What do you mean?" I asked, rhetorically.

"I only work here because I have no teeth! Otherwise, I'd be at an upscale gentleman's club. Grrrr."

Shi growls, stomping her feet.

Her little tantrums usually worked on AZ. I, on the other hand, needed rent money. I ignored her and walked to the bar ordering myself a drink.

Feeling like a fool in the doorway by herself, eventually she went to the bathroom and changed her clothes.

I waited for her to come out, knowing if I left, she'd only call home and complain. AZ would then want me to return and bring her home.

I had to agree with her. The place was a pigsty.

The bathroom was a small box with no partitions. It served as a dressing room for dancers and a bathroom for female patrons. Whenever customers wanted to use the bathroom, they had to do it in front of the dancers. The strippers usually refused to leave arguing it was their place of refuge.

Tuning everyone out, I focused on the flat screen above my head and watched the basketball game.

Thirty minutes later, Shi came out of the bathroom ready to turn up. A sexy black corset pushed her tiny boobs over the cup. Thigh high stockings made her small buttocks look firm and tight.

Shi searched for customers, but everyone was being entertained by two or more dancers. She made her way across the floor and mounted the stage. Her erotic pole dancing caught everyone's eye.

I went over and made it rain to help her money game.

When customers saw me doing this, they joined in.

Shi slid down the pole and seductively crawled to the biggest spender. She laid on her back, slowly swinging her legs open and closed, patting her vagina.

The drooling customer was clearly captivated by her table dance because he put all of his money on the stage. Shi whispered in his ear, then went to the bar with a fist full of dollars.

"Hey, Joy Joy. I bought you a double of Hennessy.

I know it's your favorite!" she said, walking over, placing the drink on the pool table in front of me.

Shi was louder than necessary, feeling cocky about her stage performance. I was playing pool by myself, so it wasn't disturbing anyone.

"Thanks, I'm always thirsty," I said, swallowing a big gulp. "I appreciate what you did for me on stage, but I didn't need your help," she said, narrowing her eyes at me. "Of course not," I said, winking at her.

She spun on her heels, proudly marching away.

I continued playing pool, thinking *even with youth and beauty on her side, she was still intimidated by me.*

I stayed at the club for Shi's entire shift.

She returned throughout the night to check on me.

Her mood lightened with every visit. Both Pisces, born three days apart, we had much in common and many similarities. We laughed and talked between her sets until the club closed.

On the ride home, she remained jovial before falling fast asleep. I was gullible enough to believe she really enjoyed our time together.

Pulling into the mansion driveway, I parked the car and shook her awake.

"Home sweet home," I said, turning down the music.

Shi slowly sat up, blinking rapidly to focus under the moonlight.

"We're here already?!"

"Yup. You passed out on me, co-pilot." I laughed and helped her get out of the car.

"Thanks for the ride. Let's smoke something later," she said while getting her work bag from the back seat.

A house full of people saw us walk through the front door like old school friends. Cute ass Mingo was playing cards at the table with KG, Uni and Rabyt. He was now welcomed at the mansion after returning AZ's truck.

"Hello, guys!" I said, on my way up the stairs.

"Hi, ladies!" Rabyt said to us.

The fellas just looked and nodded.

Rushing to my room, I sat on the bed and began rolling some weed. I was happy Shi and I finally clicked. She was actually pleasant at work -- not her usual obnoxious self.

"You busy?" KG asked, entering my room. "Oh, hi, Kay! What's on your mind?"

"I just wanted to tell you that Fredro sent out the flyer on Myspace," he said, sitting on the bed.

"Okay, cool. Now all I need to do is buy food and liquor,"

I said, folding the ends of the blunt so the weed wouldn't fall out. "Fredro, also wants us to buy some kegs of beer," he frowns. "I don't know anything about buying kegs, KG."

"Fredro said he'll order them if you pay for it.

His crowd mostly drinks beer. I didn't invite any friends myself. I don't have any," KG sighs, shrugging his shoulder.

"I don't have any friends either, Kay," I said, laughing out loud.

I lost track of the time talking to KG, not realizing.

Shi had been in her room for quite some time. In any event, when he left and I went to her room to smoke with her.

I knocked hard and loud on Shi's bedroom door. "Who is it?!" AZ shouted.

Still slightly buzzed, I turned the doorknob and walked right in without answering him.

"Bitch, close the door!" he yelled angrily at me. I froze in the doorway, shocked and embarrassed.

AZ's head was on a swivel like the chick from "The Exorcist".

He was furious when I caught them having sex.

"Shi, you gonna let her disrespect you like that?! Go beat her fucking ass!" he yelled.

Shi, stupidly obeyed the order. She jumped out of bed and quickly put her sneakers on. My reflexes were too slow to react.

I fumbled with the knob and shut the door, then ran down the hall to the safety of my room.

Inside of the room, I frantically looked for a place to hide.

My mind raced with unanswered questions.

"Why didn't they lock the door? I didn't disrespect them. Why did he answer in the first place?" BOOM!

Shi, kicked open my bedroom door. AZ was fast on her heels. I cowered by the window when they entered the room.

"Beat her fucking ass, Shi!" AZ screamed.

The two fools didn't know I was a pee wee black belt.

All through junior high school, I studied and mastered the art of Tae Kwon Do. At one hundred and twenty-five pounds, I was all muscle. I exercised daily to maintain my skill and agility.

Even with age, I was a force to be reckoned with. Shi was no match for how I was about to give it up.

The whole house heard the commotion. People came running up the steps filling my large room with blurry figures. I couldn't see exactly who because my eyes were trained on the enemy. I got into stance, bounced lightly on my toes, and blocked out their noisy cheers. My heart raced with nervous energy watching her every move.

Shi came in swinging wildly at my head.

With perfect timing, I swiftly ducked, grabbed and slammed her to the floor.

"Whoa!" The crowd groaned, engulfing our tussling bodies.

I pinned her down, ferociously punching her ribs with deafening blows. It knocked the wind out of her right away. She doubled over in pain without fighting back.

"Get her old ass, Shi!" AZ roared, standing over our struggling bodies.

Briefly looking up, I saw the hate in his eyes. "Back up! Move out the way!" AZ yelled at the crowd.

His position against me infuriated KG and Mingo.

They watched him with animosity.

"You back the fuck up!" Mingo screamed at him. "Ain't nobody jumping in!" AZ told him.

Mingo turned crimson red, pulling his T shirt up, showing AZ the gun in his waistband.

"Oh, you gangsta nigga!" Mingo screamed in his face.

I hated the idea of AZ being riddled with bullets, but I loved seeing Mingo defend me.

The fight ended when I was satisfied Shi could take no more.

She stumbled to her feet and the crowd parted, letting her and AZ through. When the room emptied, I sat on the bed to catch my breath.

Rabyt rushed to my side.

"That was fucked up." she said to me.

"Yeah, it was!" KG said, sucking his teeth, upset. "That nigga knew better than to put his hands on you with me here!" Mingo said, patting the gun on his side. "I'm alright, guys." I said, blinking back the tears.

"Okay, get some rest then. We're going back downstairs." KG said and began ushering everybody out of the room.

His brother, Born, stuck his head into the room after everyone was gone.

"Hey, Karen, this fell on the floor during the fight," he said, holding up my diamond tennis bracelet.

"Oh, snap. Thanks, Born! I paid over five thousand dollars for that bracelet. I'm so happy you found it."

"I got you."

Born smiled, gently wrapped the bracelet around my wrist and fastened the clasp.

"I can tell it's expensive by these big shiny rocks," he said, grinning wide. "Karen, tell me something. Why do you mess with that guy? Is it the big penis? 'Cause if that's the case, we all got one," he said, jokingly.

I really wasn't in the mood for his humor. Sensing this, Born backs out of the room gracefully.

"Remember our little talk," he smirks, disappearing out the door. Once he was gone, my thoughts drifted back to AZ.

Loving AZ is sucking the life out of me.

First, he wants to be a pimp. Next, he falls in love with a stripper. Now he's fighting me. It's the ultimate betrayal. I'll never forget this!

Falling back on the bed, I let the tears flow freely until my heart grew cold.

It was Saturday Morning, Labor Day weekend. Fredro's staff hastily moved around the mansion preparing for the party.

He was the event planner; therefore, I had no idea what was going on. For weeks, he had been coming to the mansion privately meeting with KG.

Today, the cute young Hispanic walked around making sure everything was perfect. All morning, I watched him from my post on the back porch. I feared disturbing him would make me seem like a control freak.

Though falling back wasn't easy either. I had too much riding on the event. The *Urban Black Country Club* depended on this party!

Fredro, walked past me with his head down. I slid the patio door open to seize the moment.

"Psst, Fredo. How are we looking tonight?" I whispered, hoping no one else heard me.

Fredro looked up from texting on his Blackberry, surprised to see me there.

"Everything's good! We got mad people coming tonight. This place is going to be lit," he said, then continued texting on his cellphone.

I wanted to question him further, but he was immediately distracted. A delivery guy came through the front door carrying a large keg of beer.

"Can we talk later? I have to go handle that," he said dismissively. "Don't worry. I got this!" he yelled over his shoulder, walking away. I was used to micromanaging and a stickler for details.

It took everything I had not to undermine his authority in front of the staff. I waved my hand pretending to be satisfied, then went back on the porch to smoke some weed.

"Somebody is going to tell me something!" I mumbled underneath my breath.

"Talking to yourself again, Karen Joy!" KG said, walking out on the porch laughing.

The interruption made me jump and choke on the blunt in my mouth.

"Yeah. You know I'm crazy." I said, giggling with him. He often caught me talking to myself.

KG was hot and sticky from working hard all day.

His dirty wife beater and cut off blue jeans were heavily soiled. He walked across the porch on his toes, dragging heavy Timberland boots.

"What's going on tonight, KG?" I asked, eager for some answers. "It's going down! My man H is bringing Maserati Fox.

You remember, he's Fiddy's man. They shooting his video here tonight. Fredro's been promoting the event on My Space all month."

Hearing KG explain the theme for the party made me content. It was comforting to know things were in order. "We are charging at the door and selling drinks.

This party should pay the rent," KG said, smiling at me with his big puppy dog eyes.

"Sounds like there's nothing left for me to do but get dressed," I said, playfully punching his arm.

"Yup, but not before we puff these trees," he grinned, taking out a fat blunt to smoke.

Leaning my elbows back on the railing, I inhaled deeply, daydreaming about the night's festivities.

Five hours later, the party was in full swing. Fredro's Hispanic friends came out in numbers. They packed the living room floor like sardines, humping and grinding to the beat.

I stood behind the kitchen counter, serving multiple cups of beer. I had to restock twice to keep the party flowing.

H arrived around eleven o'clock with his girlfriend Quashia, and Maserati Fox. H was a brown skin, well-built, easy-going guy. KG and AZ met him at Stonehedge where his girlfriend danced. The fellas became close after finding a common interest in music and strippers.

H briefly talked to KG, then made his way across the room to me.

"Hey, Karen," he says, remembering me from the strip club. "What's up, H!" I smiled at him but kept busy serving drinks. "Nice crowd you got here tonight," he chuckles.

"Thanks to you and Maserati Fox. These people mainly came out for his video. You deserve a drink for that," I said, reaching for the bottle of Hennessy which KG kept refilling with water every time it got too low. Now, the liquor in the bottle was light brown.

"I'll take a beer for me and my girl. I don't want to get too drunk. I'm working tonight. On second thought, give me a shot for Maserati," he said.

"No problem."

I handed him the drinks then quickly turned to the paying customers. "Thank you. Let me go rescue Maserati from these fans," he said, disappearing into the crowd.

Five minutes later, KG shows up to check on me.

"You straight back here?" he asks, ducking underneath the counter. "Yeah, I'm good," I say, watching Quashia talk to Mingo across the room. Her body language made me feel very uncomfortable. "KG, I need to go check on the front door," I say, removing everything but fifty dollars from the cash box.

"Okay, I got the bar," he says, measuring the level of liquor in the Hennessy bottle.

When I got to the front door, AZ was talking to some people. "How are we doing so far?" I asked, once the coast was clear. "We're doing great," he said, opening the cash box to show me the money.

I put my hand inside and took everything but a few singles. "Aye, where's my cut?" he asked, holding his hand out.

I'm hustling to pay rent. You and your non-paying friends are the reason I'm in this predicament in the first place. I thought to myself, giving him a disparaging look.

"Room and board is your cut," I snapped at him, shoving the crumpled bills into my pocket.

"I've been at this door all night," he argues, hopeful I'll change my mind.

"You're doing a great job. Keep up the free work," I say, turning on my heels, parading across the floor.

"Oh, it's like that!" he yells after me.

On my way to stash the cash, I bumped into Mazaradi and H on the dance floor.

"Hey, Karen, this is Maserati!" H yells above the loud music.

I smile at the large man and keep it moving. Little did I know, it was the last time I'd ever see him.

The following morning, I sat on the bed counting my earnings from the party. The count was a little over thirty-five hundred dollars. The amount was still not enough to pay rent.

Kal was arranging a meeting between Adriana and the music producer today. I hoped his plan would make up the difference in the short amount. My Blackberry rang as I prepared to send him a text.

"You ready?" Kal asks, in good spirits, when I pick up.

"Born ready," I say, joking with hm.

"Good, I'm downstairs in your driveway!" he says, unexpectedly. "Already?!" I jump off the bed, running to the window to check. "Okay, I'll be right down," I say, looking at his BMW idling in the driveway.

When I get downstairs, Kal is playing my favorite song,

"Mrs. Officer", by Lil Wayne featuring Bobby Valentino is blasting out the radio speakers.

I slip into the passenger seat, singing along.

The car is recently washed and freshly scented with strong cologne.

Kal is casually dressed in blue jeans with his baseball cap twisted to the side.

"Where are we going?" I ask him.

He keeps his hand on the volume, nodding to the beat until the song is over.

"We going to get this money," he says, lowering the music. "My man Special is meeting us in midtown.

He got the state-of-the-art equipment that we need to get this job done!"

Kal smirks, coasting out the driveway into the street.

The thought of him handing Adriana's money over to someone else made me cringe.

Arriving in midtown, we saw Adriana's vehicle parked in front of the restaurant. She sat alone in the SUV. I was glad she didn't bring her mortgage broker. He was a nice guy but something about him disturbed me. Kal pulled to the curb, and we got out to greet her.

"Hi, I'm glad you two could make it," Adriana said in a thick Italian accent.

As usual, she was professionally dressed in a blouse and tight-fitting skirt. I watched Kal slither over and kiss her on the cheek like they were old friends.

"Traffic wasn't too bad on the LIE," I said, giving her a warm hug. The smell of expensive perfume flared my nostrils.

"Shall we go inside!" she said, spinning on her heels, letting long blonde hair bounce off of her shoulders.

Entering the restaurant, we see Kal's two friends seated in the back by the window. The dark-skinned guy waves for us to come over.

Following behind Kal, I immediately recognize the other guy. He was Busta Rhyme's hype man, Spliff Star. The big gold chain dangling from around his neck sparkled under the light.

"Hey, Kal, you're late." The dark-skinned guy says, grinning at him.

Kal turns to us saying, "This is my man, Special." Then the two men vigorously shake hands and hug. "This is Spliff," Special says, pointing to him. "So, what's this all about, Kal?" he asks, inviting us to sit with them.

A male waiter starts to come over and take our order. Spliff gives a stern look, waives him away, then sits back folding his arms across his chest.

"We need to." Kal begins to speak but I immediately cut him off.

"Get this music project off the ground for her daughter," I say, finishing his sentence.

"Is there a budget?" Special spins his baseball cap from front to back and looks at Adriana and me for the answer.

Spliff sits there quietly listening. I figure he's just here for the comments.

"Oh, absolutely!" Adriana says, seemingly eager to give her money away.

I grimace, thinking about the thousands of dollars slipping through my fingers.

"Okay! Let's get this party started!"

Expressing excitement, Special spins his baseball cap back to the front. Without saying much else, the fellas stand to leave.

"It's been a pleasure but we gotta run. We have more meetings and more money to make. Kal, you finalize the details. You know how to get in touch with me."

Special adjourns the meeting and the two men quickly get up and exit the restaurant.

It's only then, I realize the details had already been discussed. Walking Adriana back to her car, I was pissed. I gave her the rent check, which she happily accepted before getting into her SUV and driving away.

"What just happened in there, Kal?" I ask when we are back in the BMW.

"I hooked you up. That's what happened," he says smugly.

"How is that?! You gave the money away to the next guy!" I say, annoyed by his cocky attitude.

"You still got the mansion, right? Adriana is getting a quality project for her daughter, and everybody is happy. So, let's go home."

Kal smirks, turning the ignition key.

I stare at him for signs of deceit almost certain he's getting a cut of the money but excluding me. Undisturbed by my stare, Kal keeps his eyes glued on the windshield. The confident look on his face speaks volumes.

I should've left your homeless ass in the street. I think to myself.

All the way home, I didn't utter a word. Kal made light of my silence by cracking a joke when we pulled in the driveway.

"See you later, alligator," he said, smiling at me.

"Not for a while, you slimy crocodile."

I let Kal know exactly how I felt getting out of the car.

He shook his head and sped down the driveway.

Entering the mansion, I was ambushed again. Mingo, KG, and Leah were waiting for me in the living room. I could tell they were talking about me because the room fell silent as soon as I walked in.

"Karen, we are leaving!" Leah said, sharply. KG dropped his eyes when I looked at him.

"Who's leaving?" I asked, baffled by her statement. "Me, Uni, and the rest of your tenants at the other house."

My heart sank, hearing her say this. Those were the only paying tenants I had. Their money was the reason I could afford to live in the mansion.

"Why? What's wrong?" I asked, trying not to sound too upset.

"Well, first of all, you've been neglecting your other house. You think this mansion is everything."

Listening to Leah speak, I heard the jealousy in her voice.

"Plus, me and KG are moving into our own spot," her neck swivels, looking at him to corroborate her story.

"Yeah. We are moving into a two-bedroom condo in Ridge with my brother and his girl." KG said, as a matter of fact.

I felt the blood rushing from my face.

KG, you traitor! Not only are you leaving, but you're taking my income with you.

Even though KG referred Leah to me as a tenant, I still felt betrayed by him. He, of all people, knew I needed her money to keep the mansion afloat for my country club.

"Karen, I'll rent your other house!" Mingo said, with a big grin on his face.

"Hold that thought. I'll be right back," I said, dashing out the front door with my head spinning. It was important for me to go check on my other house.

In the driveway, I was met by Ant live. He was surveying the property with two contractors. Ant was the guy who found the mansion for me.

"Hey, Karen. Where are you going?" Ant said, holding up some papers in his hand.

"I can't talk right now, Ant," I said, rushing by him.

"Wait a minute. I brought these builders to bid on the job for your country club. They have some blueprints for you to review. Their plans include an in-ground pool, tennis, and basketball courts. You'll love it," Ant said, grabbing me by the arm.

"Not now, Ant! It's a bad time!" I shouted, pulling away from him, fighting back tears.

Realizing something is wrong, Ant lets me to go.

"Okay, Karen. Maybe later, sis," he says, walking back to the porch with the contractors.

Watching him roll up those blueprints breaks my heart.

When I get into the car, I can't stop the tears from pouring down my face. I take out my cellphone and call AZ.

"Hello," he answers, still half asleep. "I can't take it anymore!" I cry out.

"What's wrong with you?" AZ asks, never hearing me break down like this before. To him, I was usually solid as a rock.

"Kal took Adraina. KG took Leah and now I have nothing!

I'm running out of options. I don't know what to do next. I've tried everything! Nothing is working!" I say in between heavy sobs.

"I told you not to trust those people. That's always your problem. You believe and trust everybody. Where are you now?" he asks after scolding me.

"I'm in the mansion driveway on my way to the other house."

"We'll think of something. We always do!" he says, making me feel better.

"Thanks, bae, I love you."

"Love you too," he says, hanging up the phone.

I dry my eyes and pull out the driveway, heading for the other house.

The house was dark and completely empty when I walked inside. Turning on the lights, I saw the living room was filthy. The carpet was badly stained and hadn't been vacuumed in months. The tenant upstairs was gone, just like Leah said she was.

I really didn't care because her social service checks stopped coming a long time ago.

Agreeing with Leah, my neglect for the house showed. I inspected the rooms, discovering the need for a paint job and garbage removal. Luckily, there was no structural damage. The only decent place was the basement.

I knew preparing for new tenants would be a lot of work. Without their money, I had to do most of it myself.

I sat on the couch and rolled a blunt, calling Uni. My call went straight to voice mail.

"Hello, Uni. I'm at the house in Coram. It's important that you call me right away."

You're supposed to be here managing the place. I think to myself.

Hanging up angry, I decided to stay the night and gather my thoughts. I lit the blunt and Mingo came to mind. Considering him for a tenant was grabbing at straws.

Though under the circumstances, I didn't have much choice. Inhaling deeply, I carefully weighed my options.

The next morning, I awoke to the sound of a honking horn. Raising the blind, Mingo was in the driveway standing beside a small white sedan. He was with a young white girl, who I believed was his girlfriend.

"Oh wow!" I said, out loud.

I forgot about the text I sent Mingo the night before.

I took off running to my bedroom to put on some sweatpants before answering the door.

"Hey, girl. What are you doing in here?

I been knocking for like ten minutes. If your car wasn't outside, I would've left." Mingo said, when I opened the front door.

His low cut ceasar accentuated creamy flawless skin.

I stared at him thinking, *even casually dressed in a peacoat and blue jeans makes him look good as hell.*

"Sorry about that. I didn't hear you knocking," I said, grinning wide.

Mingo stood there, head cocked to the side, looking at me suspiciously. His dark piercing eyes were menacing.

"You here alone?" he asked, stepping inside cautiously. Everyone I met up until this point was easily readable.

Mingo, though, was cut from a different cloth. He was a dangerous gangster who always had a hidden agenda. I would need street and book smarts to outwit him.

"Why? Did you come to see someone else?" I asked, joking with him.

His dark beady eyes stared straight through me.

Not being able to determine what he was thinking made me nervous.

"Let me show you around the place," I said, awkwardly.

Mingo gave the living room a quick look over then silently followed me around the house.

He listened intently to excuses I made about its poor condition.

Finally, we landed back in the living room.

"So, what you think?" I ask, noticing he hasn't said much during the tour.

"I'll take it. How much you charging?!" he asks, without blinking an eye.

"I'll rent you the whole house except the basement for two stacks." I say to feel him out.

His shifty eyes darted from side to side thinking about it.

I knew Mingo didn't want to pay that much. It was my angle to leverage the cost.

"Nah, two stacks is too much," he says finally.

"You staying here with your girl, right?" I ask, getting ahead of myself.

"Who said I got a girl!" he barks, shooting me a dirty look.

"I just ttthought," I stutter, embarrassed for prying. "I just need a room," he says sharply, reaching into his pants pocket, pulling out a large bank roll. "Is five hundred dollars okay?" he asks.

"Five hundred is cool." I say, desperately needing the cash.

Mingo, peels off two-hundred-dollar bills and hands them to me.

"When will I get the rest?" I ask, taking the money. "When I come back for the keys with Quashia." My mouth pops open. A hot flash comes over me.

Did I hear him correctly? Isn't Quashia H's girl?!

Mingo looks out the window for his ride and doesn't see the shock on my face.

"My ride is back. I have to go," he says, opening the front door, letting himself out.

I stand in the doorway with my mouth hung open.

AZ is going to kill me. What have I done? I just rented the crib to Mingo so he can pimp Quashia. H will think our party was a set up to steal his girl.

It's going to ruin our relationship with him. This is tragic, but I can't turn back now. I need this money! I think to myself.

After I cleaned the house, I headed back to the mansion to seek advice from AZ about my new tenant.

"Bae, I'm home!" I hollered, walking in the mansion. I was in good spirits in spite of my meeting with Mingo.

With no one in sight, I went to AZ and Shi's room.

I knocked and patiently waited this time for someone to answer.

It was a lesson well learned.

Receiving no response, I checked around on the first floor. Hearing muffled voices in the basement, I went downstairs and walked into a heated argument.

"I don't know why you brought this nigga here! You brought all kinds of people here! And none of them have any money!" AZ yelled at Cheeks.

"You ain't gotta yell, son!" Cheeks said, raising his voice. "I brought my man LB here to help YOU out! I thought he could help clean up or something," Cheeks said to support his argument.

AZ and I both knew that was a lie.

Cheeks bought LB to sling some pipe to me.

The mansion was in constant turmoil ever since that fight with me and Shi. It was a weakness everyone used to conquer and divide us.

However, AZ wasn't letting go of his gold mine so easily.

Even if it meant kicking out his friend, Mr. Cheeks.

"I don't need no damn maid! LB, got to go!" AZ yelled while Cheeks continued packing his suitcase.

LB, sat on the bed, quietly listening to them.

I crept into the room and whispered to Shi, "What's going on?" She shrugged her shoulders, but AZ answered me.

"This guy thinks I'm stupid," he said, spinning around to face me. "Say no more! We out! Bing!" Cheeks barked, continuing to stuff the overflowing suitcase with more clothes.

"Good! Be out then!" AZ said, storming out the room with Shi on his heels.

"WOW! What the hell happened? I left for one night and came back to y'all at each other's throats," I said, watching Cheeks close the suitcase and carry it up the steps into the living room.

"AZ is bugging! Everybody else is staying here! Why not my man, LB?!" he asked me.

I gave him the side eye because I certainly didn't want any more freeloaders. Cheeks already had his R&B artist, Shemar, living with us.

When we got upstairs, Shemar was on the catwalk looking over the banister.

"What's going on, Cheeks?!" he yells.

"We out this dump!" Cheeks says, hurrying out the front door with his luggage.

Shemar runs back to his room and comes out, tossing a large duffle bag over the banister.

It just misses my head by inches.

"Damn, Shemar!" I yell, ducking to avoid the blow. I was offended by his attitude. He had been living free for weeks and this is how he showed gratitude.

Shemar ran down the steps, picked up his bag and dashed out the door behind Cheeks and LB.

When they were gone, AZ came out and locked the front door.

"Everything okay out here?" KG asks, sticking his head out of his room. AZ and I were surprised to see him.

KG was quiet as a mouse throughout the whole ordeal.

AZ shook his head, returning to his room.

I went upstairs to my room without telling either of them about Mingo. It was a sad day when Cheeks left the mansion.

My continuous knocking on Mingo's bedroom door infuriated him. He snatched it open, standing before me half naked from the waist up.

"Why are you here so early?!" he barked, squinting from the bright light above my head.

His scrawny, hairless chest looked very unattractive to me. It was hard to believe this puny little body terrorized the hood. Behind him, I saw Quashia curled in a mattress on the floor.

She was wrapped in a filthy blanket covering her naked body. Her frightened little face pleaded for my help.

"Karen, what do you want?" Mingo snapped impatiently.

He was becoming agitated with my fixation on Quashia. "Huh! It's bbbeen two weeks. You still haven't paid the rest of the rent. Do you have the money now?" I asked, staring into the eyes of a dangerous man.

I had been warned about Mingo. He was a tyrant in the streets. I could only imagine what he was doing to Quashia in that room.

Mingo's breathing is heavy and uneven.

"Not yet! See me later. I'll have something for you then!" he says, slamming the door in my face.

I was able to get one last glimpse of Quashia trembling in the background. Walking back to the car, I struggled with my thoughts. The girls at the strip club were worried about her. They said Quashia hadn't been to work in days. All agreed it wasn't like her to miss money.

Rescuing Quashia was not an option for me. No one was brave enough to challenge Mingo. Not even H was willing to help her. One thing for sure! Mingo, was going to pay rent or get the hell out of my house!

Arriving back at the mansion, I was met with more problems.

AZ was in the office finishing up a call when I walked in the door.

"Karen, where have you been all morning?" he asked, hanging up the telephone.

"I left early this morning to trap Mingo off for my rent," I said, sitting in the chair beside him.

"Did you get it?" he asked, doubtful I had. "Of course not!" I frowned, lowering my head.

"That's too bad because Adriana is on her way," he said, scratching his chest.

"What do you mean?!" I sighed, feeling overwhelmed.

Knock! Knock! Knock!

"That's probably her now. She just called."

AZ smirked and went to his room to duck the unwanted company.

Opening the front door, I gasped when Kal boldly walked in first.

"Hi, Joy Joy," he says, smiling at me. Adriana and Special, who I only met once, followed behind him.

What the hell are these three doing together? I think to myself. "Hi, Joy." Adriana says, having never called me that before.

It's evident she adopted the name from Kal.

"Hi!" I say, walking behind them into the kitchen.

Special is much calmer this time. I suspect he's already begun the project for her daughter. I was certain the opportunity to build a country club was over for me.

"Adriana, what brings you here today?" I ask.

The sinister smile on her face tells me it's not a friendly visit. I inhale deeply, pausing for the worst.

"I wanted to check on my house." she says, with a smug look. "Karen, I can no longer wait for the rent."

My faces flushes when she discloses our personal business in front of everyone.

"Adriana, I just rented my whole house. I can have a check for you right away." I blurt out in despair.

Kal looks at me, surprised. He knew Mingo was only renting a room at my house. I narrow my eyes, daring him to say anything.

Adriana raises a brow staring at me intently.

I get the uneasy feeling she doesn't believe me. The mood in the room is very tense.

"Perfect! This concludes our business then," she says, grabbing her handbag off the counter. "I'll expect that check no later than next week." She walks away, clicking her heels across the hardwood floor.

At the door, she turns for one last look. Kal smirks and opens the door for her.

"Karen, I really like you, but things aren't working between us," she says, then quickly exits before I can respond.

"It's nice seeing you again," Special says, walking out last.

"The pleasure is all mine," I say sarcastically happy to see them go.

AZ comes into the room after they leave.

He and I watch through the window until their cars disappear out the driveway.

"What did Adriana say? I know it wasn't easy seeing her with Kal," he says, hugging me sympathetically. "Ya think! Your man Kal strikes again. It's depressing to lose my only investor for this country club. I'm also struggling with being kept out of the loop. More importantly, I still have to pay this rent. We better give another party," I say, sulking.

AZ puts his arm around my shoulder, walking me to the fridge. "I have a better idea! I just spoke to Erin on the phone.

She's leaving Big Will and flying back to New York in the morning. Erin, is a money-making machine!"

He grins, going to the refrigerator, taking out two beers.

My expression is guarded. Erin's arrival may be a little too late.

"Don't worry, Shi is going to work tonight. That will give us some twos and fews," he says, handing me a beer.

Early the next morning, Erin's cab drives slowly up the winding driveway. AZ anxiously waits for her on the front porch. After paying the cab driver, Erin wiggles out the back seat. She looks completely different from the last time I saw her. Watching from the second-floor window, I see her hop into AZ's arms for a long embrace. Happy she's here, I run downstairs to welcome her.

"Oh my gosh! Erin, it's so great to see you!" I say, entering the kitchen.

AZ lags behind, carrying her heavy luggage. "Hi, Karen!" she says, hugging me tightly.

She looked fantastic and smelled even better.

Red lipstick accentuated a sassy blonde hair cut. The sex red outfit and expensive stilettos gave her a classy look.

Life with Big Will had definitely done her some justice. "I have something special for you, daddy."

Erin, reached in her bra coming out with a wad full of cash.

She handed the money to AZ. It was customary for a girl to give all of her money to her new pimp. It was called breaking yourself.

AZ's eyes lit up. He hadn't seen this much money since he began pimping.

"Thanks, bae!" he said, shoving the money into his pants pocket.

"Where's my sister wife?" Erin gloated.

"Shi's asleep. Let me show you to your room," AZ said, rushing her up the steps.

"This is a beautiful home you have here. It reminds me of mansions in Miami," she says, following him upstairs.

I watched AZ whisk Erin away to get into her panties.

I knew he wanted to thank her before Shi woke up. Shi was very jealous of other women. AZ had to sneak around to have sex with them.

"See you later, Erin," I said, before retiring to my room.

I was super stressed and tired of worrying about paying rent for two houses. I laid on the bed, looking at the ceiling, thinking about the long night ahead.

Erin's arrival meant it was time to execute a plan against Mingo. His actions made it very clear. He was never going to pay me rent. Besides with Erin here, I wouldn't need him anymore. Tonight, I was going to put an end to Mingo!

I propped a pillow under my head, relaxing until the time came.

It was almost daybreak when I woke up and drove to Coram. I parked a block away from the house and walked briskly down the street.

Arriving out front, I was hoping Mingo and Quashia were still asleep. I crept around to the side of the house and hid in the bushes until the coast was clear. It was a grimy plan, but someone had to do it.

Sneaking inside of the basement, my stomach muscles twist and turn. Using a flashlight to navigate through the dark, I located the circuit breakers. Swallowing the lump in my throat, I flipped the main switch to cut off the power. I darted back outside successfully completing the mission.

If Mingo suspected anything, it was a perilous move. Driving fast and recklessly, I was unsure about the decision. Ten minutes later, my tires came to a halt in the mansion driveway. I jumped out, running scared to my room. I dove on the bed, pulled the pillow over my head, allowing sleep to overcome me.

Rrrrinngggg!

The cell phone was so loud, I thought it was a damn dream.

I woke up, realizing it wasn't.

"Hello! Who is this?" I asked the heavy breather. "It's me, Mingo! The lights are off over here!" he had nerve to say.

I covered my mouth to stop myself from laughing out loud.

"The lights are off!" I repeated as if clueless. "That's what I said!" he answered, annoyed. "Alright, let me get myself together. I'll come check it out," I said, knowing damn well I wasn't going over there. I waited about twenty minutes before calling Mingo back.

"Hello!" he answered quickly, sounding very upset. "Mingo, I just spoke with the utility company. They cut off the lights this morning for non-payment."

After some thought, he inhaled deeply saying, "I'm coming to the mansion."

"Okay." I said, not knowing what his intentions were. The idea of facing him alone made me panic.

Hanging up, I went right downstairs to find AZ.

Shi, Erin, and AZ were the only ones living in the mansion with me. Everyone else either left or were kicked out.

When I got downstairs, Erin was on the back porch smoking a cigarette.

"Good morning, Karen. It's so peaceful out here," she said, watching a family of deer grazing on the lawn.

"Yes, it is. Where's AZ?" I asked, anxiously.

"He's probably still asleep with Shi. I haven't seen him since last night," Erin said, sucking her teeth.

She had the same problem they all had. Once AZ got their money, he never spent any time with them. He ran straight to Shi like a whipped little puppy.

Erin clung to my arm batting long eyelashes.

"Karen, can you please take me to get something to eat? There's nothing in that refrigerator!"

She gave me the perfect excuse to leave before Mingo arrived. "Of course, I will. Just let me shower and dress."

Knowing Mingo didn't have a car, I rationalized it would take him some time to get to the mansion.

Fifteen minutes later, Erin and I left out the driveway.

"Are you okay?" she asked, watching me speed down the street in the rental. I had recently crashed my Maxima into a snowbank.

"I'm fine, just hungry for some I HOP?" I said, driving as fast as possible.

"Yayy, I HOP!" Erin said, happy about my choice of restaurants.

Sitting in I HOP for what seemed like an eternity, I kept looking at my cellular waiting for Mingo to call.

"I'm stuffed. These eggs and pancakes really hit the spot," Erin said, leaning back rubbing her stomach.

"Did you enjoy your meal, Karen? she asked, noticing I hadn't touched my plate.

"Yeah, it's good." I said, too nervous to eat anything, thinking about Mingo. "I'll take a doggy bag to go. Why don't you order some food for your daddy?" I suggested to further our wait.

"Good idea!" Erin said, waving for the waitress.

Hours later, I drove slowly back to the mansion relieved Mingo hadn't called me. Walking in the front door, I was stunned to see Quashia sitting at the table.

"Is Mingo here?!" I asked with my head on a swivel. "No. He brought me over here to take a shower. There's no lights or hot water at the other house. AZ let us in."

Quashia looked from side to side then motioned for me to come closer.

"Karen, I got to get away from Mingo. Please call H for me," she whispered in my ear.

I knew Mingo probably took her cellphone.

He was a master at the game.

"Say no more. There's a phone in the computer room.

Go use it!" I said, terrified of him myself.

"What's wrong with her?" Erin asked, watching Quashia tremble with fright.

"Nothing. I'll explain later," I said, moving fast across the room to stand vigilant at the window. There was a chance Mingo would return catching Quashia on the call.

Bang! Bang! Bang!... Bang! Bang! Bang!

Ten o'clock that night, I cringed underneath my blanket, listening to loud thrashing at the front door. I was too petrified to go answer it. Instincts told me it was Mingo downstairs. He had been calling for Quashia all day. After she contacted H, he came and got her right away.

My bedroom door slowly creaked open. "Are you awake? AZ whispered in the dark.

I removed my head from underneath the blanket to peek at him.

"Yes, I am. Who can sleep with that loud banging outside?" I said, trembling beneath the cover.

"It's Mingo! You better go handle that," AZ said, reluctant to do it himself.

"Why me? Why don't you go do it?" I whimpered, already knowing he was scared too.

"I'm not the one who let Quashia call H. You did!" AZ said, turning the room light on.

"Alright, alright! I'll go. But if he kills me, it's your fault," I pouted, flipping off the blanket to put my slippers on.

"Just don't open the door. Talk to him through it!" AZ suggested, appearing nervous himself. I walked out the room, rolling my eyes at him.

Downstairs, Mingo was glaring through the glass at me.

I walked slowly to the door taking my time. "Where's my bitch, Karen?!" he shouted at me.

I rubbed my eyes, pretending to be sleepy.

"She's not here, Mingo," I said, yawning loudly.

"Gimme my bitch! I'm not playing no games with you!" he said, banging hard on the glass with both fists to intimidate me.

"Quashia is gone," I whimpered, careful not to upset him.

Mingo peered through the glass, narrowing his eyes at me.

He foamed at the mouth, clutching the butt of his gun so tightly I could see the white of his knuckles.

"Give me my bitch! Give me my bitch! Give me my bitch!" The deranged look on his face rattled my nerves.

Fearful he might shoot me through the door, I remained calm, searching for the right words.

"Quashia called H. He came and got her. I had nothing to do with it," I said bravely, backing away from him.

Even with a door between us, I knew what he was capable of doing to me.

After a few more futile attempts at turning the knob, Mingo walked away frustrated.

I rushed back upstairs to my room where AZ waited behind the door. We hugged tightly, both glad he was gone. After that night, I stayed clear of the strip club and my other house.

A few days later, there was a loud knock on the mansion door. When I looked outside it was Uni standing there. I hadn't seen him for weeks. He disappeared after Cherry went to jail.

"Karen, what happened between you and Mingo?" he asked, sitting in his usual seat at the kitchen table. He had a blunt in one hand and a Coors light in the other.

I leaned across the table, glaring into his eyes. "What the hell happened between you and me?!

You walked away from that other house, leaving me to deal with the devil!" I snapped at him.

Uni shrugged his shoulders.

"I had some business to take care of. But I have something special for you," he said, dropping two sets of keys on the table. "Mingo was mad at you for helping Quashia. He wanted to shoot you that night."

Uni chuckled, slurping on the can of beer.

"Mingo, gave you my house keys?" I asked, nervously. picking them up.

"Yup! You can thank me later."

He stood up grinning and walked out slamming the door behind him.

It was satisfying to know I could return to my house.

I speculated Mingo had no use for the keys now that Quashia was gone. In the end my plan had worked. Book smarts prevailed over street smarts.

I smirked to myself, happy to be done with that problem.

When nightfall came, AZ and I went to the strip club.

We drank heavily to celebrate Mingo's eviction.

On the ride home, everyone was sloppy drunk.

AZ drove, while I rode shot gun with Shi in the back seat. I love hard so my feelings die slow.

But once I stop caring, you'll never get them back. I hadn't crossed that threshold with AZ yet.

However, this night put my love to the test.

"So, you really meant what you said tonight?" I ask AZ, revisiting a conversation we had earlier in the club.

"Damn right! I don't care about nothing but my hoes and my money." AZ answers, stupidly.

"You don't care about me after all I've sacrificed for you, nigga?!"

I was hurt hearing him say this.

"You followed me into this game. I never asked you to!" he says, real slick out the mouth. Looking in his eyes, I saw the hate again.

"I'm a pimp! I don't care about nothing but money," he barks at me.

It's the straw that breaks the camel's back.

I blow up in a jealous rage, believing once again AZ is putting Shi before me.

I unbuckle the seat belt, jump swiftly to my knees, and violently throw a flurry of haymakers to his face and head.

"OUCH! What the fuck are you doing?! I'm going to crash!" AZ screams and ducks, attempting to block my blows with one hand.

Enraged with anger, I continue landing as many punches as possible. I didn't care that we were swerving all over the highway at seventy miles per hour.

Shi knew our lives were in danger. Her eyes widened with fear.

"Stop it! Stop it!" she yelled, taking off her spike heels.

Due to the liquor, I couldn't feel her repeatedly hitting me in the face with her shoe. Blinded by rage,

I continued punching AZ until warm blood oozed from the gaping wounds and trickled down my cheek.

Seeing the front of my white wife beater saturated in blood, infuriated me. I pounced on Shi like a savage.

"Ouch! Ouch! Stop it!" she screamed, as I wrestled the shoe from her grip.

Terribly winded from tussling with them both, I had no more fight left in me. I sat back in my seat, deviously plotting the whole ride home.

When we arrive at the mansion, I swing open the passenger door and hop out before the car comes to a full stop.

AZ slams on the brakes, jumping out with me.

The look on his face tells me I'm badly hurt. He rushes over with a towel in his hand to wipe away my dripping blood.

Thinking quickly, I stop him to keep the evidence.

Pushing him aside, I run in the house, heading straight for the bathroom.

Looking in the mirror, I gasp at my swollen bloody face.

There is so much blood, it's even caked in my hair.

I immediately reach for my cellphone to call the police.

When the operator answers, I cry out frantically. "Please help me! Come quickly! They're trying to KILL ME!"

The 911 operator expeditiously takes my name and address. I stay in the bathroom until I hear loud knocking and police radios outside. Running to the door, wildly swinging it open, I know my swollen face and bloody tee will be shocking. "Help me!" I cry out to the two policer officers standing in the doorway.

Four cop cars sit idling in the driveway with their headlights beaming at me.

"Who did this to you, Miss?!" The female officer cringes at the sight of my bloody face.

Still furious, I point in the direction of Shi and AZ's room.

"They did!" I moan, holding my jaw in agony. "Where are they?" she asks, rushing in to my aid.

The other officers got out of their cars, entering the house in search of the culprits. I recognized some from prior calls placed by our neighbors. Every time we had a wild party, the neighbors would complain about the loud music.

Hearing the police commotion, Shi and AZ came slowly into the living room.

"There's that bitch and bastard!" I said, pointing to them.

AZ's eyes popped out of the socket. He was surprised by the presence of so many police officers. A black man with a record was an easy target. Shi wasn't happy to see them either. She had her own bad experience with the police.

"Turn around and face the wall!" one officer commanded, keeping his hand on the gun in his holster.

Shi and AZ were promptly handcuffed and made to sit on the living room floor.

I was questioned by the female officer while the house underwent a search. Frazzled and confused, I just wanted them taken away and arrested.

The police, however, were tossing the whole house looking for evidence to arrest all of us.

At this point, I noticed AZ becoming very nervous. "Karen, don't let them search my room. I have a gun in there. We'll all go to jail," he whispered when the female officer turned her back.

This got my full attention. I spun into action, stopping the officers. "Hey wait a minute! What are y'all doing in there?

I didn't give permission to search the premises!" I yelled, making the officers come out of AZ's room.

One of them became very hostile with me.

"Well, what the hell are we doing here?! You want the m arrested or not?!"

I flung my arms into the air, acting crazy and belligerent to distract him.

"Just get them out of here! I don't care what you do with them!" I said, irritating him more.

Disappointed for ending the search, they storm out the mansion, taking Shi and AZ with them.

When they were gone, I breathed a heavy sigh of relief.

It was a close call knowing I could've been leaving in handcuffs too.

Still pissed from the fight, I called the Bronx and reached out to my hitters.

"Karen, it's four o'clock in the morning. You alright?" Hearing my friend's voice makes me break out in tears. "G man, they hurt me." I say, balling hard, releasing all of my anguish.

"Who the hell hurt you?!" G man asks, now wide awake. In between crying, I try explaining what happened to me.

I heave and choke so badly he can hardly understand me. Finally, I wipe away the tears and speak clearly.

"G man, I need your help. I'm coming to get you." I softly whimper, exhausted from the turn of events.

"Say no more. Me and the wife are getting dressed now!" G man was my longtime friend. He was like family to me.

I knew him since elementary school. He was a small piece of leather but well put together and no joke in my old neighborhood.

He was shot twice, surviving both incidents. If I was going to retaliate against AZ, I wanted him on my side.

I climbed into the rental car, drunk and tired, heading straight to the city. Ten minutes later, I jumped on interstate 495 and sped to the Bronx.

We arrived back at the mansion, eight o'clock in the morning.

It was very disappointing to discover G man and his wife weren't as eager for war as I was.

"So, why did they jump you again? I don't understand why my man AZ would do something this stupid!"

G man said, trying to make me repeat a story I had already told him four times in the car.

"It's like I told you before. I don't know why they jumped me. I was whupping his ass when Shi caught me with a shoe to the face. I had to fight them both!" I said, sticking to my story.

"It doesn't matter why! They shouldn't have done that to her anyway, G man!" his wife interjects, taking my side.

Mo was no joke either. She'd kick G man's ass if the opportunity presented itself.

"AZ has it made living here. This place is crazy dope. I can't see a man messing that up."

G man raises an eyebrow still doubting my story.

"Ma, look at this mansion," he said, grabbing his wife's hand, walking her around the place.

They entered Shi and AZ's bedroom.

"This shower is big enough to fit seven people," G man shouted, from the master bathroom.

"That's Shi and AZ's room. You can sleep there tonight if you like. They won't be back anytime soon."

The thought of AZ and Shi leaving in handcuffs brought a smile to my face.

"Erin is probably asleep in her room. That's AZ's other bitch.

Don't worry about her. Make yourself at home," I said, turning the can of beer up to my lips.

"Okay, we'll do that. You just get some rest. It's a long ride back to the city, and we have to go home soon," G man said before I heard the shower running.

I picked up my Blackberry off the kitchen counter and went to my room to text KG. I couldn't wait to tell him the awful story.

KG now lived a few miles down the road in a condo with Leah. He immediately returned my text.

"You let her get you back?!"

I laid in bed reading his text message without responding. I tried to go to sleep but the red eyes and horns reappeared. My eyes popped open too afraid to look at them. I, instead, stared at the ceiling until drifting into unconsciousness.

During the next couple of days, I played it cool at the mansion.

I stayed in my room away from Shi and AZ.

When the cops took them off the premises that night, they were never arrested. They came back and hid in the basement all night. They resurfaced when I drove G man and his wife back to the city.

As a result of the fight, Adriana never received a check from me.

I made plans for a New Year's Eve party to pay her. Luckily, Uni rented my other house again. His money was a tremendous help paying the bills over there.

Home alone on Friday night, I looked out the window and saw two headlights coming up the driveway. When the doorbell rang, I jumped out my seat to answer it.

I was ecstatic to see Rabyt and KG standing on the porch.

"Boy, am I glad to see you two," I said, giving them both a big hug.

"What the hell happened to your face?!" Rabyt asks, alarmed by my bruises.

KG shakes his head, already knowing the story. "Rabyt, I did something real dumb. I got into another fight with AZ and Shi. This time, I came out on the losing end," I say sadly.

"WOW, I can see that!" she says, squinting to get a better look at my wounds.

"These marks are very deep. I don't think they'll ever come out. Shi hit me with the spike of her heel," I say, pointing to my deepest scar.

"I told you to watch your back," KG sighs, frustrated with me.

"Those scars will heal. Just put some cocoa butter on them.

I had scars worst than that. See!" Rabyt shows me some light scratches on her face. "Mine cleared up," she says, making me feel better.

"I have something for those bruises." KG grins and takes out a blunt of weed.

"And I got something to numb your pain," Rabyt holds up a bottle of liquor, then goes to the kitchen for some cups.

I smile to myself, feeling like they never left.

"We came by to help you organize this New Year's Eve party.

Everybody in the neighborhood is talking about it. Word travels fast," KG says, taking a seat on the windows ill behind the computer.

He sparks the blunt, inhaling deeply.

"That's good to hear because I'm having a hard time advertising on Myspace. I don't know nothing about this website."

"Really? Let me help you. My kids keep me up on this social media stuff," Rabyt says, entering the room with three red plastic cups. She sits down and begins eagerly typing on the keyboard. KG leans over her shoulder to watch.

"Don't forget that Mr. Cheeks is performing. Will C of Streetheat is the videographer, and the music is by DJ Wade. Use the same flyer on Fredro's page," he says, offering his assistance.

"Karen, make yourself useful and pour us some drinks," Rabyt chuckles, twisting and popping her neck.

I was happy they came. Seeing us all together again completely changed the mood.

On New Years Eve the mansion was popping! My mind was fuzzy from all of the strong drinks.

I placed a hand on the bathroom sink to steady myself while looking in the mirror at the bruises on my face. Overcome with anger, I put the dark shades back on and marched out the bathroom vowing venegence.

"It's about time! I almost pissed myself," said the teenage girl waiting outside.

"Sorry about that. The bathroom is all yours," I said, brushing past her.

The crowd was much younger this time. There were drunk teenagers groping and kissing everywhere.

I bypassed several on my way down the hall to my room.

Most were too young to be drinking alcohol.

I knew if the cops came it could mean big trouble for me. The last party was invites only. This party was open to the public.the mansion was full to capacity with people I didn't even know.

Entering my room, I closed the door and leaned up against it breathing a heavy sigh of relief.

These kids wouldn't be here if I wasn't so desperate to pay rent. I thought to myself.

The music was so loud, I barely heard the soft tapping on the other side of the door. I apprehensively cracked it open and Rabyt peeked through the slit. "Girl, get in here!" I said, quickly snatching her inside.

I was relieved to see a familiar face.

Rabyt was gorgeous from head to toe. She had on a tight black spandex dress with matching heels and purse. Her makeup was flawless as usual.

I was embarrassed to be standing before her with a hoodie pulled over my curls.

"Karen, what are you doing hiding up here? The party is jumping downstairs! Cheeks just got here!" she says, flipping her bangs to one side.

The heavy perfume she wore had a hard time concealing the liquor on her breath.

"Cheeks came with some chick named Miss Parker. She's supposed to be his new manager or something."

Rabyt twists her neck and rolls her eyes.

Shrugging my shoulders, I sat on the bed and reached for the blunt in the ashtray.

"I'm not messing with those people downstairs," I say, lighting the blunt, taking a long pull.

"Who you talking about, AZ and Shi?" Rabyt giggles, drunk from the liquor.

"Yeah! Where they at anyway?" I ask, narrowing my eyes.

"AZ is collecting money at the front door.

KG is at the bar. I didn't see Shi. She's probably in her room. Come downstairs and get a drink or something," she says, pulling the short dress over thick thighs.

Distracted, I gaze out the window at the incoming cars.

"Listen, Rabyt, I want you to be my eyes and ears tonight.

First go get me some more Hennessy. I need a drink to strategize my next move."

"You know I got you!" she says, opening the door, slipping outside.

I locked it behind her and went back to the window. It was frustrating to watch cars park on the grass because no space was left in the driveway.

After ten minutes, I grew impatient waiting for Rabyt to return. I opened the bedroom door, observing more people on the catwalk than I thought it could support.

Rabyt eagerly pushed through the crowd, holding two plastic cups in her hand.

"Karen, you got to come downstairs! I think AZ is fighting!" she says, eyes wide with fright.

"Who's fighting?!" I ask, grabbing the cup from her, taking a big gulp.

"I think it's AZ!" she says, jumping up and down, excited.

"Oh, shit! Let's go!"

I feared AZ was being robbed for my rent money! Panicking, we ran downstairs, bolting into the kitchen.

"KG, what's going on?!" I ask, breathing heavy.

"I don't know. I can't leave the bar to go see," he says, excited. Rabyt and I race out the kitchen, running to the front door.

When we get there, AZ is sprawled out on the floor, violently fighting some guy in a full-length fur coat.

AZ is beating the crap out of the guy but still securely holding the cash box.

I bend down to remove it. In the confusion, he fights me off and scrambles to his feet fleeing with it.

"Did you see that? AZ was thumping with the money in his hand!" Rabyt says, chuckling.

"Yeah, AZ is no joke. He's a wild boy!" I say, breathing heavy from all the excitement.

"Let me go find out if he's okay. You think you can handle this situation at the door?" I ask, gesturing at the drunk guy laid out on the floor in a ruffled coat.

Rabyt gazes down at him.

"I can handle this," she says, confidently.

AZ's in his bedroom talking to Shi when I walk in.

He's still clutching the box of money to his chest.

"You alright?" I ask, walking over to relieve him of the cash box.

"Yeah, I'm good. It's the other guy you need to worry about," he says, relaxing his grip, allowing me to take the cash box.

"As soon as dude started talking shit, *BAM!* I bashed him in the face with the cash box. *BOOM*, dude hit the floor.

It was all over after that."

Still hyper from the fight, AZ bounces around on his toes, shadow boxing to demonstrate his skills.

"That's right, bae!" Shi leaps off the bed, clapping her hands to commend his victory.

AZ grins, poking his chest out.

Touching my face, I instantly grow angry from the memory of our fight.

Hope these idiots don't think our beef is over yet.

If so, they are sadly mistaken.

"Okay, Rocky. You should get back to the front door," I say, emptying the cash box, handing it back to him.

Leaving the room, I move inconspicuously across the living room floor before someone grabs my arm.

"Hey, Karen. Is that you?" Nettles asks, pulling me in close for a bear hug.

Nettles was an old-time friend I met years ago at KG's studio.

We became close after that. He was one of the few people I actually liked on Long Island. Even in disguise, he recognizes me.

"Hey Nettles! When did you get back in town?" I ask, smiling at him.

Releasing me, he keeps one arm draped over my shoulder.

I hated for people to touch me but cordially allowed him to escort me across the room this way.

"I just got in from North Carolina. I heard about your party tonight, so I came!" Nettles gushes.

His jolly demeanor always made me happy. I was glad he did come.

"It's good to see you, Nettles. You've been gone for a minute."

"Yeah, I miss my people! I heard you guys are doing big things. KG got a CLK. AZ has the Armada, and you got this big ass mansion. What's good?!"

Nettles grins at me. Normally, I would've gloated. But now I felt like more money more problems.

"All that glitters isn't gold," I say, looking down at my feet. I was ashamed by the hardships endured with this mansion. Those cars were repossessed for non-payment, and I was being evicted. There was nothing to celebrate.

"Why are you wearing a hood and dark shades?" Nettles chuckles, touching the glasses on my face.

"It's a long story when I have time to tell it," I say, inhaling deeply. Nettles glares at me strangely.

"I hear that. Where's the drinks? I'm ready to party he says, turning his attention to some honeys dancing against the wall.

"Oh, hell NO!" I yell, looking at the big black stain behind them. "What's the matter?" Nettles asks me.

"These people have no damn home training! They are ruining the damn property by rubbing their big asses on that wall!"

I point to the black mark behind the girls.

"I need a drink!" I say, grabbing my head with both hands. "Let's go get one. You can clean that wall later," he says with little regard for the damage.

Entering the kitchen, I think about all the damage done to the mansion since we got here.

When we first arrived, Shi broke a large expensive mirror, during a fight with AZ. Subsequently, she locked herself in the bathroom in an attempt to get away from him. He kicked the door clean off the hinges. It completely ruined the door frame.

If that wasn't enough, one day he and Cheeks dragged a TV across the living room. This resulted in a long deep scratch on the hardwood. Tonight, KG drilled holes in the crown molding to erect a stripper pole in the basement.

"Ugh!" *Adriana's going to kill me! I can't pay rent and now I've destroyed her property.*

Doomsday finally arrived. It was two days after the New Year's Eve party.

Kicking AZ, Shi, and Erin out of the mansion was little satisfaction for me. I had the rent money but was too afraid to call Adriana. Earlier in the day, I received a text message that she was coming to collect it. I scrambled around the mansion in an attempt to fix the damage before she arrived.

Hearing the doorbell ring in the middle of repairs, I knew it was too late. Peeking through the window, I saw Adriana and company on the front porch. I dropped what I was doing and hurried to open it.

"Hello, Karen!" Adriana says, shivering in the bitter cold.

She gathers the lapels on her coat, pulling them close to her face.

"Hi," I say, surprised by the intrusion of so many people.

Adriana steps inside followed by a group of men dressed like construction workers. They carried heavy ladders and toolboxes inside with them.

"Why is it so cold in here, Karen?" she asks, twisting her face with concern.

"Well, Adriana, I'm having a little trouble with your boiler," I whimper, not being completely honest with her. Actually, I had let the oil run out. Now the boiler needed to be bled before refueling.

Adriana turns her nose up and continues walking around inspecting the place.

"Oh my gosh! What happened to this wall, Karen?! It's completely ruined!" she yells, staring at the big black stain in the living room.

"It's nothing a little paint can't fix," I say, running over spraying the spot with a bottle of Fantastic. Having no success with wiping it clean, I stupidly grin at her.

Adriana nods to one of the men carrying a clip board.

He quickly jots something on the piece of paper.

She leaves us standing there and strolls into the kitchen. "Oh no! What the hell happened to my stove?!"

I rush in the kitchen to see Adriana gawk at the scratches on the stove.

"This is a glass top stove! What did you do to it?!"

I had no idea what she was talking about. I was not familiar with this type of stove or any of the fancy things in this house.

I knew nothing about crown molding, glass top stoves, hard wood floors, brick fireplaces or jacuzzi tubs. My eyes were full of sorrow.

"I cleaned it with comet and brillo pads. I scrubbed it from top to bottom. Is it not clean enough for you?" I asked, naively.

Adriana opens the oven door discovering more damage.

She blankly stares with her mouth hung open. I had no clue what the problem was. I did however know if she thought this was bad, wait until she saw the rest of the house.

There were broken mirrors, damaged doors, and busted crown molding everywhere.

"Karen, I think you need to get your stuff and leave my house right now!" Adriana screams at me with fire in her eyes.

"Hello, People!" Kal suddenly walks in the door with a silly grin on his face.

What's he doing here?! Adriana must've called him.

How else would he know to come? I think to myself, frowning.

The last time I saw Kal was at the New Year's Eve party.

I was charging at the front door, but he was sneaking his friends in through the basement to avoid paying.

"Adriana, I know this looks bad. I promise to fix it," I say, embarrassed.

"Karen, you haven't fixed anything since you've been here!" she shouts, eyes dark with anger.

"I know, but things got so hectic for me," I stutter, trying to find the right words.

"Looks like all you did was throw wild parties and ruin my property. Just get out of here!" she yells, opening the front door for me to leave.

"You can come back later for the rest of your things." she says, holding the door wide open.

Walking outside backwards, I trip down the steps trying to explain myself.

"But Adriana, I tried..."

"Karen, just leave!" Kal yells at me.

I was shocked looking at him. I couldn't believe his trifling ass was siding with her against me.

"Can't you see she wants you to get out!" he says to further humiliate me. Now I knew why he was here. He came to help her put me out.

Dropping my head between my shoulders, I slowly turned around and walked away.

"I'll be back later for the rest of my things." I said over my shoulder.

Opening the car door, I flopped into the driver's seat blinded with rage.

How could Kal be so insensitive toward me?

I was the person who gave him a roof over his head when he was homeless. It's because of bums like him I'm in this predicament in the first place.

This is the end of my Urban black country club!

I drove home feeling defeated with tears rolling down my face.

CHAPTER XI
DEAR DIARY

Dear diary, it's June 18, 2013.

It's only two days after Father's Day. A lot has happened in the five months since Suga left with the police. We haven't heard from her bum ass, but Facebook reveals she's pregnant with twin girls. It's probably DJ's seeds.

AZ has moved on to recruit Suga's best friend named Vanilla.

The white girl makes good money, but she's a basket case just like Suga.

When Vanilla first came in late April, AZ took all of the girls to Miami. He invited Gator along for male companionship. We drove down in two cars for the trip. The girls thought they were going on a vacation, but AZ had other plans. He wanted Shi, Nina, Vanilla and Lexx to work at strip clubs the entire time.

On the ride there, Lexx was very upset with AZ. He stayed in the truck with Shi and Vanilla instead of switching vehicles to be with her. She sent him angry text messages every five minutes to drive him crazy. I was miserable listening to her complain for twenty-four hours. The whole ride was a nightmare.

Arriving in Miami, AZ took us straight to South Beach.

We waited in the cars while he booked two hotel rooms across from the ocean. The spot was a dump, but AZ bragged it was a tourist spot near Wet Willie's and the Versace mansion.

As soon as we found parking, he and Lexx began to argue, and she took off running down the street. AZ was so flustered he didn't know what to do. He spent over an hour calling her on the cell phone. Finally, she answered revealing her location.

She was sitting on a bench across from the hotel watching us. AZ had me go over and talk with her.

I got the lucky task of convincing a teenager to come back to the hotel with us. The drama didn't end there.

When Lexx and I walked into the hotel room, AZ and Shi were there alone. This sets her off again.

"Buy me a plane ticket. I want to go home, AZ!" she shouts, walking around in circles, kicking a bag of luggage on the floor.

AZ was still pissed at her for running off. He sat on the bed rolling a blunt trying to ignore her. Realizing she wasn't getting his attention, she jumped up and down screaming, "Give me my bags and my stuff, AZ! I want to leave this place right now!"

Then, she stupidly makes the mistake of picking up a bag and tossing it at his head. Even though he ducks in time, AZ is infuriated by this.

Shi, anticipating the trouble, quickly exits to the bathroom.

I stayed to run interference because both rooms were registered in my name.

AZ jumped up and knocked Lexx face down on the floor.

She was only ninety pounds soaking wet but this didn't stop the assault. He proceeds to stomp her head into the ground until she begs for mercy. Thinking she got the message, he steps over the body and walks out of the room.

Lexx remains on the floor sobbing inconsolably.

Shi peeks into the room while I'm helping Lexx up off the floor. "You are ruining everyone's vacation. Why can't you just leave him alone?" I ask, forgetting Lexx is bipolar.

"I told him; I didn't want to come here. I knew he was going to be all squared up with Shi. I don't want to see that bullshit."

Watching Lexx cry, I understood her frustration.

AZ did favor Shi. Supposedly, because she was his bottom chick. Lexx, however, felt entitled to the crown considering she made the most money.

After we talked a while, Lexx switched back to her normal self.

We all got dressed and went out to the beach to enjoy the sun. That first night dictates how the rest of the trip would be.

We spent two days on South beach before AZ moved us to a roach motel in Fort Lauderdale. It rained most of the time we were there though this didn't stop our fun. During the bad weather we went to the Hard Rock Café. We either ate dinner or watched the playoff games between the Knicks and the Pacers.

On other days, Shi and I would awake early and sit pool side drinking liquor while she enjoyed tanning. This, of course, was all compliments of Lexx. Shi and I had the pleasure of sharing a room with her crazy ass. Every morning, Lexx would call her parents around six o'clock begging them to buy her a ticket home. The loud commotion usually forced us out of the room.

At night, AZ always popped in to check on us. If he so much as looked at Shi, Lexx would go into a frenzy.

One morning, Lexx could stand no more. She had a customer fly her back to New York. It was right before we had to leave, which really pissed AZ off. He needed her to help us drive home.

In addition, AZ was broke. He spent all of his money because no one would work in Miami but Nina.

Fortunately, he was able to bag another dancer. She was a pretty young girl from Tennessee that he met in the strip club.

He convinced her to come back to New York with us. She gave him two thousand dollars to cover the cost of the trip.

However, right before our departure the girl fell ill. She contracted a bad throat infection, I believed from fellatio. AZ had to spend most of the money on a doctor.

In any event, we all made it safely back to New York, minus Lexx who boarded a flight. The Tennessee girl only stayed a week with us before returning home. AZ didn't mind because she served her purpose.

Dear diary, it's July 6, 2013.

Round and round we go, where this dangerous game ends, nobody knows.
I used to have a lovely home in New York. Now, it was a turnstile for crazy misguided bitches. Once believing I could help them, now I realize they need real psychiatric care.
The girls have their own agenda no matter what you try to preach or teach them.
It was little over two months since our return from Miami. Crazy ass Lexx and Vanilla had both disappeared. AZ had a general idea where they were. Vanilla was somewhere in a hotel posting on Back page. She was beautiful busty blonde who had many customers. Her phone never stopped ringing.
Lexx was living with a drug dealer two towns over. AZ basically was done with both of them. Luckily, he still had Shi and Nina. They were his ride or die chicks.
When Gator calls AZ about a new girl, it quickly piques his interest. AZ was always in hot pursuit of a prostitute.
Ironically, the girl had the same government name as Lexx.
But she called herself Ally.
AZ, picked Ally up from a hotel where she was hanging out with Gator.
The Italian chick was tall and thick. Young, dumb and full of cum, exactly how AZ liked them.

Dear Diary, it's July 9th, 2013.

Thinking business as usual, I never could've imagined it would be the worst day of our lives. I woke up this day at one o'clock in the afternoon. I got dressed and headed to the Pineapple Dreamz store.

AZ arrived an hour after me. I was sitting at the computer when he walked in the store rearranging clothes on the racks.

"Take me to the junkyard. I need a part for my truck," he commands, in a cocky manner.

"I just got here," I say, rolling my eyes at him.

"Just close the store and come with me. You don't make any money anyhow," he says, sarcastically.

I stare at him, looking dumb founded.

Poor sales are not my fault. You chose this bad location and cheap inventory.

There was no arguing with AZ. I got my handbag from underneath the counter and followed him out of the store.

I locked up, waved to the barbers next door, and hopped in the car.

We rode a few miles to an industrial area.

Stopping at the first junk yard we saw, AZ jumped out in search of the part.

Having no luck, he returned to the car frustrated. "I'm hungry. Take me to get some seafood," he said, slipping back into the passenger seat.

I looked at him thinking, *you have no patience when it comes to accomplishing goals.*

"Okay, let's get out of here," I said, spinning a u-turn.

We went to a nearby restaurant, stuffing our faces with steak and crab cakes. AZ made small talk about the truck until our meal was done.

It was seven thirty in the evening when we arrived back at the house.

Vanilla was in the driveway waiting for us in her car. "Hi, daddy.

I miss y'all!" she said, hopping out with a big grin on her face.

"Hi, Vanilla," AZ said dryly.

He had called Vanilla earlier that week when he was desperate for money. Afterwards, he regretted it. He knew Vanilla was more problems than she was worth.

The three of us marched into the house, entering the kitchen. "Let me go wake up these girls for work," AZ says, going to Shi's room first. Vanilla watches him with envious eyes.

"If I was your bottom bitch, I'd already be awake!" she yells after him, hoping Shi will hear her.

"Vanilla, I'm going to call my sister," I said, leaving her alone to pout.

On the phone with my sister, I hear AZ's loud screams. "Aiieee... Oh God! Someone call the ambulance!"

I race into Shi's room just in time to see him drop her limp body on the bed. I freeze in the doorway unable to comprehend what's wrong.

"Shi is dead!" AZ screams, running from the room, holding his head.

I stare at Shi in disbelief. Seeing death up close and personal wasn't natural for me. I was too afraid to go over and touch her motionless body.

"What did AZ say?! I know he didn't say Shi is dead!" my sister yells in my ear, bringing me back to reality.

"Dee, I have to go!"

In a fog, I disconnect the call and dial 911.

Vanilla runs in the room, shoving my stiff body aside. "OH NO! This can't be!"

Panicking, she pushes and pulls on Shi's lifeless body. "Shi! Wake up! Wake up! Please wake UP!" she screams, over and over again.

Gasping for air, I speak slowly to the 911 operator.

"Plea.. Please send help. She's unconscious, not breathing. I think she's deceased," I say faintly.

AZ was pacing back and forth in the kitchen talking to himself. "Baby girl, what did you do to yourself?"

Ally, comes flying into the kitchen, asking him a bunch of dumb questions. The ditzy young broad didn't know what to do with herself.

"Mam, what's your name and address?" the operator asks me.

By now we are all hysterical. Vanilla is tweaking over Shi's body trying to revive her.

"Mam, do you know how to do CPR?" she asks me. "No, I don't," I say, without hearing myself speak. "Place the body flat on the floor to perform CPR."

Shaken to the core, I listen carefully and give Vanilla the instructions.

"Vanilla, the operator says we need to do CPR to get Shi breathing again. Move her to the floor."

Immediately going into action, Vanilla grabs hold of Shi's upper body, gently sliding it off the bed.

"Karen, please help me!" she says, struggling with the dead weight.

Too afraid to touch Shi, I lean over and quickly flip her feet to the floor.

"Now, what do I do?!" Vanilla asks me, looking at the body squeamishly.

"Don't blow in her mouth; just do chest compressions," I say, repeating what the operator tells me.

Vanilla kneels over Shi, ferociously pumping on her chest.

I pray silently the entire time, begging God to bring her back to life.

Five minutes later, first responders bust through the bedroom door.

The 911 operator hears the police entering the room. "Okay, I'm hanging up now," she says, disconnecting the call. Even though the line went dead, I continued holding the phone to my ear.

Seconds later, two paramedics rushed in the room, dropping to their knees. They began feverishly working on Shi while asking us a bunch of questions about her physical state.

"Did she take anything? How long has she been this way? When did you find her? Do we need to use Narcan?"

Watching everything unfold was so surreal. It felt like an out of body experience to me. I barely heard any of their questions. Vanilla had to respond to them.

"I don't know! I don't know! She was like this when we found her!"

Ally came in Shi's room full of nervous energy.

She bounced around annoying everyone with the same questions the paramedics were asking.

Vanilla shot her a dirty look.

"Shut the hell up and go sit your ass down somewhere!" she snapped at her.

Ally quickly exited the room allowing paramedics to do their job.

Given insulin, oxygen, and CPR for ten minutes, Shi was still unresponsive.

"We can't find a pulse," the female paramedic says, looking at us sadly.

We are taking her to the hospital. Somebody has to accompany the body," the male paramedic says, then quickly packs the equipment and puts an oxygen mask over Shi's face.

When they place her body on the stretcher, my mouth goes dry. There are no tears, no feeling at all, just shock watching them carry her away.

"I'll go with Shi!" I say, feeling dizzy and confused.

Grabbing my purse off the dresser, I follow the paramedics out the door. AZ quietly comes along, nervously dialing on his cell phone.

One of the officers stops us on the porch.

"This is a crime scene! Nobody leaves until we process the evidence!" he barks, holding his arm up to block our path. AZ, out of his mind with grief, just blankly stares at him.

The officer stands there, glaring at us for signs of guilt.

"Sir, please! Someone has to go to the hospital with Shi." I say, managing a weak rebuttal.

Vanilla appears in the doorway just in time to rescue us. "Karen, I'll stay with the police. You and AZ, go to the hospital."

In the midst of confusion, the officer nods his head, reluctantly agreeing to let us pass. Ally runs out of the house and jumps in the car with us.

"Can I come too?" she asks, eyes wide with curiosity.

When I pull out of the driveway, AZ battles me about following the ambulance.

"Where's Nina?! I can't go anywhere without her. Why is her cellphone going straight to voice mail?" he whimpers, knees drawn to his chest, holding his legs. Through my peripheral, I see the fear in his eyes.

"We have to go to the hospital and help Shi," I say to him. It was very unsettling to watch him act this way.

Ally was yacking so much in the back seat it makes me even more nervous. I breathe heavily, staring at the flashing lights in the distance. Tuning them both out, I focus on the ambulance ahead and begin praying for Shi's survival.

Please, Lord, let Shi live. The hospital has a defibrillator.
They can shock her. She'll be fine once we get her there.

"Where's Nina?!" AZ blurts out, again.

"I don't know where Nina is," I say, watching him twist and turn in the seat, sweating profusely.

"We have to find Nina!" he says adamantly.

"AZ, we have to go to the hospital for Shi," I plead, keeping my eyes on the road ahead.

"No! We have to find Nina! Turn this car around at the end of the block!" he demands defiantly.

Sucking my teeth, I reluctantly turn at the corner.

After circling the block a few times, Nina finally answers her cell phone.

"Nina, where are you?! Shi is dead!"

AZ manages to say before the line drops. He calls her right back but loses the signal again.

"I'm not going to the hospital without Nina!" he says pouting with the cell phone to his ear.

I continue circling the block until suddenly Nina appears. "There she is!" AZ says, pointing to Nina walking two blocks away with her dog.

Speeding down the street, I slam on the brakes and Nina hops in the back seat with Ally.

"What happened to Shi?! Are you sure Shi is dead?!" she asks, breathing heavy from the walk.

Clearly upset about the news, Nina looks to us for answers though none of us respond.

"Can we go to the hospital now?" I ask rhetorically, pushing the pedal to the medal.

Arriving at the hospital, I park behind the ambulance.

We all jump out of the car, but AZ stops and leans against it.

"Bae, I can't go in there." he says to me, legs wobbling. I look at Nina, and her eyes begin to water.

"I'll stay with him," she says, trembling to get a cigarette out of the pack.

"I'll go in with you!" Ally says, bubbling with excitement. Unlike us, she's a burst full of energy.

Not given a choice, I slowly begin the dreaded walk toward the emergency entrance. Ally quietly tags along with me.

Inside, we're promptly met by a doctor and some hospital personnel.

The doctor's eyes are stern and controlling.

"Come right this way," he says, ushering us through a long corridor into a conference room.

Before I have a chance to take my seat, he delivers the bad news.

"Don't worry her death was sudden and painless," he blurts out, then quickly exits the room.

His blunt demeanor stifles me. I flop into a nearby cushioned chair with the walls closing in on me. Blood rushes from my face.

Enveloped in sorrow, I gag to catch my breath. It made me angry, sad and confused all at once.

Ally remains standing with her mouth hung open.

I wanted to run after the doctor. I wanted him to check Shi again! He had to help her! It was his job to save people!

The walk back to the car seemed like forever. It was long and agonizing, especially with Ally talking the whole way there.

I dragged myself through the corridor, unable to believe Shi was really gone. She was only twenty-eight years old. It was unimaginable to die that young.

Exiting the hospital doors, my head hung low.

It sucked any ray of hope from AZ and Nina's eyes.

AZ banged his fist on the hood of the car. Nina rushed over to comfort him.

"Bae, let's go home. There's nothing else we can do for Shi," she said, holding his elbow, helping him into the car.

We all piled in feeling lost.

Even though the doctor never said so, I assumed Shi had died from a cardiac arrest. As dysfunctional as we were, losing a family member really hurt us.

On the ride home everyone was in deep thought.

The mood was sad and somber. I reflected back on a conversation Shi and I once had in the Pineapple Dreamz store.

"*Karen, when I became a stripper, I thought I'd be making a lot of money. I thought I'd earn enough to pay for law school. Funny how life doesn't always turn out like we plan.*"

Shi glared at me, sipping on her cup of liquor.

Without interruption, I let her speak. I acknowledged the fact that she was ruminating a painful part of her past.

"*Karen, what I learned from this game is that you get trapped and the fast money overcomes you. The more you make, the more you think it will never end. Though it does end. It ends that day the rent is due, and you only made ten dollars at the club.*"

Shi's eyes grew dark with her voice trailing off.

"*It's the day you accept an offer from the slimy truck driver in the corner. The man who's been propositioning you to do something strange for a little bit of change.*" *She glanced at me, then looked out into space.*

"*You take his money and let greasy palms run all over you doing the unthinkable.*"

She gagged, pretending to throw up from the memory.

Exhaling with deep regret, she looked at me with tears in her eyes.

"*It's the day a beautiful dancer becomes a prostitute. Going home, you cry in the shower, trying to scrape off his filth. He's the first, but he's definitely not the last,*" *she mumbled to herself taking another sip of the drink.*

"*Hmmm, the girls at the club call them dates. I call them filthy pedophiles. The old dirty bastards hold back tips until young girls are desperate enough to let them climb on top of them and defecate!*"

Shi trembled with anger. I nodded, unsure how to respond. "*After the first one, there's another and another, until you eventually lose count. Everybody wants a piece of you. There's lurking pimps, sleezy club owners, husbands and sometimes even wives.*"

Shi shook her head, letting it drop between her shoulders. "Shortly after this, you start self-medicating. You take any and everything to get out of your body and mind when they touch you." She stared at me blankly with tears in her eyes. Knowing the liquor was talking, living vicariously through her, I tried to understand the affliction. I never imagined she felt this way.

"What's up, boy boy?" AZ said, snapping me back to reality. He was sniffling back tears talking to someone on his cell phone.

"Shi is gone! I mean really gone, man. She is dead!" he emphasized, talking to the person on the other end.

AZ briefly listened, then hung up to make another call.

I thought this call might be to Lexx. She was living somewhere in a trap house with a drug dealer.

AZ frowned when the call went unanswered.

Turning in the driveway, we saw cops were still inside of the house.

Kal and his wife, Shirley, waited on the lawn with the rest of our friends.

AZ stepped out of the vehicle as soon as he saw them Kal immediately rushed over to him.

"Man, what the hell happened?!" he asks, concerned.

AZ gives him a pound saying, "Shit's crazy, man!

I found her dead in the bed. It happened out of nowhere."

Feeling drained, I stepped out of the car and stood beside them.

Shirley curls the corners of her mouth and sympathetically batting long eyelashes at me.

"Hi, Kal. Hi, Shirley," I say, courteously nodding at them. Shirley musters a weak smile and gently rubs my arm.

"I'm so sorry for your loss," she says, then quickly clasps her hands back together again.

"Now you guys got to sell this place," Kal says, giving me a crooked apologetic smile.

I wrinkle my brow, annoyed by the suggestion. *Sell my house! Never!*

Nina and Ally walk past us to greet the other mourners. AZ and Kal step to the side to continue their talk.

"I got someone you can speak to about Shi's death," Kal tells him. "Word?!" AZ says, showing some interest.

"I know this old Haitian lady; she sees things," Kal says, excitedly. "You mean like a psychic?" AZ asks, narrowing his eyes.

"Yeah, she's the real deal! Right, babe?" Kal glances at his wife who nods to confirm.

Listening to their conversation made me uncomfortable.

I did not want to talk to dead people!

AZ quickly dismisses the idea. "Nah man, I'm good. I think I'll pass," he says.

"Listen, she's coming to our house for a reading this week. Just come by and see for yourself," Kal insists, extending his hand for AZ to take.

AZ, reluctantly shakes it, accepting the invitation.

Soon after the cops come out of our house.

Tired and weary, I'm glad to see them leave.

"You are free to go inside now," one officer says to us. The other passing officers give their condolences.

"Okay, thanks," AZ mumbles, then turns around to address the crowd. "There's liquor inside. Let's go numb this pain!" he says, allowing everyone to follow us into the house.

My heart is pounding hard and loud when we turn into Kal and Shirley's driveway. Glancing at AZ, he's unbothered about seeing the psychic. He clutches the steering wheel and reverses into a parking space behind Shirley's black Cadillac.

When the car comes to a halt, I stumble out of the passenger side. The freshly cut grass makes my nostrils flare. Kal's well manicured lawn looked nothing like my leaf littered, weather beaten property. He clearly had a landscaper on the job.

Kal was smoking a cigarette in front of the house.

Seeing us, his face brightened with a smile. I walked toward him, unsteady on my feet. "Hey, guys. Glad you could make it!"

Kal kisses me on the cheek and shakes AZ's hand.

I nervously smile at him unable to share the sentiment. "What's going on in there?" AZ asks, taking a backwood from the pack.

It's a séance for dead people, dummy! I answer, in my head. "Everybody just got here," Kal says, bending to put his cigarette out.

AZ opens the backwood and tosses the guts into the mulch.

I frown, embarrassed by his poor manners. Kal, notices but says nothing.

"I see you're about to smoke a blunt. Come inside when you get ready," he says, opening the door, disappearing inside.

I stayed outside with AZ. Even though I didn't smoke anymore,

I enjoyed the aroma. He rolled the blunt, lit it and took a few pulls. Coughing violently, he spits out the nasty phlegm.

"You ready?" he asks me.

"Ready as I'll ever be," I say, frowning at him.

AZ, put the blunt out and opened the front door for us.

Walking inside everything seemed normal. Yet, I got an eerie feeling standing in the foyer.

Kal was nowhere in sight. His wife, Shirley, her sister and another female were seated in the kitchen at the table.

"Hello, guys! Come in. We've been waiting for you." Shirley beamed, motioning for us to come into the kitchen. "Have a seat," she said, pointing to some chair s at the counter.

I hopped on an empty stool while AZ stood, hands in pocket, nervously looking around.

From what I could see the two-story home was beautifully decorated with expensive furniture. "You guys already know my sister.

This is my friend..." Shirley begins to say, before being cut off by Kal.

"Who's next? She's waiting," he whispers, tip toeing into the room.

We all look at each other, waiting for someone to respond. "I'll go," AZ volunteers, surprising me.

My eyes grow wide with fear watching him and Kal walk into the unknown.

Shirley leaps off the high stool.

"I've already had my reading. I'm going outside to smoke a cigarette," she says.

The friend follows Shirley into the backyard, leaving me and the sister alone.

"AZ will be fine," the sister says, noticing I'm very nervous.

"Oh, I'm not worried." I say, with my stomach doing somersaults.

"It doesn't take very long. I've been here before for a reading.

In the middle of my session, I received a phone call. She told me who was on the line before I even answered it. She's amazing!" the sister says and smiles reassuringly.

The door opens in the foyer and AZ pops out.

Shirley and her friend come back inside to hear about his experience.

"Everything okay?" Kal asks from his seat on the couch in the living room.

AZ looks bewildered but remains tight-lipped. "Yeah, I'm good," he says, reaching into his pocket, taking out his wallet to pay for the session.

"We got you," Kal says, waving for him to put the wallet away. "Karen, you should go next," Kal says out of nowhere.

Hearing my name makes a hot flash rush over me.

"Who me?" My heartbeat begins to accelerate. "Nah, I'm just here to support AZ." *hmmm, I want no part of this devil worshipping.*

"You really should go hear what she has to say," Shirley insists.

Feeling trapped, I look at AZ.

He shrugs, leaving the decision up to me.

I take a deep breath trying to convince myself.

Karen, you can do this, I think, rising slowly from the chair.

It takes all of my energy to walk into that room.

Once inside, I find a harmless old lady seated behind a large desk with two chairs in front. Her colorful dress matches the turban on her head. The atmosphere in the room is very relaxing. I stand in the doorway waiting for her to pull out a crystal ball or something.

"Sit down!" she commands sharply in a Haitan accent.

I quickly plop into one of the hard wooden chairs. "You don't believe in this," she says calmly, eyes fixated on me.

"I don't know what to believe," I say, nervously fidgeting with my fingers.

She gently closes her eyes, seemingly ignoring me. Not knowing what else to do, I begin talking.

"My mom passed away," I say, trying to make conversation.

Her eyes quickly pop open.

"Your mother is with her mother. She's not around you. You're surrounded by Indians," she scowls, annoyed by the interruption.

"Do you know someone named Jimmy?"

I gasp because I did!" *My father was from Trinidad.*

My mother always called him Jimmy, but his real name was James. He was dead but somehow the psychic knew his name!

Her eyes narrow and the focal point is now on my mid-section. "You need surgery," she says to me.

I quickly fold my arms across my stomach to block her apparent x-ray vision.

"Surgery?!" I ask, pretending to be baffled. *Doctors already told me years ago I had fibroids. I needed surgery to remove them.*

I withhold this information from her.

"Yes, surgery! And what's wrong there?" she asks, pointing to my left shoulder.

Rubbing my shoulder, I forgot it was injured in a fall while fighting one of my tenants. I gawk, amazed she knows so much. "Just reading you. Just reading you," she repeats, rocking back and forth, hands folded in her lap.

Amused by my startled look, she went on to tell me everything about my health, relationship, and recent home renovations.

She stopped talking when I asked her about Shi.

"Can you tell me what happened to my friend who just died?"

I ask, feeling goose bumps rise on my arm.

She wrinkles her brow. "Your friend is fine. It was her heart. It is you that should be concerned!" she scorns.

My back stiffens and beads of sweat form on my forehead, fearing the worst.

"You're doing nothing with your life!" she barks at me. "But we can fix you."

I exhaled and she watched the fear disappear from my face. "Here take this!"

Her hand comes from underneath the table with a bottle of clear liquid. My eyes widen with curiosity. *Does she expect me to drink that?*

"Rub it all over your body in the shower. You'll be fine," she says, voice softening.

Already standing, I reach for the bottle she gives me.

"Okay, thanks." I say, feeling like I'm being dismissed.

I turn to leave, relieved the worst is over. Closing the door behind me, I realize she was referring to my heavy drinking.

I had acid reflex whenever I drank too much. Also true, I was doing nothing with my business degree. I smiled to myself, making a mental note to do better. *Coming to see the psychic wasn't so bad after all.*

On the ride home, I glance to see if AZ's in a talkative mood.

He continues staring out the windshield like a zombie.

Clearing my throat, he only frowns.

"Well!" I say, trying to engage him. "Well, what?!" he snaps at me.

"Is she convincing?"

He only shrugs when I ask this. It's like pulling teeth to get AZ to reveal what the clairvoyant told him.

Unbuckling the safety strap, I kneeled in the seat to face him.

"Tell me what happened in there!" I urge, desperately wanting to know.

Briefly gazing at me, AZ sees there's no avoiding my questions. Inhaling deeply, he slows the car down.

"Well, when I sat in the chair, she said two women were standing beside me. One was a thin Asian girl with dark hair from New Hampshire. The other woman was older. She was holding her breast."

My mouth drops open when he describes Shi and his mother. "She said Shi was upset about having the abortion. My mom said, to take care of her baby"

Drifting into thought, AZ's mouth tightens in a hard line.

His eyes reveal deep anguish.

At this point, I stop pressuring him. I sit back in the seat and place a bottle of ice firmly against my aching back.

It dulls the pain from my herniated disc.

A feeling of guilt overcomes me wishing I'd done more to protect these girls. If only I had, Shi might still be alive. The seer was right. I needed to do something more constructive with my life. From this day on, I would not indulge in any fornication, drinking or smoking.

I pledged to do my best to help other people.

Dear Lord, I repent of my sins. I was lost but now I'm found.

Please let me be your humble servant.

I dedicate this book in loving memory to Shi and Gator.

Rest in Paradise my friends.

KAREN JOY

WE ARE SURVIVORS

#METOO

If you or someone you know is in need of help contact the
following helplines.
Survivetothriveglobal.org
Helpline: 1-800-799-SAFE

Meierclinics.org
Helpline: 1-855-821-1230

Taffidollar.org/ Lady of Prestige
Helpline: 1-800-910-1707

WAHIDA CLARK PRESENTS INNOVATIVE PUBLISHING

EROTICA
LIT
SERIES

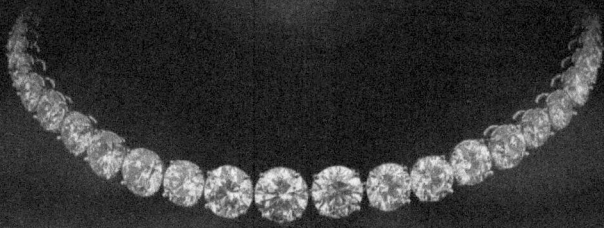

WAHIDA CLARK PRESENTS

DIARY
OF A *Pimp &*
WIFE

CAUTIONARY TALE BASED ON A TRUE STORY

KAREN JOY
FEATURING
MR. CHEEKS

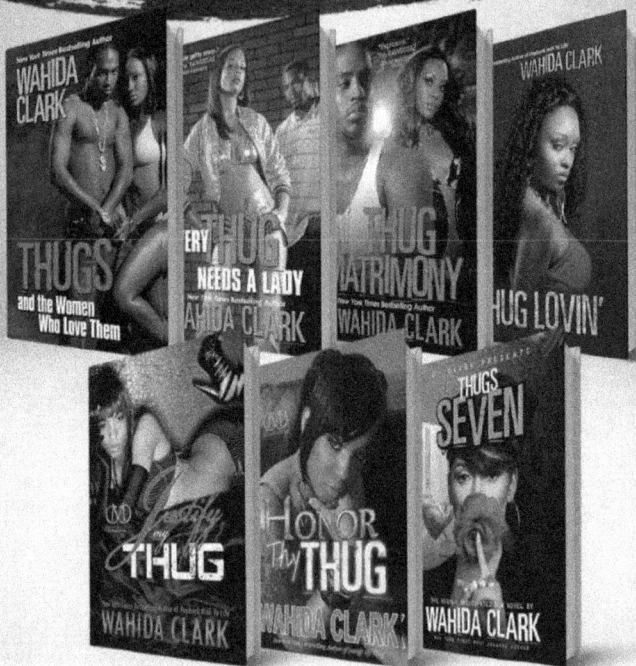

i WAHIDA CLARK
P R E S E N T S
INNOVATIVE PUBLISHING

CLASSIC
STREET LIT
—S—E—R—I—E—S—

FROM WAHIDA CLARK PRESENTS
INNOVATIVE PUBLISHING